WELSH
FOOTBALL
TABLES
1893-2018

EDITOR
Michael Robinson

FOREWORD

We are indebted to Dave Collins and Mel Thomas who act for the Welsh Football Data Archive (www.welshsoccerarchive.co.uk) which provided the bulk of the information contained within this book. This includes the brief written histories which have been added to enable a better appreciation of football within the Principality in the areas covered.

Regrettably, not all final tables are available for some of the leagues covered in this book and, where this is the case, it is noted within the text. If readers have any information which might help to complete some of the missing statistics, please contact the Welsh Football Data Archive via their web site.

British Library Cataloguing in Publication Data
A catalogue record for this book is available from the British Library

ISBN: 978-1-86223-360-7

Copyright © 2018   Soccer Books Limited, 72 St. Peters Avenue, Cleethorpes, DN35 8HU, United Kingdom   (01472 696226)

Printed in the UK by 4edge Ltd

CONTENTS

WELSH PREMIER LEAGUE

Formation

The Welsh Premier League was born out of political necessity in 1992.

Welsh football had lost a (British) championship and not yet found a role. This situation was being exploited in FIFA circles by African and Asian nations who resented the independent status of the four British associations, and who saw the participation of the senior Welsh clubs in English football as a contradiction of that status. Alun Evans, the Secretary General of the Football Association of Wales (FAW) believed that the future of the Welsh national team was at risk as long as Wales lacked its own national championship, something which had previously been prevented by the problems set by local geography and the economy, together with the presence of its powerful English neighbour. Evans therefore led the FAW to take the initiative in 1992 and the League of Wales was founded.

The 20 original members were drawn on a roughly equal basis from all parts of the country, and from the Welsh League and Cymru Alliance League in particular, Bangor and Newtown joining from the Northern Premier League.

However, the formation of this new national league for Wales saw the start of a bitter dispute between the FAW and those non-league clubs who wanted to remain part of the English football pyramid. The 'Irate Eight', as they were dubbed, consisted of Bangor City, Barry Town, Caernarfon Town, Colwyn Bay, Merthyr Tydfil, Newport, Newtown and Rhyl. At the time, Cardiff City, Swansea City and Wrexham were long-established Football League clubs, and the FAW decided to allow those teams to continue to play in the English system.

Before the League of Wales commenced, Bangor City, Newtown and Rhyl all agreed to play in the new competition, albeit somewhat reluctantly. However, as Rhyl's application to join was late, they were placed in the second level of the Welsh pyramid system. The remaining five clubs who wished to play in English football were then forced to play their home matches in England due to sanctions imposed by the FAW. Following a season in exile at Worcester City, five became four, as Barry Town joined the League of Wales.

Following a court ruling in 1995, the remaining four clubs were allowed to return to Wales to play their home matches while still remaining within the English non-league pyramid but, despite this victory, Caernarfon Town decided to join the League of Wales. Newport County, Colwyn Bay and Merthyr Town continue to play in the English football pyramid to this day. Newport County currently play in the Football League though Wrexham have dropped into English non-League. In 1996, a club transferred the opposite direction as the English team Oswestry Town (now sadly defunct) were accepted by the League of Wales and The New Saints are now based in Oswestry (having moved from Llansantffraid, Powys in 2007).

The League of Wales was renamed the Welsh Premiership in 2002 and then took the current title, the Welsh Premier League, two years later in 2004.

The League of Wales/Welsh Premier League was played as a standard league format with each team playing their opponents home and away until a reorganisation in 2010. Since then, teams have played each other twice on a home and away basis, before the league is split into two groups with the top six playing each other twice to decide the title and the bottom six playing each other twice to decide relegation.

WELSH PREMIER LEAGUE 1992-93

Cwmbran Town	38	26	9	3	69	22	87
Inter Cardiff	38	26	5	7	79	36	83
Aberystwyth Town	38	25	3	10	85	49	78
Ebbw Vale AFC	38	19	9	10	76	61	66
Bangor City	38	19	7	12	77	58	64
Holywell Town	38	17	8	13	65	48	59
Conwy United	38	16	9	13	51	51	57
Connahs Quay Nomads	38	17	4	17	66	67	55
CPD Porthmadog	38	14	11	13	61	49	53
Haverfordwest County	38	16	5	17	66	66	53
Caersws FC	38	14	10	14	64	60	52
Afan Lido FC	38	14	10	14	64	65	52
Mold Alexandra	38	16	3	19	63	69	48
Llanelli AFC	38	11	8	19	49	64	41
Maesteg Park AFC	38	9	13	16	52	59	40
Fflint Town United	38	11	6	21	47	67	39
Briton Ferry Athletic	38	10	9	19	61	87	39
Newtown AFC	38	9	9	20	55	87	36
Llanidloes Town	38	7	9	22	48	93	30
Abergavenny Thursdays	38	7	7	24	36	76	28

Mold Alexandra had 3 points deducted

WELSH PREMIER LEAGUE 1993-94

Bangor City	38	26	5	7	82	26	83
Inter Cardiff	38	26	3	9	97	44	81
Ton Pentre AFC	38	21	8	9	62	37	71
Fflint Town United	38	20	6	12	70	47	66
Holywell Town	38	18	10	10	74	57	64
Newtown AFC	38	18	9	11	52	48	63
Connahs Quay Nomads	38	16	11	11	59	47	59
Cwmbran Town	38	16	9	13	51	46	57
Ebbw Vale AFC	38	16	9	13	68	66	57
Aberystwyth Town	38	15	10	13	57	56	55
CPD Porthmadog	38	14	7	17	90	71	49
Llanelli AFC	38	14	4	20	76	100	46
Conwy United	38	13	6	19	55	70	45
Mold Alexandra	38	12	7	19	59	75	43
Haverfordwest County	38	10	10	18	40	81	40
Caersws FC	38	9	12	17	39	56	39
Afan Lido FC	38	8	15	15	52	66	39
Llansantffraid FC	38	9	7	22	46	77	34
Maesteg Park AFC	38	8	9	21	43	71	33
Briton Ferry Athletic	38	8	9	21	53	84	33

WELSH PREMIER LEAGUE 1994-95

Bangor City	38	27	7	4	96	26	88
Afan Lido FC	38	24	7	7	60	36	79
Ton Pentre AFC	38	23	8	7	84	50	77
Newtown AFC	38	20	8	10	78	47	68
Cwmbran Town	38	20	7	11	69	49	67
Fflint Town United	38	20	3	15	77	60	63
Barry Town	38	16	11	11	71	57	59
Holywell Town	38	16	10	12	62	55	58
Llansantffraid FC	38	15	10	13	57	57	55
Inter Cardiff	38	14	11	13	58	43	53
Rhyl FC	38	16	5	17	74	69	53
Conwy United	38	14	7	17	60	65	49
Ebbw Vale AFC	38	12	9	17	51	57	45
Caersws FC	38	11	11	16	57	64	44
Connahs Quay Nomads	38	12	7	19	57	79	43
CPD Porthmadog	38	11	7	20	57	73	40
Aberystwyth Town	38	9	12	17	57	75	39
Llanelli AFC	38	10	6	22	64	104	36
Mold Alexandra	38	10	4	24	57	90	34
Maesteg Park AFC	38	2	6	30	23	113	12

WELSH PREMIER LEAGUE 1995-96

Barry Town	40	30	7	3	92	23	97
Newtown AFC	40	23	11	6	69	25	80
Conwy United	40	21	13	6	101	58	76
Bangor City	40	21	6	13	72	65	69
Fflint Town United	40	19	9	12	76	57	66
Caernarfon Town	40	16	13	11	77	59	61
Cwmbran Town	40	14	15	11	58	49	57
Inter Cardiff	40	14	12	14	62	62	54
Caersws FC	40	15	9	16	81	97	54
Connahs Quay Nomads	40	13	14	13	68	63	53
Ebbw Vale AFC	40	14	11	15	59	56	53
Llansantffraid FC	40	14	10	16	66	57	52
CPD Porthmadog	40	13	11	16	56	62	50
Aberystwyth Town	40	13	9	18	60	68	48
Cemaes Bay FC	40	13	7	20	63	80	46
Holywell Town	40	12	7	21	53	74	43
Briton Ferry Athletic	40	11	9	20	64	91	42
Rhyl FC	40	11	9	20	47	83	42
Ton Pentre AFC	40	8	16	16	46	65	40
Afan Lido FC	40	9	9	22	33	71	36
Llanelli AFC	40	8	9	23	50	88	33

WELSH PREMIER LEAGUE 1996-97

Barry Town	40	33	6	1	129	26	105
Inter Cardiff	40	26	6	8	80	32	84
Ebbw Vale AFC	40	23	9	8	87	40	78
Caernarfon Town	40	23	9	8	81	58	78
Newtown AFC	40	22	5	13	74	49	71
Total Network Solutions	40	19	12	9	78	54	69
Conwy United	40	20	8	12	66	44	68
Bangor City	40	20	5	15	82	62	65
Cwmbran Town	40	19	8	13	71	61	65
Porthmadog FC	40	18	8	14	64	60	62
Connahs Quay Nomads	40	16	9	15	62	64	57
Cemaes Bay FC	40	13	10	17	62	72	49
Aberystwyth Town	40	13	8	19	67	82	47
Caersws FC	40	11	9	20	53	77	42
Flint Town United	40	11	8	21	48	76	41
Carmarthen Town	40	11	7	22	41	79	40
Welshpool Town	40	10	9	21	50	80	39
Ton Pentre AFC	40	12	3	25	59	99	39
Rhyl FC	40	10	8	22	51	71	38
Holywell Town	40	7	8	25	52	81	29
Briton Ferry Athletic	40	5	1	34	39	129	16

WELSH PREMIER LEAGUE 1997-98

Barry Town	38	33	5	0	134	31	104
Newtown AFC	38	23	9	6	101	47	78
Ebbw Vale AFC	38	22	11	5	94	55	77
Inter Cardiff	38	23	5	10	58	28	74
Cwmbran Town	38	22	7	9	78	47	73
Bangor City	38	20	8	10	72	54	68
Connahs Quay Nomads	38	18	12	8	75	54	66
Rhyl FC	38	17	10	11	61	49	61
Conwy United	38	15	8	15	66	59	53
Aberystwyth Town	38	13	13	12	64	63	51
Caersws FC	38	14	4	20	64	71	46
Carmarthen Town	38	11	11	16	57	72	44
Caernarfon Town	38	12	7	19	57	66	43
Total Network Solutions	38	9	15	14	54	67	42
Rhayader Town	38	11	6	21	55	78	39
Haverfordwest County	38	10	8	20	54	87	38
Porthmadog FC	38	10	5	23	55	77	35
Flint Town United	38	9	7	22	50	77	34
Welshpool Town	38	6	7	25	55	97	25
Cemaes Bay FC	38	2	3	33	30	155	9

WELSH PREMIER LEAGUE 1998-99

Barry Town	32	23	7	2	82	23	76
Inter Cardiff	32	19	6	7	61	26	63
Cwmbran Town	32	17	6	9	73	44	57
Aberystwyth Town	32	16	9	7	59	47	57
Caernarfon Town	32	13	11	8	45	46	50
Newtown AFC	32	13	10	9	45	35	49
Conwy United	32	14	7	11	54	49	49
Total Network Solutions	32	12	11	9	55	42	47
Carmarthen Town	32	13	8	11	46	46	47
Caersws FC	32	12	8	12	49	55	44
Bangor City	32	11	6	15	44	49	39
Connahs Quay Nomads	32	10	8	14	43	46	38
Haverfordwest County	32	9	7	16	43	60	34
Afan Lido	32	7	10	15	28	46	31
Rhayader Town	32	5	11	16	29	54	26
Rhyl FC	32	7	2	23	40	80	23
Holywell Town	32	3	9	20	38	86	18

WELSH PREMIER LEAGUE 1999-2000

Total Network Solutions	34	24	4	6	69	37	76
Barry Town	34	23	5	6	98	34	74
Cwmbran Town	34	21	6	7	71	37	69
Carmarthen Town	34	22	3	9	68	42	69
Llanelli AFC	34	21	3	10	76	46	66
Aberystwyth Town	34	19	4	11	70	46	61
Connahs Quay Nomads	34	17	6	11	57	35	57
Newtown AFC	34	14	6	14	48	41	48
Bangor City	34	15	3	16	56	61	48
Afan Lido FC	34	12	10	12	45	43	46
Rhyl FC	34	13	5	16	40	60	44
Caersws FC	34	11	8	15	49	50	41
NEWI Cefn Druids	34	13	2	19	44	63	41
Rhayader Town	34	9	7	18	35	48	34
Inter Cardiff AFC	34	8	6	20	30	62	30
Haverfordwest County	34	6	11	17	37	65	29
Conwy United	34	6	5	23	33	96	23
Caernarfon Town	34	1	8	25	21	81	11

WELSH PREMIER LEAGUE 2000-01

Barry Town	34	24	5	5	84	30	77
Cwmbran Town	34	24	2	8	71	34	74
Carmarthen Town	34	17	7	10	68	39	58
Newtown AFC	34	18	4	12	48	37	58
Caersws FC	34	16	9	9	72	39	57
Aberystwyth Town	34	15	10	9	64	42	55
Rhyl FC	34	16	6	12	74	52	54
Total Network Solutions	34	15	9	10	64	47	54
Connahs Quay Nomads	34	14	8	12	45	47	50
Haverfordwest County	34	14	7	13	56	55	49
Afan Lido FC	34	13	8	13	42	37	47
Rhayader Town	34	10	10	14	54	65	40
NEWI Cefn Druids	34	11	5	18	60	70	38
Bangor City	34	10	7	17	56	84	37
Oswestry Town	34	10	6	18	40	74	36
Port Talbot Town	34	10	5	19	49	77	35
Llanelli AFC	34	9	2	23	57	97	29
Inter Cardiff AFC	34	3	4	27	26	104	13

WELSH PREMIER LEAGUE 2001-02

Barry Town	34	23	8	3	82	29	77
Total Network Solutions	34	21	7	6	65	33	70
Bangor City	34	21	6	7	83	38	69
Caersws FC	34	18	4	12	65	44	58
Afan Lido FC	34	18	4	12	42	36	58
Rhyl FC	34	17	5	12	53	45	56
Cwmbran Town	34	17	4	13	66	53	55
Connahs Quay Nomads	34	14	9	11	56	46	51
Aberystwyth Town	34	14	9	11	53	46	51
Carmarthen Town	34	13	9	12	51	37	48
Caernarfon Town	34	12	8	14	64	64	44
Port Talbot Town	34	12	7	15	44	55	43
Newtown AFC	34	9	11	14	35	44	38
NEWI Cefn Druids	34	8	8	18	49	79	32
Llanelli AFC	34	8	7	19	41	64	31
Oswestry Town	34	8	6	20	39	84	30
Haverfordwest County	34	6	10	18	45	76	28
Rhayader Town	34	3	6	25	29	89	15

WELSH PREMIER LEAGUE 2002-03

Barry Town	34	26	5	3	84	26	83
Total Network Solutions	34	24	8	2	68	21	80
Bangor City	34	22	5	7	75	34	71
Aberystwyth Town	34	17	9	8	54	38	60
Connahs Quay Nomads	34	18	5	11	55	46	59
Rhyl FC	34	17	7	10	52	33	58
Afan Lido FC	34	14	10	10	44	34	52
Caersws FC	34	15	6	13	57	52	51
Cwmbran Town	34	14	8	12	51	40	50
Newtown AFC	34	12	6	16	48	54	42
Port Talbot Town	34	11	6	17	36	51	39
NEWI Cefn Druids	34	11	5	18	37	51	38
Haverfordwest County	34	10	5	19	40	68	35
Caernarfon Town	34	8	10	16	43	53	34
Carmarthen Town	34	9	5	20	33	66	32
Oswestry Town	34	6	10	18	36	67	28
Welshpool Town	34	7	7	20	30	62	28
Llanelli AFC	34	4	5	25	42	89	17

WELSH PREMIER LEAGUE 2003-04

Rhyl FC	32	23	8	1	76	26	77
Total Network Solutions	32	24	4	4	77	28	76
Haverfordwest County	32	17	11	4	40	23	62
Aberystwyth Town	32	18	5	9	59	39	59
Caersws FC	32	15	10	7	63	41	55
Bangor City	32	16	6	10	72	47	54
Cwmbran Town	32	15	3	14	51	44	48
Connahs Quay Nomads	32	11	9	12	58	55	42
Caernarfon Town	32	11	9	12	65	65	42
Newtown AFC	32	12	5	15	43	50	41
Port Talbot Town	32	11	6	15	41	51	39
Porthmadog FC	32	11	3	18	41	55	36
NEWI Cefn Druids	32	11	2	19	44	59	35
Afan Lido FC	32	8	8	16	31	54	32
Welshpool Town	32	6	9	17	35	71	25
Carmarthen Town	32	3	11	18	28	69	20
Barry Town	32	3	7	22	30	77	16

WELSH PREMIER LEAGUE 2004-05

Total Network Solutions	34	23	9	2	83	25	78
Rhyl FC	34	23	5	6	70	31	74
Bangor City	34	20	7	7	73	44	67
Haverfordwest County	34	17	12	5	50	28	63
Caersws FC	34	19	5	10	67	39	62
Carmarthen Town	34	17	10	7	60	34	61
Cwmbran Town	34	15	8	11	52	47	53
Aberystwyth Town	34	15	8	11	45	40	53
Welshpool Town	34	14	9	11	55	46	51
Newtown AFC	34	13	7	14	49	55	46
Porthmadog FC	34	11	12	11	38	39	45
Connahs Quay Nomads	34	9	9	16	48	58	36
Port Talbot Town	34	6	11	17	36	49	29
Llanelli AFC	34	8	5	21	42	84	29
Caernarfon Town	34	7	7	20	28	72	28
Airbus UK	34	5	9	20	36	76	24
NEWI Cefn Druids	34	5	7	22	30	72	22
Afan Lido FC	34	6	6	22	29	52	21

Afan Lido had 3pts deducted

WELSH PREMIER LEAGUE 2005-06

The New Saints	34	27	5	2	87	17	86
Llanelli AFC	34	21	5	8	64	28	68
Rhyl FC	34	18	10	6	65	30	64
Carmarthen Town	34	17	6	11	62	42	57
Port Talbot Town	34	15	11	8	47	30	56
Technogroup Welshpool	34	15	9	10	59	48	54
Aberystwyth Town	34	14	10	10	59	48	52
Haverfordwest County	34	12	14	8	49	36	50
Bangor City	34	14	3	17	51	54	45
Caersws FC	34	11	12	11	44	56	45
Porthmadog FC	34	12	8	14	57	59	44
Gap Connahs Quay	34	10	8	16	36	46	38
Caernarfon Town	34	9	10	15	47	55	37
Elements Cefn Druids	34	7	11	16	42	58	32
Airbus UK Broughton	34	8	8	18	35	60	32
Newtown AFC	34	10	6	18	42	61	31
Cwmbran Town	34	8	8	18	42	73	19
Cardiff Grange Harlequins	34	4	4	26	23	110	15

Cwmbran Town had 13 points deducted.

WELSH PREMIER LEAGUE 2006-07

The New Saints	32	24	4	4	81	20	76
Rhyl FC	32	20	9	3	67	35	69
Llanelli AFC	32	18	9	5	72	33	63
Technogroup Welshpool	32	17	9	6	54	33	60
Gap Connahs Quay	32	16	8	8	49	40	56
Port Talbot Town	32	15	6	11	42	39	51
Carmarthen Town	32	14	8	10	57	50	50
Aberystwyth Town	32	13	9	10	47	37	48
Bangor City	32	14	6	12	55	47	48
Haverfordwest County	32	10	9	13	49	46	39
Porthmadog FC	32	8	11	13	40	52	35
Airbus UK Broughton	32	7	8	17	40	67	29
Elements Cefn Druids	32	7	7	18	41	66	28
Caersws FC	32	6	9	17	34	59	27
Caernarfon Town	32	6	8	18	41	73	26
Newtown AFC	32	6	6	20	30	63	24
Cwmbran Town	32	4	8	20	36	75	20

WELSH PREMIER LEAGUE 2007-08

Llanelli AFC	34	27	4	3	99	35	85
The New Saints	34	25	3	6	85	30	78
Rhyl FC	34	21	6	7	60	24	69
Port Talbot Town	34	17	8	9	57	48	59
Bangor City	34	15	10	9	62	31	55
Carmarthen Town	34	15	9	10	59	47	54
Neath FC	34	15	9	10	57	52	54
Haverfordwest County	34	14	5	15	61	59	47
Aberystwyth Town	34	13	7	14	57	45	46
Technogroup Welshpool	34	12	10	12	49	52	46
Airbus UK Broughton	34	11	9	14	36	44	42
Elements Cefn Druids	34	12	2	20	45	66	38
Newtown AFC	34	9	10	15	47	66	37
Caernarfon Town	34	10	6	18	42	74	36
Gap Connahs Quay	34	9	7	18	42	85	34
Porthmadog FC	34	7	6	21	48	70	27
Caersws FC	34	6	8	20	37	72	26
Llangefni Town	34	7	3	24	39	82	24

WELSH PREMIER LEAGUE 2008-09

Rhyl FC	34	29	3	2	95	29	90
Llanelli AFC	34	26	5	3	98	38	83
The New Saints FC	34	20	11	3	79	27	71
Carmarthen Town	34	19	5	10	62	47	62
Port Talbot Town	34	16	8	10	57	48	56
Bangor City	34	16	7	11	58	40	55
Haverfordwest County	34	16	7	11	53	39	55
Aberystwyth Town	34	12	10	12	51	50	46
Gap Connahs Quay	34	12	5	17	49	65	41
Newtown AFC	34	10	10	14	46	54	40
Technogroup Welshpool	34	11	7	16	48	70	40
Airbus UK Broughton	34	12	3	19	47	57	39
NEWI Cefn Druids	34	9	7	18	57	74	34
Neath FC	34	10	4	20	43	65	34
Prestatyn Town	34	8	9	17	48	70	33
CPD Porthmadog	34	10	2	22	57	91	32
Caersws FC	34	6	7	21	38	61	25
Caernarfon Town	34	5	8	21	32	73	20

Caernarfon Town had 3 points deducted

WELSH PREMIER LEAGUE 2009-10

The New Saints	34	25	7	2	69	13	82
Llanelli	34	25	5	4	79	26	80
Port Talbot Town	34	19	8	7	56	23	65
Aberystwyth Town	34	19	7	8	54	41	64
Bangor City	34	19	6	9	75	45	63
Rhyl	34	18	8	8	74	43	62
Airbus UK Broughton	34	12	13	9	49	37	49
Prestatyn Town	34	12	12	10	53	53	48
Neath	34	12	11	11	41	38	47
Carmarthen Town	34	12	9	13	45	38	45
Bala Town	34	12	9	13	39	47	45
Haverfordwest County	34	11	11	12	43	47	44
Newtown	34	10	11	13	54	57	41
Gap Connahs Quay	34	11	8	15	31	42	41
Porthmadog	34	6	6	22	23	66	24
Technogroup Welshpool	34	6	5	23	30	70	23
Caersws	34	3	4	27	26	94	13
Elements Cefn Druids	34	1	6	27	16	77	9

WELSH PREMIER LEAGUE 2010-11

Championship Conference

Bangor City	32	22	4	6	80	44	70
The New Saints	32	20	8	4	87	34	68
Neath	32	16	10	6	62	41	58
Llanelli	32	15	8	9	58	41	53
Prestatyn Town	32	10	10	12	44	46	40
Port Talbot Town	32	8	12	12	37	48	36

Play-Off Conference

Aberystwyth Town	32	11	9	12	42	54	42
Airbus UK Broughtonn	32	11	8	13	53	53	41
Newtown	32	8	11	13	40	55	35
Carmarthen Town	32	10	5	17	39	64	35
Bala Town	32	10	3	19	41	57	33
Haverfordwest County	32	5	4	23	30	77	19

WELSH PREMIER LEAGUE 2011-12

Championship Conference

The New Saints	32	23	5	4	75	31	74
Bangor City	32	22	3	7	72	45	69
Neath	32	18	8	6	60	36	62
Llanelli	32	18	5	9	63	37	59
Bala Town	32	14	7	11	48	41	49
Prestatyn Town	32	8	4	20	41	63	28

Play Off Conference

Airbus UK Broughton	32	10	9	13	48	50	39
Aberystwyth Town	32	8	10	14	47	59	33
Port Talbot Town	32	8	9	15	39	51	33
Afan Lido	32	7	11	14	40	55	32
Carmarthen Town	32	10	2	20	33	67	32
Newtown	32	7	5	20	44	82	23

Aberystwyth Town had 1 point deducted
Newtown had 3 points deducted

WELSH PREMIER LEAGUE 2012-13

Championship Conference

The New Saints	32	24	4	4	86	22	76
Airbus UK Broughton	32	17	3	12	76	42	54
Bangor City	32	14	9	9	64	52	51
Port Talbot Town	32	13	8	11	51	52	47
Prestatyn Town	32	11	7	14	62	79	40
Carmarthen Town	32	10	7	15	36	50	37

Play-Off Conference

Bala Town	32	17	5	10	62	41	56
Gap Connahs Quay	32	12	5	15	62	69	40
Newtown	32	10	7	15	44	54	37
Aberystwyth Town	32	9	10	13	40	59	37
Llanelli	32	10	6	16	41	69	36
Afan Lido	32	8	3	22	43	79	27

Gap Connahs Quay had one point deducted

WELSH PREMIER LEAGUE 2013-14

Championship Conference

The New Saints	31	22	7	3	87	20	73
Airbus UK Broughton	32	17	9	6	56	34	59
Carmarthen Town	32	14	6	12	54	51	48
Bangor City	32	14	6	12	47	50	48
Newtown	32	12	6	14	46	58	42
Rhyl	32	11	5	16	43	49	38

Play-Off Conference

Aberystwyth Town	32	15	9	8	72	48	51
Bala Town	32	13	6	13	61	45	45
Port Talbot Town	32	10	8	14	45	53	38
Gap Connahs Quay	32	10	8	14	47	65	38
Prestatyn Town	32	9	8	15	42	47	35
Afan Lido	32	3	6	23	21	100	15

Airbus UK Broughton had 1 point deducted
Aberystwyth Town had 3 points deducted

WELSH PREMIER LEAGUE 2014-15

Championship Conference

The New Saints	32	23	8	1	90	24	77
Bala Town	32	18	5	9	67	42	59
Airbus UK Broughton	32	18	4	10	62	34	58
Aberystwyth Town	32	14	10	8	69	61	52
Port Talbot Town	32	13	4	15	54	59	43
Newtown	32	10	8	14	52	65	38

Play-Off Conference

Gap Connahs Quay	32	11	10	11	44	53	43
Rhyl	32	11	9	12	41	49	42
Carmarthen Town	32	12	6	14	48	57	42
Bangor City	32	9	8	15	48	62	35
Cefn Druids	32	7	6	19	38	64	27
Prestatyn Town	32	4	6	22	43	86	18

WELSH PREMIER LEAGUE 2015-16

Championship Conference

The New Saints	32	18	10	4	72	24	64
Bala Town	32	15	12	5	48	27	57
Mbi Llandudno	32	15	7	10	53	46	52
Gap Connahs Quay	32	15	3	14	50	42	48
Newtown	32	11	9	12	46	54	42
Airbus UK Broughton	32	12	6	14	46	55	42

Play-Off Conference

Carmarthen Town	32	14	5	13	45	52	47
Aberystwyth Town	32	13	7	12	51	47	46
Bangor City	32	13	6	13	49	52	45
Port Talbot Town	32	10	9	13	39	56	39
Rhyl	32	5	12	15	36	50	27
Haverfordwest County	32	5	6	21	27	57	21

WELSH PREMIER LEAGUE 2016-17

Championship Conference

The New Saints	32	26	1	3	101	26	85
Gap Connahs Quay	32	16	10	6	45	24	58
Bala Town	32	16	9	7	61	46	57
Bangor City	32	16	4	12	53	53	52
Carmarthen Town	32	10	9	13	40	46	39
Cardiff Met University	32	10	6	16	41	41	36

Play-Off Conference

Newtown AFC	32	12	9	11	59	41	45
Cefn Druids	32	9	12	11	40	48	39
Llandudno FC	32	7	14	11	31	45	35
Aberystwyth Town	32	10	4	18	41	63	34
Rhyl FC	32	8	6	18	38	76	30
Airbus UK	32	5	6	21	37	78	21

WELSH PREMIER LEAGUE 2017-18

Championship Conference

The New Saints	32	23	5	4	83	32	74
Bangor City	32	19	3	10	49	32	60
Connahs Quay Nomads	32	17	6	9	46	29	57
Barry Town	32	16	5	11	39	31	53
Bala Town	32	15	4	13	37	48	49

Play-Off Conference

Cefn Druids	32	12	8	12	38	41	44
Cardiff Met University	32	12	7	13	46	41	43
Newtown AFC	32	12	4	16	52	55	40
Aberystwyth Town	32	10	7	15	47	56	37
Llandudno FC	32	9	9	14	40	44	36
Carmarthen Town	32	8	5	19	35	62	29
Prestatyn Town	32	4	7	21	27	68	19

CYMRU ALLIANCE

Formation

Prior to February 1990, there had been attempts by various bodies in North and Mid Wales at forming a joint League covering their area. Progress was impeded by arguments and disagreements and was about to come to nothing when the FAW intervened by formulating a plan to initialise a fully national League by the 1992-93 season.

As an interim measure and part of a structured pyramid system, the formation of a North & Mid-Wales premier league was essential and a meeting of interested clubs was arranged on Sunday 12th February at Flint. FAW Secretary Alun Evans outlined the proposals and stated that, "There WILL be a North Wales equivalent to the Welsh Football League in the South next season".

Mr Evans continued, "Some leagues will be ruffled by what is going to happen but soccer in this region has been stagnating for too long. It is a bold step forward which is being imposed on those who could not previously agree."

Welsh Alliance secretary Trefor Lloyd Hughes added, "I am wholeheartedly behind this plan and I say that as secretary of a League that is likely to lose most clubs". Mr Hughes was also active within the FAW in support of the plan.

Sixteen of the eighteen clubs present indicated strong interest to join from what would be the new league's feeder leagues in the proposed pyramid system – the Welsh Alliance, Central Wales League and the Welsh National League (Wrexham Area).

The setting up of the new League was administered by the FAW – under the control of Mr Evans – and application forms were circulated to all clubs that voiced interest.

Twenty-two clubs eventually applied to join the new league and prior to selection were asked to complete a questionnaire before the final sixteen chosen by the FAW. Clubs had to satisfy the governing body that they recognised the responsibility of membership as being part of the creation of a National League in two years time and aimed at criteria that would fall in line with that proposal.

The sixteen teams selected were:

Caersws FC, Carno FC, CPD Penrhyncoch, Llanidloes Town, Welshpool AFC from the Central Wales League

Bethesda Athletic, Connah's Quay Nomads, Conwy United, CPD Porthmadog, Flint Town United, Holywell Town and Nantlle Vale FC from the Welsh Alliance

Brymbo Steelworks, Gresford Athletic and Mold Alexandra from the Welsh National League (Wrexham Area).

Elfed Ellis became the Chairman of the League with John Eifion Lloyd as Vice-Chairman and the role of Treasurer taken by J.O. Hughes.

Terrence Hewitt was released from his duties with the WNL (Wrexham Area) to become League Secretary.

Since then the Cymru Alliance has established itself as the second tier of the pyramid in the North with regular promotion and relegation between it and the Welsh Alliance and WNL (Wrexham Area) leagues.

Mid-Wales clubs in membership have dwindled finding the cost of travelling too high especially to Anglesey and the coast where most of the current membership are based.

CYMRU ALLIANCE 1990-91

Flint Town United	26	22	1	3	78	25	67
Caersws FC	26	19	3	4	66	26	60
Connahs Quay Nomads	26	16	3	7	54	36	51
Lex XI FC	26	14	6	6	59	41	48
Conwy United	26	12	6	8	54	35	42
CPD Porthmadog	26	12	5	9	65	40	41
Welshpool AFC	26	11	7	8	54	40	40
Mostyn FC	26	8	7	11	37	60	31
Holywell Town	26	6	6	14	29	40	24
Llanidloes Town	26	6	6	14	24	51	24
Carno FC	26	7	2	17	26	56	23
Mold Alexandra	26	6	5	15	27	66	23
Gresford Athletic	26	4	8	14	27	52	20
CPD Penrhyncoch	26	4	5	17	27	59	17

CYMRU ALLIANCE 1991-92

Caersws FC	30	15	10	5	65	27	55
Llansantffraid FC	30	15	8	7	58	34	53
CPD Porthmadog	30	14	10	6	63	43	52
Flint Town United	30	14	9	7	58	37	51
Conwy United	30	15	5	10	62	45	50
Connahs Quay Nomads	30	11	12	7	41	33	45
Mostyn FC	30	13	6	11	52	56	45
Lex XI FC	30	11	10	9	44	52	43
CPD Penrhyncoch	30	11	7	12	53	51	40
Mold Alexandra	30	12	3	15	40	47	36
Holywell Town	30	7	10	13	48	49	31
Llanidloes Town	30	8	7	15	37	57	31
Gresford Athletic	30	8	6	16	34	55	30
Carno FC	30	5	2	23	28	69	17
Brymbo	30	4	2	24	29	108	14
Welshpool AFC	30	20	7	3	74	23	1

Mold Alexandra had 3 points deducted.
Welshpool AFC had 66 points deducted.

CYMRU ALLIANCE 1992-93

Llansantffraid FC	28	23	3	2	89	34	72
Welshpool AFC	28	21	2	5	92	34	65
Rhyl FC	28	20	4	4	74	22	64
Wrexham Reserves	28	19	4	5	81	34	61
Lex XI FC	28	14	8	6	60	42	50
Carno FC	28	9	11	8	44	56	38
Cefn Druids	28	10	5	13	46	41	35
CPD Penrhyncoch	28	10	5	13	56	71	35
Ruthin Town	28	9	7	12	43	58	34
Rhos Aelwyd	28	7	6	15	37	67	27
Knighton Town	28	7	6	15	48	82	27
Mostyn FC	28	7	3	18	35	64	24
Rhayader Town	28	6	5	17	32	66	23
Gresford Athletic	28	6	1	21	36	76	19
Brymbo	28	3	8	17	40	66	17

CYMRU ALLIANCE 1993-94

Rhyl FC	34	28	3	3	110	28	87
Welshpool AFC	34	26	3	5	93	29	81
Wrexham Reserves	34	20	6	8	83	38	66
Llandudno FC	34	20	5	9	91	48	65
Mostyn FC	34	20	3	11	85	67	63
Brymbo	34	15	10	9	52	34	55
Cemaes Bay FC	34	15	9	10	61	43	51
Cefn Druids	34	14	5	15	74	72	47
Lex XI FC	34	13	7	14	47	53	46
CPD Penrhyncoch	34	12	8	14	51	60	44
Carno FC	34	12	6	16	57	76	42
Buckley Town	34	10	11	13	47	55	41
Rhayader Town	34	10	5	19	50	86	35
Llanidloes Town	34	8	10	16	42	71	34
Ruthin Town	34	8	8	18	49	79	32
Knighton Town	34	6	8	20	39	78	26
Rhos Aelwyd	34	6	6	22	30	81	24
Gresford Athletic	34	4	5	25	36	99	17

Cemaes Bay FC had 3 points deducted.

CYMRU ALLIANCE 1994-95

Cemaes Bay FC	34	29	3	2	117	24	90
Brymbo	34	26	2	6	81	35	80
Wrexham Reserves	34	24	5	5	101	39	77
Llandudno FC	34	23	5	6	88	32	74
Cefn Druids	34	19	3	12	73	51	60
Carno FC	34	18	4	12	63	61	58
Llandrindod Wells	34	12	11	11	71	60	47
Lex XI FC	34	13	8	13	47	58	47
Welshpool AFC	34	13	7	14	57	61	46
Ruthin Town	34	10	9	15	41	51	39
Rhayader Town	34	11	6	17	48	66	39
Penycae FC	34	11	6	17	47	74	39
Knighton Town	34	10	6	18	37	71	36
Rhos Aelwyd	34	9	7	18	45	72	34
Llanidloes Town	34	6	6	22	41	86	24
Buckley Town	34	6	5	23	41	80	23
Mostyn FC	34	3	4	27	46	111	10
CPD Penrhyncoch	34	12	5	17	53	65	2

Mostyn FC had 3 points deducted. CPD Penrhyncoch had 39 points deducted.

CYMRU ALLIANCE 1995-96

Oswestry Town	36	25	3	8	84	41	78
Welshpool AFC	36	23	7	6	83	40	76
Brymbo	36	23	4	9	81	57	73
Llandudno FC	36	21	9	6	94	42	72
Rhydymwyn FC	36	21	8	7	73	40	71
Rhayader Town	36	20	5	11	66	44	65
CPD Penrhyncoch	35	18	10	7	74	45	64
Cefn Druids	36	19	4	13	82	57	61
Lex XI FC	36	18	4	14	67	49	58
Penycae FC	36	13	8	15	58	71	47
Llandrindod Wells	36	11	11	14	50	58	44
Mostyn FC	36	13	4	19	78	78	43
Knighton Town	36	11	2	23	52	83	35
Mold Alexandra	36	10	6	20	61	90	33
Ruthin Town	36	9	6	21	42	71	33
Rhos Aelwyd	35	10	5	20	47	74	32
Llanidloes Town	36	8	5	23	34	70	29
Buckley Town	36	7	6	23	38	107	27
Carno FC	36	6	3	27	42	89	21

Mold Alexandra and Rhos Aelwyd both had 3 points deducted.

CYMRU ALLIANCE 1996-97

	P	W	D	L	F	A	Pts
Rhayader Town	34	21	12	1	79	25	75
Rhydymwyn FC	34	20	8	6	75	48	68
Llandudno FC	34	19	9	6	83	30	66
Oswestry Town	34	19	9	6	79	31	66
Cefn Druids	34	19	8	7	74	50	65
Knighton Town	34	19	6	9	68	46	63
Llandrindod Wells	34	16	7	11	67	44	55
CPD Penrhyncoch	34	15	9	10	71	56	48
Brymbo Broughton	34	10	14	10	47	48	44
Lex XI FC	34	12	4	18	54	72	40
Denbigh Town	34	11	5	18	60	70	38
Mold Alexandra	34	12	5	17	51	64	38
Buckley Town	34	10	5	19	39	64	35
Llanidloes Town	34	9	7	18	36	77	34
Mostyn FC	34	8	9	17	46	67	33
Penycae FC	34	9	3	22	40	99	30
Ruthin Town	34	7	3	24	39	68	24
Rhos Aelwyd	34	7	3	24	42	91	24

Mold Alexandra had 3 points deducted.
CPD Penrhyncoch had 6 points deducted.

CYMRU ALLIANCE 1997-98

	P	W	D	L	F	A	Pts
Rhydymwyn FC	36	25	6	5	86	34	81
Holywell Town	36	24	5	7	72	29	77
Cefn Druids	36	21	12	3	100	30	75
Knighton Town	36	21	8	7	74	41	71
CPD Glantraeth	36	18	6	12	88	63	60
CPD Penrhyncoch	36	16	8	12	72	67	56
Denbigh Town	36	15	8	13	82	79	53
Oswestry Town	36	17	11	8	72	49	50
Llandudno FC	36	14	7	15	60	66	49
Llandrindod Wells	36	12	11	13	54	55	47
Lex XI FC	36	12	11	13	64	66	47
Ruthin Town	36	12	9	15	57	54	45
Brymbo Broughton	36	12	9	15	39	41	45
Mostyn FC	36	11	8	17	42	65	41
Buckley Town	36	11	8	17	62	88	41
Penycae FC	36	10	6	20	52	95	36
Chirk A.A.A.	36	10	4	22	46	74	34
Llanidloes Town	36	4	7	25	54	110	19
Mold Alexandra	36	2	6	28	32	102	12

Oswestry Town had 11 points deducted

CYMRU ALLIANCE 1998-99

	P	W	D	L	F	A	Pts
Flexsys Cefn Druids	30	22	3	5	105	36	69
Rhydymwyn FC	30	17	6	7	66	36	57
Flint Town United	30	14	6	10	60	44	48
Oswestry Town	30	15	3	12	67	53	48
CPD Glantraeth	30	13	7	10	57	47	46
Cemaes Bay FC	30	12	9	9	53	48	45
CPD Porthmadog	30	12	7	11	52	49	43
Welshpool Town	30	11	9	10	47	39	42
Llandudno FC	30	11	7	12	50	48	40
Lex XI FC	30	11	7	12	48	62	40
Holyhead Hotspur	30	11	6	13	49	62	39
Denbigh Town	30	11	4	15	53	66	37
Ruthin Town	30	7	15	8	36	37	36
Buckley Town	30	9	6	15	48	75	33
Brymbo Broughton	30	8	7	15	28	44	31
Mostyn FC	30	1	8	21	26	99	11

CYMRU ALLIANCE 1999-00

	P	W	D	L	F	A	Pts
Oswestry Town	32	21	4	7	64	43	64
CPD Glantraeth	32	18	7	7	81	40	61
Cemaes Bay FC	32	17	8	7	74	44	59
Welshpool Town	32	17	6	9	60	41	57
CPD Porthmadog	32	17	5	10	64	40	56
Flint Town United	32	16	8	8	65	43	56
Llandudno FC	32	16	5	11	71	58	53
Rhydymwyn FC	32	15	5	12	55	54	50
Llangefni Town	32	13	10	9	60	43	49
Buckley Town	32	13	8	11	53	44	47
Ruthin Town	32	13	7	12	55	46	46
Holyhead Hotspur	32	9	6	17	52	67	33
Lex XI FC	32	9	3	20	55	92	30
Brymbo Broughton	32	7	8	17	32	49	29
Denbigh Town	32	8	5	19	36	79	29
Holywell Town	32	7	4	21	41	69	25
Corwen Amateurs	32	5	3	24	25	91	18

Oswestry Town had 3 points deducted.

CYMRU ALLIANCE 2000-01

	P	W	D	L	F	A	Pts
Caernarfon Town	32	24	4	4	105	29	76
Llangefni Town	30	20	5	5	67	34	65
Welshpool Town	32	19	7	6	86	35	64
Cemaes Bay FC	32	17	9	6	64	38	60
Buckley Town	31	17	7	7	66	29	58
CPD Porthmadog	31	16	6	9	62	37	54
Llandudno FC	32	14	6	12	46	52	48
Lex XI FC	31	12	4	15	68	84	40
Halkyn United	30	11	6	13	47	55	39
Holywell Town	32	11	6	15	47	69	39
Airbus UK	31	10	7	14	54	63	37
Ruthin Town	32	10	7	15	48	60	37
Holyhead Hotspur	31	10	6	15	59	76	36
CPD Glantraeth	25	7	5	13	40	60	26
Denbigh Town	32	5	5	22	32	84	20
Brymbo Broughton	30	5	4	21	34	78	19
Flint Town United	32	6	4	22	43	85	13

Flint Town United had 9 points deducted
Many fixtures were not completed due to the impact of the Foot and Mouth Disease outbreak across the country.

CYMRU ALLIANCE 2001-02

	P	W	D	L	F	A	Pts
Welshpool Town	34	25	5	4	101	29	80
Llangefni/Glantraeth	34	24	3	7	76	36	75
Cemaes Bay FC	34	23	4	7	81	45	73
CPD Porthmadog	34	20	8	6	88	45	68
Buckley Town	34	21	4	9	72	38	67
Ruthin Town	34	17	7	10	76	51	58
Halkyn United	34	17	7	10	58	43	58
Airbus UK	34	16	6	12	55	55	54
Holyhead Hotspur	34	15	4	15	72	78	49
Llandudno FC	34	12	3	19	55	80	39
Gresford Athletic	34	10	7	17	47	59	37
Llanfairpwll FC	34	10	6	18	59	81	36
Flint Town United	34	8	7	19	40	58	31
Lex XI FC	34	13	4	17	67	87	31
Guilsfield FC	34	8	6	20	49	82	30
Holywell Town	34	8	5	21	50	85	29
Brymbo Broughton	34	6	5	23	40	80	23
Denbigh Town	34	5	5	24	29	83	17

Denbigh Town had 3 points deducted.
Lex XI FC had 12 points deducted.

CYMRU ALLIANCE 2002-03

	P	W	D	L	F	A	Pts
CPD Porthmadog	32	28	2	2	106	19	86
Llandudno FC	32	20	7	5	81	41	67
Buckley Town	32	19	7	6	86	34	64
Llangefni/Glantraeth	32	21	1	10	78	39	64
Airbus UK	32	17	5	10	70	50	56
Ruthin Town	32	17	3	12	79	45	54
Halkyn United	33	14	10	9	56	57	52
Lex XI FC	32	13	5	14	83	72	44
Amlwch Town	32	11	9	12	45	55	42
Holyhead Hotspur	32	11	8	13	60	62	41
Flint Town United	32	11	7	14	50	61	40
Mold Alexandra	32	8	7	17	35	56	31
Gresford Athletic	32	8	6	18	52	64	30
Llanfairpwll FC	32	8	5	19	35	66	29
Guilsfield FC	32	7	7	18	43	86	28
Cemaes Bay FC	32	7	3	22	41	130	24
Holywell Town	32	4	5	23	33	96	8

Holywell Town had 9 points deducted

CYMRU ALLIANCE 2003-04

	P	W	D	L	F	A	Pts
Airbus UK	32	27	4	1	88	31	85
Buckley Town	32	20	6	6	74	33	66
Ruthin Town	32	19	7	6	78	48	64
CPD Glantraeth	32	18	8	6	74	44	62
Llangefni Town	32	15	7	10	71	54	52
Guilsfield FC	32	15	7	10	68	56	52
Llandudno FC	32	15	6	11	63	50	51
Halkyn United	32	15	5	12	64	57	50
Llanfairpwll FC	32	12	7	13	51	52	43
Flint Town United	32	10	9	13	61	62	39
Holyhead Hotspur	32	10	8	14	51	67	38
Lex XI FC	32	9	8	15	77	85	35
Gresford Athletic	32	10	4	18	48	64	34
Holywell Town	32	8	8	16	38	61	32
Mold Alexandra	32	6	6	20	43	84	24
Cemaes Bay FC	32	5	7	20	37	70	22
Amlwch Town	32	2	5	25	34	102	11

CYMRU ALLIANCE 2004-05

	P	W	D	L	F	A	Pts
Buckley Town	34	23	8	3	77	36	77
CPD Glantraeth	34	21	7	6	84	33	70
Llangefni Town	34	21	5	8	69	33	68
Bala Town	34	18	6	10	60	41	60
Lex XI FC	34	16	8	10	86	60	56
Llandyrnog United	34	16	4	14	71	58	52
Guilsfield FC	34	14	8	12	78	66	50
Gresford Athletic	34	15	5	14	70	62	50
Holywell Town	34	13	7	14	77	64	46
Halkyn United	34	13	6	15	71	74	45
Holyhead Hotspur	34	12	6	16	46	63	42
Llanfairpwll FC	34	11	9	14	55	73	42
Ruthin Town	34	11	7	16	57	70	40
CPD Penrhyncoch	34	9	12	13	62	71	39
Flint Town United	34	9	11	14	50	57	38
Llandudno FC	34	12	10	12	66	61	37
Mold Alexandra	34	7	7	20	51	78	28
Cemaes Bay FC	34	1	2	31	31	161	2

Llandudno had 9 points deducted
Cemaes Bay had 3 points deducted

CYMRU ALLIANCE 2005-06

	P	W	D	L	F	A	Pts
Glantraeth	34	21	7	6	83	36	70
Buckley Town	34	20	7	7	85	52	67
Flint Town United	34	19	12	3	77	40	66
Guilsfield FC	34	16	12	6	73	44	60
Llangefni Town	34	17	7	10	68	46	58
Llandudno	34	17	8	9	64	42	56
Bala Town	34	14	9	11	63	52	51
Lex XI	34	13	9	12	72	75	48
Bodedern	34	13	6	15	40	58	45
Penrhyncoch	34	13	4	17	62	78	43
Queens Park	34	11	8	15	36	59	41
Llanfairpwll FC	34	11	6	17	58	73	39
Llandyrnog United	34	10	8	16	51	64	38
Gresford Athletic	34	9	9	16	45	64	36
Ruthin Town	34	7	13	14	43	55	34
Holyhead Hotspur	34	8	9	17	44	67	33
Holywell Town	34	5	12	17	49	72	24
Halkyn United	34	5	8	21	47	83	23

Flint Town United, Llandudno and Holywell Town each had 3 points deducted.

CYMRU ALLIANCE 2006-07

	P	W	D	L	F	A	Pts
Llangefni Town	34	21	9	4	68	33	72
Bala Town	34	21	7	6	80	31	70
Flint Town United	34	20	7	7	70	36	67
Prestatyn Town	34	20	4	10	98	46	64
CPD Glantraeth	34	17	6	11	83	69	57
Llanfairpwll FC	34	17	6	11	69	59	57
Holyhead Hotspur	34	16	5	13	63	51	53
Mynydd Isa	34	15	8	11	57	45	53
Buckley Town	34	14	10	10	57	53	52
Llandudno FC	34	14	6	14	67	59	48
Guilsfield	34	14	5	15	58	64	47
Gresford Athletic	34	12	3	19	50	64	39
CPD Penrhyncoch FC	34	10	8	16	70	75	38
CPD Bodedern	34	11	5	18	49	62	38
Llandyrnog United	34	9	9	16	58	77	36
Ruthin Town	34	8	5	21	41	71	29
Lex XI FC	34	7	7	20	49	96	28
Queens Park FC	34	3	4	27	40	134	10

Queens Park had 3 points deducted

CYMRU ALLIANCE 2007-08

	P	W	D	L	F	A	Pts
Prestatyn Town	32	24	4	4	96	31	76
Bala Town	32	19	4	9	71	43	61
Flint Town United	32	16	10	6	61	42	58
Llandudno	32	16	8	8	58	35	56
Holyhead Hotspur	32	15	9	8	76	53	54
Gap Queens Park	32	15	10	7	82	46	52
Glantraeth	32	15	6	11	64	55	51
Denbigh Town	32	13	7	12	52	50	46
Guilsfield	32	12	5	15	57	62	41
Llanfairpwll	32	10	10	12	61	74	40
Mynydd Isa	32	10	9	13	45	51	39
Llandyrnog United	32	10	8	14	54	60	38
Ruthin Town	32	10	6	16	41	63	36
Buckley Town	32	8	9	15	45	80	30
Penrhyncoch	32	6	8	18	38	66	26
Lex XI	32	6	7	19	44	85	22
Gresford Athletic	32	4	6	22	32	72	18

Gap Queens Park, Buckley Town and Lex XI each had 3 points deducted

CYMRU ALLIANCE 2008-09

Team	P	W	D	L	F	A	Pts
Bala Town	32	23	6	3	81	23	75
Holyhead Hotspur	32	23	3	6	71	36	72
Llangefni Town	32	20	7	5	74	27	67
Mynydd Isa FC	32	19	4	9	73	51	61
Llandudno FC	32	16	9	7	65	33	57
Ruthin Town	32	18	3	11	56	50	57
Flint Town United	32	16	9	7	81	52	54
Buckley Town	32	12	5	15	45	64	41
Lex XI FC	32	12	7	13	58	62	40
Mold Alexandra	32	10	9	13	62	71	39
Llanfairpwll FC	32	9	9	14	47	67	36
Denbigh Town	32	9	8	15	40	49	35
Guilsfield FC	32	11	1	20	52	67	34
CPD Penrhyncoch	32	10	5	17	41	72	32
Gresford Athletic	32	7	6	19	32	63	27
CPD Glantraeth	32	4	6	22	40	82	18
Llandyrnog United	32	3	3	26	33	82	12

Flint Town United, Lex XI and CPD Penrhyncoch each had 3 points deducted.

CYMRU ALLIANCE 2009-10

Team	P	W	D	L	F	A	Pts
Llangefni Town	32	25	4	3	95	27	79
Flint Town United	32	23	6	3	84	29	75
Llandudno	32	19	8	5	73	31	65
Buckley Town	32	17	9	6	57	30	60
Penrhyncoch	32	16	7	9	51	46	55
Guilsfield	32	12	9	11	54	54	45
Ruthin Town	32	13	5	14	48	61	44
Holyhead Hotspur	32	13	4	15	53	52	40
Bethesda Athletic	32	10	9	13	70	59	39
Denbigh Town	32	10	9	13	56	56	39
Llangollen Town	32	11	3	18	59	78	36
Berriew	32	10	5	17	50	74	35
Mold Alexandra	32	11	2	19	53	81	35
Lex XI	32	9	7	16	45	70	34
Llanfairpwll	32	9	5	18	38	60	32
Caernarfon Town	32	8	5	19	50	69	26
Gresford Athletic	32	5	5	22	28	87	20

Holyhead Hotspur and Caernarfon Town both had 3 points deducted.

CYMRU ALLIANCE 2010-11

Team	P	W	D	L	F	A	Pts
Gap Connahs Quay	30	23	2	5	89	33	71
Rhyl FC	30	19	5	6	73	32	62
Cefn Druids	30	18	6	6	60	29	60
Rhos Aelwyd	30	15	6	9	68	64	51
Caersws FC	30	15	5	10	59	49	50
Llandudno	30	13	10	7	50	35	49
Flint Town United	30	13	7	10	64	55	46
Porthmadog FC	30	14	4	12	59	53	46
Buckley Town	30	13	6	11	46	48	45
Llangefni Town	30	11	4	15	67	64	37
Penrhyncoch	30	9	10	11	49	56	37
Ruthin Town	30	11	4	15	39	58	37
Guilsfield	30	8	6	16	43	56	30
Rhydymwyn FC	30	4	6	20	27	82	18
Rhayader Town	30	4	3	23	34	76	15
Technogroup Welshpool	30	5	6	19	39	76	0

Technogroup Welshpool had all 21 of their points won deducted.

CYMRU ALLIANCE 2011-12

Team	P	W	D	L	F	A	Pts
Gap Connahs Quay	30	21	5	4	89	23	68
Rhyl FC	30	19	5	6	80	22	62
Buckley Town	30	19	4	7	67	43	61
Porthmadog FC	30	19	5	6	68	41	59
Penrhyncoch	30	17	4	9	56	44	55
Cefn Druids	30	17	3	10	58	42	54
Caersws FC	30	17	4	9	68	49	52
Llandudno	30	14	7	9	55	40	49
Flint Town United	30	13	6	11	58	47	45
Conwy United	30	10	7	13	59	65	37
Guilsfield	30	10	4	16	41	58	34
Ruthin Town	30	6	7	17	28	60	25
Penycae FC	30	7	4	19	30	76	25
Llanrhaeadr	30	3	9	18	40	77	18
Rhos Aelwyd	30	3	6	21	29	75	15
Llangefni Town	30	4	2	24	32	96	14

Porthmadog and Caersws both had 3 points deducted.

CYMRU ALLIANCE 2012-13

Team	P	W	D	L	F	A	Pts
Rhyl FC	30	24	6	0	100	24	78
Cefn Druids	30	22	3	5	79	32	69
Conwy Borough	30	18	7	5	57	37	61
Caersws FC	30	18	3	9	90	42	57
Buckley Town	30	13	10	7	60	35	49
Flint Town United	30	14	6	10	61	51	48
Holyhead Hotspur	30	13	4	13	51	55	43
Guilsfield	30	12	6	12	61	54	42
Porthmadog FC	30	11	5	14	48	52	38
Penrhyncoch	30	9	7	14	50	63	34
Rhayader Town	30	9	6	15	44	66	33
Llandudno	30	8	8	14	36	59	32
Penycae FC	30	7	5	18	49	84	26
Rhydymwyn FC	30	6	8	16	49	96	26
Llanrhaeadr	30	4	7	19	29	87	19
Ruthin Town	30	3	7	20	47	74	16

CYMRU ALLIANCE 2013-14

Team	P	W	D	L	F	A	Pts
Cefn Druids	30	22	7	1	90	20	73
Conwy Borough	30	19	6	5	66	35	63
Caernarfon Town	30	18	8	4	80	32	62
Caersws FC	30	17	10	3	56	32	61
Llandudno	30	12	9	9	55	42	45
Guilsfield	30	10	12	8	44	41	42
Porthmadog FC	30	12	6	12	55	53	42
Flint Town United	30	12	5	13	46	53	41
Holyhead Hotspur	30	9	10	11	53	57	37
Penycae FC	30	10	4	16	47	64	34
Rhayader Town	30	8	9	13	41	61	33
Buckley Town	30	6	13	11	42	54	31
Llanidloes Town	30	8	6	16	43	64	30
Rhydymwyn FC	30	8	4	18	43	64	28
Penrhyncoch	30	5	8	17	35	59	23
Llanrhaeadr	30	5	1	24	32	87	13

Llanrhaeadr had 3 points deducted

CYMRU ALLIANCE 2014-15

	P	W	D	L	F	A	Pts
Llandudno	30	22	5	3	96	27	71
Caernarfon Town	30	20	6	4	82	25	66
Guilsfield	30	19	6	5	68	33	63
Buckley Town	30	15	7	8	69	47	52
Holyhead Hotspur	30	15	6	9	49	38	51
Porthmadog FC	30	15	5	10	63	35	50
Denbigh Town	30	14	6	10	54	51	48
Caersws FC	30	13	8	9	61	47	47
Mold Alexandra	30	13	5	12	57	48	44
Flint Town United	30	13	5	12	39	45	44
Conwy Borough	30	12	5	13	52	46	41
Rhayader Town	30	8	6	16	41	53	30
Llanidloes Town	30	8	5	17	56	78	29
Penycae FC	30	6	4	20	46	78	22
Llandrindod Wells	30	5	3	22	32	103	18
Rhydymwyn	30	1	0	29	21	132	0

Rhydymwyn had 3 points deducted.

CYMRU ALLIANCE 2015-16

	P	W	D	L	F	A	Pts
Caernarfon Town	30	24	3	3	95	23	75
Cefn Druids	30	21	3	6	62	33	66
Denbigh Town	30	20	3	7	72	46	63
Guilsfield	30	17	2	11	60	44	53
Holywell Town	30	15	7	8	55	34	52
Gresford Athletic	30	15	4	11	45	44	49
Holyhead Hotspur	30	13	7	10	44	40	46
Prestatyn Town	30	14	3	13	61	50	45
Flint Town United	30	13	3	14	54	45	42
Porthmadog FC	30	13	2	15	46	54	41
Conwy Borough	30	11	3	16	47	54	36
Buckley Town	30	9	5	16	45	65	32
Mold Alexandra	30	9	4	17	38	59	31
Caersws FC	30	8	2	20	40	67	26
Llanfair United	30	7	0	23	35	69	21
Rhayader Town	30	4	3	23	24	96	15

CYMRU ALLIANCE 2016-17

	P	W	D	L	F	A	Pts
Prestatyn Town	30	26	2	2	114	35	80
Caernarfon Town	30	19	7	4	83	45	64
Gresford Athletic	30	18	2	10	67	47	56
Porthmadog	30	16	2	12	64	48	50
Holywell Town	30	14	8	8	52	45	50
Flint Town United	30	14	6	10	62	47	48
Caersws	30	15	3	12	61	59	48
Guilsfield	30	12	7	11	54	46	43
Holyhead Hotspur	30	12	6	12	57	52	42
Denbigh Town	30	10	8	12	57	62	38
Ruthin Town	30	10	3	17	49	72	33
Penrhyncoch	30	9	7	14	39	48	31
Llanfair United	30	7	4	19	36	69	25
Mold Alexandra	30	7	4	19	44	91	25
Conwy Borough	30	7	3	20	53	83	24
Buckley Town	30	6	4	20	38	81	22

Penrhyncoch had 3 points deducted.

CYMRU ALLIANCE 2017-18

	P	W	D	L	F	A	Pts
Caernarfon Town	28	19	8	1	98	31	65
Denbigh Town	28	19	3	6	69	43	60
Airbus UK Broughton	28	17	3	8	67	42	54
Guilsfield	28	15	8	5	54	38	53
Holywell Town	28	14	8	6	75	37	50
Rhyl	28	13	8	7	62	45	47
Porthmadog	28	13	5	10	70	46	44
Gresford Athletic	28	12	6	10	57	57	39
Penrhyncoch	28	10	9	9	45	46	39
Ruthin Town	28	10	5	13	51	49	35
Flint Town United	28	10	6	12	49	42	30
Holyhead Hotspur	28	9	3	16	40	57	30
Caersws	28	5	3	20	39	72	18
Queens Park	28	2	3	23	26	110	9
Llandudno Junction	28	1	4	23	28	115	7

Gresford Athletic had 3 points deducted.
Flint Town United had 6 points deducted.

WELSH LEAGUE SOUTH

Formation

In April 1904 the Merthyr Express newspaper reported that a new football league would be formed in addition to the South Wales League which had been in existence since 1891.

This new competition would be named the Rhymney Valley League and the reason for its creation was due to the South Wales League being 'overly dominated by Cardiff clubs', though the number of teams from Cardiff barely numbered more than a couple in any one season.

Interest in the new league was high and the formation of three divisions attracted no fewer than 25 clubs, including Corinthians from Cardiff.

Seven clubs formed the new top division and Aberdare were crowned as the inaugural champions, four points clear of Ebbw Vale following the round of 12 matches.

The league is now made up of three divisions (named the Welsh Football League Division One, the Welsh Football League Division Two and the Welsh Football League Division Three) each having 16 clubs. There is promotion and relegation between the divisions, with the top two or three teams in each division being promoted to the one above and the bottom two or three being relegated to the one below. The winner of the First Division may be promoted to the national Welsh Premier League (subject to ground facilities), the highest level of Welsh football.

The bottom three teams in the Third Division may be relegated to the appropriate parallel regional league running below the Welsh Football League, subject to champions of the feeder leagues being promoted, again assuming ground criteria being met. This number totalled four in 2011, despite only two teams being promoted, in order for the three divisions to number 16 clubs.

Since its inception in 1904, the Welsh League South has always been the top flight of the Welsh League for the teams located in South Wales. This division has changed its name on numerous occasions.

WELSH LEAGUE SOUTH 1904-1915

Unfortunately, no tables have yet been located for the Welsh League South from formation to the 1914-15 season when the League was suspended due to the onset of war.

WELSH LEAGUE SOUTH 1919-20

Division 1

Mid Rhondda	30	23	2	5	76	23	48
Cardiff City	30	22	2	6	73	37	46
Ton Pentre	30	18	6	6	76	36	42
Swansea Town	30	15	8	7	53	33	38
Llanelli	30	16	3	11	70	38	35
Pontypridd Town	30	16	3	11	60	54	35
Merthyr Town	30	13	7	10	73	47	33
Maerdy	30	14	5	11	40	40	33
Barry	30	11	6	13	62	50	28
Ebbw Vale	30	12	3	15	52	58	27
Bargoed	30	10	4	16	58	66	24
Aberaman	30	9	6	15	48	48	24
Caerau	30	10	4	16	44	47	24
Porth	30	8	3	19	45	85	19
Caerphilly	30	6	2	22	33	98	14
Chepstow	30	4	3	23	34	122	11

Division 2

Aberdare Amateurs	16	12	3	1	46	12	27
Llanbradach	16	10	4	2	34	14	24
Mardy Reserves	15	10	0	5	35	13	20
Treharris Athletic	15	10	0	5	31	17	20
Aberaman Reserves	15	7	2	5	17	24	16
Ton Pentre Reserves	16	6	0	10	30	34	14
Cardiff Harlequins	16	4	0	12	18	41	8
Cwmpark	16	2	2	12	13	53	4
Nelson	15	2	2	11	16	39	3

Not all fixtures were completed.

WELSH LEAGUE SOUTH 1920-21

Division 1

Aberdare	42	27	7	8	90	37	61
Pontypridd	42	26	9	7	109	49	61
Swansea Town II	42	25	10	7	86	35	60
Caerphilly	42	26	7	9	96	41	59
Ebbw Vale	42	25	7	10	93	39	57
Porth	42	23	7	12	84	53	53
Mid Rhondda	42	21	7	14	69	33	49
Cardiff City II	42	23	3	16	100	56	49
Barry Town	42	18	9	15	66	60	45
Merthyr Tydfil	42	16	9	17	67	70	41
Ton Pentre	42	17	6	19	78	67	40
Aberaman	42	16	7	19	62	69	39
Mardy	42	12	13	17	56	73	37
Newport County II	42	16	5	21	57	78	37
Bridgend	42	16	3	23	76	85	35
Caerau Athletic	42	14	6	22	66	80	34
Llanelly	42	14	6	22	68	88	34
Pembroke Dock	42	11	10	21	621	8	32
Bargoed Town	42	11	5	26	56	98	27
Llanbradach	42	9	9	24	42	124	27
Treherbert	42	9	7	26	48	95	25
Chepstow	42	7	6	29	38	110	22

Aberdare, Mid Rhondda and Treherbert were relegated.

Division 2

Rhymney	32	22	3	7	90	35	47
Troedyrhiw	32	20	7	5	76	33	47
Penrhiwceiber	32	21	5	6	85	42	47
Aberdare Reserves	32	22	2	8	92	27	46
Abercynon	32	21	4	7	76	36	46
Cwmparc	32	14	7	11	42	38	35
Mardy	32	12	9	11	66	37	33
Bargoed	32	15	1	16	62	64	31
Aberfan	32	12	6	14	49	47	30
Treharris Athletic	32	11	7	14	35	41	29
Gilfach Goch	32	12	4	16	35	58	28
Trelewis	32	12	4	16	50	76	28
Pontycynon	32	8	8	16	37	59	24
Abergavenny	32	6	10	16	32	62	22
Nantymoel	32	8	3	21	49	92	19
Ynysybwl	32	4	8	20	37	97	16
Pengam	32	5	3	24	22	78	13

Other divisional tables have not yet been located.

WELSH LEAGUE SOUTH 1921-22

Division 1

Porth	40	24	11	5	89	39	59
Cardiff City II	40	22	11	7	80	31	55
Bridgend	40	20	12	8	95	53	52
Aberaman	40	19	12	9	75	40	50
Ton Pentre	40	21	8	11	69	41	50
Ebbw Vale	40	19	11	10	74	33	49
Caerphilly	40	21	6	13	94	54	48
Pontypridd	40	21	6	13	75	43	48
Pembroke Dock	40	20	7	13	80	59	47
Swansea Town II	40	16	12	12	65	48	44
Merthyr Tydfil	40	17	7	16	69	71	41
Llanelly	40	15	9	16	58	67	39
Barry Town	40	14	8	18	55	66	36
Caerau Athletic	40	13	9	18	67	65	35
Rhymney	40	12	11	17	62	81	35
Abertilly	40	13	8	19	50	82	34
Mardy	40	7	10	23	51	91	24
Chepstow	40	9	6	25	54	99	24
Newport County II	40	7	10	23	42	98	24
Bargoed Town	40	8	6	24	43	115	24
Llanbradach	40	8	6	26	45	108	22

Chepstow and Llanbradach were relegated.
Other divisional tables have not yet been located.

WELSH LEAGUE SOUTH 1922-23

Division 1

Cardiff City II	40	35	2	3	140	22	72
Swansea Town II	40	28	6	6	120	41	62
Llanelly	39	28	5	6	101	32	61
Ebbw Vale	40	21	10	9	81	38	52
Newport County II	40	24	4	12	119	52	52
Pontypridd	40	20	8	12	98	56	48
Caerau Athletic	40	19	7	14	70	64	45
Aberdare	40	19	6	15	92	94	44
Aberaman	38	17	8	13	83	76	42
Bridgend	40	17	8	15	85	67	42
Barry Town	40	17	6	17	62	60	40
Merthyr Tydfil	40	18	5	17	70	82	41
Pembroke Dock	39	17	5	17	86	78	38
Rhymney	40	15	8	17	74	78	38
Mardy	40	16	3	21	65	95	35
Caerphilly	40	8	9	23	41	103	25
Ton Pentre	37	9	6	22	47	106	24
Bargoed Town	39	8	7	24	40	75	23
Porth	40	5	8	29	29	102	16
New Tredegar	39	5	6	28	39	135	16
Abertilly	35	4	1	30	37	162	9

Rhymney, Caerphilly, Ton Pentre, Bargoed Town, Porth,
New Tredegar and Abertilly were all relegated
It is believed that not all fixtures were completed.

Division 2 – Section A

Penrhiwceiber	28	23	4	1	101	22	50
Aberpergwm	28	17	5	6	70	49	39
Trecynon	28	15	7	6	68	36	37
Treharris	27	16	3	8	54	37	35
Llandbradach	28	13	8	7	60	41	34
Troedyrhiw	28	11	6	11	51	48	28
Abercynon	28	11	8	9	43	51	30
Aberaman	28	8	9	11	48	43	25
Pengam	28	9	7	12	42	57	25
Aberfan	28	10	4	14	44	54	24
Brecon	28	9	6	13	39	54	24
Dowlais	28	9	6	13	35	58	24
Fleindre	28	7	9	12	46	50	23
Talywain	27	6	1	20	35	95	13
Hirwain	28	2	7	19	26	70	11

Abercynon appeared above Troedyrhiw in the final published
table.
Not all fixtures were completed.

Division 2 – Section B

Cwmparc	24	18	4	2	83	27	40
Ferndale	24	18	2	4	68	31	38
Wattstown	24	14	3	7	75	41	31
Tylorstown	24	11	9	4	58	41	31
Nantymoel	23	12	2	9	47	56	26
Abertridwr	23	10	5	8	57	46	25
Pontypridd	21	11	2	8	35	53	24
Ton Pentre	21	7	3	11	36	47	17
Barry	24	8	1	15	37	54	17
Ystrad Mynach	21	4	6	11	31	62	14
Port Talbot	18	4	5	9	24	37	13
Cilfynnydd	22	5	2	15	26	45	12
Gilfach Goch	19	2	2	15	18	64	6

Not all fixtures were completed.

WELSH LEAGUE SOUTH 1923-24

Division 1

Pontypridd	30	24	3	3	110	34	51
Swansea Town II	30	23	2	5	86	18	48
Mid Rhondda	30	19	5	6	98	29	43
Cardiff City II	30	17	5	8	68	41	38
Newport County II	30	17	4	9	63	40	38
Llanelly	30	14	5	11	62	51	33
Ebbw Vale	30	14	3	13	58	44	31
Bridgend	30	12	5	13	42	38	29
Aberdare	30	13	3	14	43	57	29
Barry Town	30	11	5	14	40	53	27
Penrhiwceiber	30	9	6	15	48	66	24
Mardy	30	10	3	17	41	81	23
Merthyr Tydfil	30	9	3	18	42	85	21
Aberaman	30	8	4	18	27	65	20
Caerau Athletic	30	5	6	19	25	66	16
Pembroke Dock	30	3	4	23	35	104	10

Mardy were relegated.
Other divisional tables have not yet been located.

WELSH LEAGUE SOUTH 1924-25

Division 1

Swansea Town II	32	24	4	4	75	18	52
Cardiff City II	32	19	8	5	66	25	46
Mid Rhondda	32	18	8	6	58	24	44
Lovells Athletic	32	18	5	9	43	32	41
Newport County II	32	14	8	18	50	47	36
Pontypridd	32	14	6	12	50	33	34
Ebbw Vale	32	15	4	13	54	48	34
Cardiff Corinthians	32	13	5	14	47	49	31
Barry Town	32	13	4	15	45	57	30
Bridgend	32	11	6	15	46	44	28
Penrhiwceiber	32	9	9	14	44	59	27
Merthyr Tydfil	32	12	3	17	54	71	27
Llanelly	32	9	7	16	47	67	25
Pembroke Dock	32	10	4	18	39	47	24
Aberaman	32	8	8	16	32	50	24
Aberdare	32	10	2	20	40	67	22
Caerau Athletic	32	7	4	21	33	82	18
					823	820	

Goals for and against do not tally in the available table.

Llanelly and Caerau Athletic were relegated.
Other divisional tables have not yet been located.

WELSH LEAGUE SOUTH 1925-26

Division 1

Swansea Town II	28	23	2	3	95	32	48
Cardiff City II	28	16	4	8	60	36	36
Mid Rhondda	28	17	2	10	65	44	36
Pembroke Dock	28	15	5	8	69	37	35
Barry Town	28	15	5	8	48	32	35
Newport County II	28	13	4	11	55	37	30
Lovells Athletic	28	9	11	8	47	55	29
Ebbw Vale	28	12	5	11	53	63	29
Merthyr Tydfil	28	8	8	12	65	70	24
Penrhiwceiber	28	7	8	13	55	65	22
Cardiff Corinthians	28	6	10	12	51	70	22
Aberdare	28	7	8	13	44	71	22
Bridgend Town	28	6	7	15	46	78	18
Pontypridd	28	5	8	15	30	66	18
Aberaman	28	4	8	16	45	76	16

Pontypridd and Aberaman were relegated.

Division 2 – Section A

Llanbradach	32	25	4	3	121	40	54
Pontlottyn	32	25	2	5	105	48	52
New Tredegar	32	24	3	5	124	32	51
Aberbargoed	32	20	4	8	119	61	44
Treharris	32	18	7	7	79	38	43
Ystrad Mynach	32	16	4	12	87	69	36
Risca Town	32	16	3	14	85	60	35
Abergavenny	32	15	4	13	85	67	34
Bargoed Athletic	32	15	4	13	74	88	34
Fleur-de-Lis	32	15	2	15	69	68	32
Trethomas	32	12	6	14	53	62	30
Pengam	32	12	3	17	71	74	27
Markham	32	8	6	18	40	73	22
Caerphilly	32	7	4	21	47	111	18
Abertysswg	32	6	3	23	48	117	15
Gelligaer	32	4	4	24	40	111	12
Tredomen	32	1	2	29	21	143	4

Division 2 – Section B

Troedyrhiw Welfare	24	17	5	2	77	22	39
Troedyrhiw Carl	24	16	5	3	64	27	37
Wattstown	24	18	0	6	76	40	36
Ferndale	24	15	4	5	58	25	34
Ynysybwl	24	12	4	8	44	47	28
Cardiff Camerons	24	12	3	9	55	46	27
Abercynon	24	8	4	12	45	68	20
Aberfan	24	7	5	12	54	54	19
Ton Pentre Amateurs	24	7	5	12	39	59	19
Cambrian Welfare	24	7	3	14	48	59	17
Nantymoel	24	7	1	16	58	64	15
Kenfig Hill	24	5	3	16	27	68	13
Aberaman	24	3	2	19	40	82	8

WELSH LEAGUE SOUTH 1926-27

Division 1

Barry Town	24	16	5	3	87	35	37
Swansea Town II	24	17	3	4	68	30	37
Lovells Athletic	22	15	3	4	52	25	33
Cardiff City II	23	15	2	6	63	24	32
Newport County II	24	12	2	10	52	48	26
Aberdare	24	11	3	10	48	52	25
Ebbw Vale	24	10	2	12	78	46	22
Bridgend Town	23	8	4	11	33	54	20
Cardiff Corinthians	24	6	3	15	37	56	15
Merthyr Tydfil	22	6	3	13	42	62	15
Mid Rhondda	22	6	1	15	32	60	13
Pembroke Dock	15	5	1	9	26	53	11
Penrhiwceiber	23	3	3	17	35	180	9

Pembroke Dock were suspended during the season and their
record was included in the table. The Championship was
awarded to Barry by an Appeal Committee.

Division 2 – Section A

Ystrad Mynach	24	18	0	6	78	35	36
Dowlais Town	24	14	6	4	55	33	34
Llanbradach	24	16	1	7	91	39	33
Pontlottyn	24	13	6	5	69	31	32
New Tredegar	24	13	5	6	77	32	31
Abertysswg	24	14	2	8	65	62	30
Abergavenny	24	13	3	8	56	51	29
Treharris	23	8	4	11	31	47	20
Gelligaer	24	6	2	16	40	77	14
Cwm	23	6	1	16	41	74	13
Trethomas	24	3	7	14	37	96	13
Bargoed Athletic	23	2	8	13	31	68	12
Pengam	23	5	1	17	36	71	11

Division 2 – Section B

Troedyrhiw	14	11	1	2	36	18	23
Wattstown	14	9	1	4	49	25	19
Cardiff Camerons	12	8	1	3	35	22	17
Aberfan	14	6	2	6	39	30	14
Cambrian Welfare	14	4	3	7	25	35	11
Hirwaun	10	2	2	6	14	33	6
Penygraig	10	1	2	7	16	27	4
Nantymoel	8	1	0	7	4	27	2

Not all fixtures were completed.

WELSH LEAGUE SOUTH 1927-28

Division 1

Newport County II	24	21	1	2	102	38	43
Cardiff City II	24	17	4	3	81	31	38
Ebbw Vale	24	15	4	5	79	38	34
Aberdare	24	16	0	8	87	42	32
Swansea Town II	24	11	6	7	82	45	28
Lovells Athletic	24	9	5	10	54	50	23
Barry Town	24	10	1	13	60	68	21
Merthyr Tydfil	24	8	4	12	47	57	20
Penrhiwceiber	24	9	1	14	45	57	19
New Tredegar	24	6	3	15	32	87	15
Cardiff Corinthians	23	5	4	14	32	61	14
Bridgend Town	24	4	4	16	32	88	12
Mid Rhondda	23	5	1	17	23	75	11

Not all fixtures were completed.
Aberdare, Bridgend Town and Mid Rhondda were relegated.
Other Divisional tableshave not yet been located

WELSH LEAGUE SOUTH 1928-29

Division 1

Cardiff City II	20	16	1	3	64	19	33
Ebbw Vale	20	12	3	5	57	46	27
Lovells Athletic	20	10	4	6	48	31	24
Swansea Town II	20	8	4	7	51	42	22
Newport County II	20	9	4	7	47	39	22
Llanelly	20	9	4	7	49	56	22
Cardiff Corinthians	20	7	5	8	40	39	19
New Tredegar	20	8	2	10	52	55	18
Barry Town	20	6	5	9	25	37	17
Merthyr Tydfil	20	6	3	11	42	39	15
Penrhiwceiber	20	0	3	17	26	83	3

Division 2

Abertysswyg	24	13	8	2	61	26	34
Gilfach Albions	24	13	7	4	78	43	33
Troedyrhiw	24	14	3	7	68	38	31
Bargoed Athletic	24	13	3	8	40	41	29
Llanbradach	24	11	5	8	51	63	27
Rhymney	23	9	7	7	49	38	25
Treharris	21	9	5	7	41	51	23
Gelligaer	24	9	4	11	45	49	22
Dowlais Town	24	8	5	11	45	55	21
Hirwaun	22	5	7	10	39	52	17
Pontlottyn	20	7	2	11	34	50	16
Tredomen	23	3	8	12	32	57	14
Fleur-de-Lis	24	3	4	17	33	82	10

Not all fixtures were completed.

WELSH LEAGUE SOUTH 1929-30

Division 1

Llanelly	20	14	5	1	65	27	33
Cardiff City II	20	13	5	2	84	33	31
Swansea Town II	20	8	5	7	47	38	21
Lovells Athletic	20	7	6	7	49	42	20
Merthyr Tydfil	20	7	6	7	55	51	20
Newport County II	20	8	4	8	51	52	20
Cardiff Corinthians	20	8	3	9	39	40	19
Barry Town	20	7	4	9	47	45	18
Ebbw Vale	20	7	4	9	49	57	18
Penrhiwceiber	20	4	4	12	38	78	12
New Tredegar	20	4	0	16	39	101	8

Other divisional tables have not yet been located.

WELSH LEAGUE SOUTH 1930-31

Division 1

Merthyr Tydfil	20	14	1	5	69	33	29
Llanelly	20	14	1	5	73	39	29
Cardiff City II	20	12	2	6	52	33	26
Swansea Town II	20	12	2	6	60	40	26
Barry Town	20	10	2	8	48	45	22
Lovells Athletic	20	9	2	9	60	51	20
Newport County II	20	8	3	9	45	59	19
Cardiff Corinthians	20	6	3	11	31	36	15
Penrhiwceiber	20	7	0	13	25	64	14
Ebbw Vale	20	6	1	13	32	55	13
Aberaman	20	2	3	15	28	66	7

Other divisional tables have not yet been located.

WELSH LEAGUE SOUTH 1931-32

Division 1

Lovells Athletic	20	18	2	0	79	23	38
Newport County II	20	10	7	3	54	32	27
Swansea Town II	20	10	5	5	46	28	25
Llanelly	20	11	1	8	53	34	23
Merthyr Tydfil	20	10	1	9	55	58	21
Cardiff Corinthians	20	9	2	9	42	46	20
Cardiff City II	20	9	1	10	35	42	19
Barry Town	20	8	1	11	48	65	17
Penrhiwceiber	20	5	2	13	39	60	12
Aberaman	20	3	4	13	31	63	10
Ebbw Vale	20	3	2	15	32	60	8

Division 2

Troedyrhiw	20	17	0	3	85	14	34
Rhymney	20	15	1	4	66	18	31
Nantymoel	17	10	4	3	42	44	24
Bargoed Har	17	10	2	5	39	41	22
Treharris	19	8	1	10	39	41	17
Tredomen Welfare	18	5	5	8	32	55	15
Onllwyn Welfare	19	5	3	11	36	53	13
Caerau	20	4	4	12	35	53	12
Tirphil Welfare	15	6	0	9	22	55	12
Llanbradach	20	5	1	14	33	57	11
Abertysswg	18	4	3	11	20	51	11

Not all fixtures were completed.

WELSH LEAGUE SOUTH 1932-33

Division 1

Llanelly	22	19	0	3	100	16	37
Swansea Town II	22	13	7	2	65	25	33
Lovells Athletic	22	14	1	7	56	33	29
Merthyr Tydfil	22	14	1	7	60	38	29
Troedyrhiw	22	9	5	8	56	54	23
Newport County II	22	9	4	9	49	68	22
Cardiff City II	22	7	4	11	47	69	18
Aberaman	22	8	1	13	44	72	17
Ebbw Vale	22	11	4	12	30	54	16
Barry Town	22	7	2	13	47	72	16
Cardiff Corinthians	22	4	5	13	25	48	13
Penrhiwceiber	22	4	2	16	44	78	10

Division 2 – Western Section

Llanelly A	22	20	0	2	95	30	40
Gwynfi Welfare	22	12	4	6	42	32	28
Nantymoel	22	11	5	6	54	38	27
Britol Ferry Athletic	22	11	3	8	51	47	25
Ammanford	22	10	3	9	55	53	23
Caerau Athletic	22	9	5	8	37	44	23
Skewen Athletic	22	8	5	9	46	46	21
Sea Side Athletic	22	7	7	8	42	45	21
Aberavon Quins	22	6	7	9	34	35	19
Swansea A	22	4	8	10	34	47	16
Glyncorrwg	22	5	6	11	28	47	16
Onllwyn Welfare	22	1	3	18	16	68	5

Division 2 – Eastern Section

Gelli Colliery	26	18	5	3	82	37	41
Abertysswg	26	17	5	4	88	39	39
Treorchy	26	15	5	6	71	51	35
Trethomas	26	14	5	7	77	55	33
Gilfach & Bargoed	26	12	6	8	73	69	30
Ton Pentre Town	26	13	3	10	65	45	29
Treharris Athletic	26	13	2	11	59	52	28
Trelewis Welfare	26	11	3	12	67	61	25
Aberbargoed	26	11	3	12	55	57	25
Caerphilly United	26	10	1	15	62	67	21
Caerphilly W V	26	8	4	14	70	75	20
Aber Stars	26	5	6	15	41	74	16
Llanbradach	26	5	4	17	35	105	14
Tredomen Works	26	2	4	20	41	103	8

Subsidiary Competition

Aberaman	8	7	0	1	38	11	14
Penrhiwceiber	8	4	1	3	15	14	9
Treharris	6	3	1	2	15	14	7
Nantymoel	6	2	0	4	9	15	4
Onllwyn	8	1	0	7	9	32	2

Two matches were not played.

WELSH LEAGUE SOUTH 1933-34

Division 1

Swansea Town II	24	15	4	5	76	39	34
Llanelly	24	11	9	4	41	26	31
Lovells Athletic	24	12	4	8	49	45	28
Newport County II	24	11	4	9	57	53	26
Merthyr Tydfil	24	10	5	9	49	44	25
Barry Town	24	9	7	8	49	55	25
Aberaman	24	10	4	10	55	49	24
Troedyrhiw	24	10	4	10	58	55	24
Penrhiwceiber	24	9	4	11	40	45	22
Cardiff Corinthians	24	9	4	11	33	50	22
Porth United	24	9	2	13	46	50	20
Cardiff City II	24	8	3	13	49	63	19
Ebbw Vale	24	3	4	17	29	56	10

Merthyr Tydfil were relegated.
Other divisional tables have not yet been located.

WELSH LEAGUE SOUTH 1934-35

Division 1

Swansea Town II	24	22	2	0	85	15	46
Barry Town	24	13	7	4	64	36	33
Cardiff City II	24	14	2	8	74	38	30
Newport County II	24	13	3	8	57	42	29
Porth United	24	10	6	8	53	56	26
Lovells Athletic	24	9	6	9	53	50	24
Cardiff Corinthians	24	8	6	10	45	47	22
Troedyrhiw	24	7	6	11	49	67	20
Aberaman	24	8	3	13	54	51	19
Aberdare Town	24	6	5	13	37	49	17
Ebbw Vale	24	5	7	12	42	68	17
Llanelly	24	6	3	15	25	64	15
Penrhiwceiber	24	3	8	13	37	85	14

Ebbw Vale were relegated.
Other divisional tables have not yet been located.

WELSH LEAGUE SOUTH 1935-36

Division 1

Swansea Town II	32	23	6	3	94	32	52
Cardiff City II	32	21	5	6	118	54	47
Newport County II	32	19	6	7	105	63	44
Aberdare Town	32	21	1	10	106	60	43
Treharris Athletic	32	16	9	7	96	64	41
Lovells Athletic	32	15	8	9	102	61	38
Barry Town	32	15	8	9	86	52	38
Caerau Athletic	32	13	10	9	77	88	36
Gwynfi Welfare	32	14	3	15	72	75	31
Caerphilly Town	32	12	6	14	62	66	30
Aberaman	32	13	3	16	82	74	29
Gelli Colliery	32	11	6	15	62	85	28
Cardiff Corinthians	32	9	3	20	46	84	21
Porth United	32	8	5	19	61	104	21
Troedyrhiw	32	7	2	23	55	116	16
Llanelly	32	5	5	22	43	98	15
Penrhiwceiber	32	5	4	23	39	103	14

Gelli Colliery were relegated.
Other divisional tables have not yet been located.

WELSH LEAGUE SOUTH 1936-37

Division 1

Newport County II	32	21	5	6	114	59	47
Aberaman	32	21	3	8	107	59	45
Swansea Town II	32	20	3	9	104	50	43
Cardiff City II	31	18	5	8	96	44	41
Caerau Athletic	32	19	2	11	86	87	40
Barry Town	32	13	12	7	65	35	38
Gwynfi Welfare	32	15	6	11	73	62	36
Lovells Athletic	32	15	6	11	50	45	36
Tredomen Works	32	14	4	14	63	71	32
Troedyrhiw	32	11	8	13	70	78	30
Aberdare Town	31	11	7	13	82	83	29
Treharris Athletic	31	12	4	15	71	82	28
Porth Town	32	12	3	17	64	84	27
Caerphilly Town	32	9	2	21	63	105	20
Llanelly	31	7	6	18	51	95	20
Penrhiwceiber	32	7	4	21	52	104	18
Cardiff Corinthians	32	3	5	24	34	94	11

Tredomen Works, Porth Town and Penrhiwceiber were relegated.

Division 2 – Eastern Section

Abercynon	20	14	3	3	57	35	31
Oakdale United	20	13	4	3	76	32	30
Trethomas	18	12	2	4	52	33	26
Nantymoel	20	10	2	8	47	31	22
Dowlais Welfare	20	9	2	9	45	44	20
Treorchy Boys	20	8	4	8	40	42	20
Caerphilly United	20	7	5	8	38	50	19
Ton Pentre Town	20	4	8	8	43	42	16
Trelewis Welfare	18	4	7	7	27	35	15
Trecynon	19	4	2	13	31	61	10
Bedlinog	19	2	1	16	24	74	5

Not all fixtures were completed.

Division 2 – Western Section

Milford Haven	24	21	1	2	109	34	43
Caerau Villa	24	17	4	3	81	33	38
Haverfordwest	24	13	6	5	86	47	32
Skewen Athletic	24	12	4	8	54	59	28
Glynneath	24	11	2	11	55	47	24
Gilbertsons	24	8	6	10	45	57	22
Elba Welfare	24	10	2	12	51	66	22
Grovesend Welfare	24	8	5	11	65	60	21
Garw Stars	24	7	7	10	55	66	21
Britol Ferry Athletic	24	8	3	13	58	72	19
Aberavon Quins	24	4	9	11	38	64	17
Glyncorrwg	24	5	5	14	37	74	15
Ynystawe	24	3	4	17	29	91	10

WELSH LEAGUE SOUTH 1937-38

Division 1

Lovells Athletic	32	23	4	5	109	31	59
Cardiff City II	32	23	4	5	94	44	50
Swansea Town II	32	20	7	5	84	44	47
Aberaman	32	18	5	9	94	54	41
Barry Town	32	17	7	8	74	59	41
Caerau Athletic	32	17	4	11	82	59	38
Newport County II	32	16	4	12	79	54	36
Gwynfl Welfare	32	13	8	13	73	66	32
Haverfordwest	32	13	6	13	74	78	32
Troedyrhiw	32	13	5	14	63	72	31
Llanelly	32	12	6	14	70	86	30
Aberdare Town	32	11	7	14	65	80	29
Milford United	32	10	7	15	70	67	27
Treharris Athletic	32	6	7	IS	56	83	19
Caerphilly Town	32	6	6	20	30	81	18
Cardiff Corinthians	32	5	5	22	59	131	13
Ebbw Vale	32	4	1	27	31	125	9

Caerphilly Town were relegated.
Other divisional tables have not yet been located.

WELSH LEAGUE SOUTH 1938-39

Division 1

Lovells Athletic	34	27	4	3	116	31	58
Cardiff City II	34	20	7	7	88	51	47
Milford United	34	21	5	8	115	76	47
Aberaman	34	22	3	9	107	75	47
Caerau Athletic	34	20	5	9	99	86	45
Swansea Town II	34	19	4	11	93	50	42
Haverfordwest	34	17	4	13	74	76	38
Gwynfl Welfare	34	16	3	15	58	82	35
Tredomen Works	34	16	2	16	86	68	34
Barry Town	34	14	6	14	75	83	34
Newport County II	34	14	4	16	90	71	32
Nantymoel	34	12	3	17	75	90	29
Aberdare Town	34	11	3	20	71	81	28
Treharris Athletic	34	10	5	19	53	96	25
Ebbw Vale	34	11	3	20	56	83	25
Troedyrhiw	34	10	1	23	67	93	21
Cardiff Corinthians	34	6	4	24	46	114	16

The Welsh League South was suspended between the years of 1939 and 1945 following the onset of war.

WELSH LEAGUE SOUTH 1945-46

Division 1

Lovells Athletic	36	31	3	2	171	43	65
Merthyr Town	36	27	3	6	187	62	57
Milford United	36	23	5	8	113	73	51
Troedyrhlw	36	20	10	6	109	56	50
Aberaman Athletic	36	20	4	12	100	80	44
Cardiff City II	36	19	3	14	99	97	41
Swansea Town II	36	16	6	13	99	90	38
Ebbw Vale	36	17	3	15	116	90	37
Tredomen Works	36	16	4	16	101	104	36
Gwynfl Welfare	36	16	4	16	97	105	36
Barry Town	36	15	5	16	84	91	35
Nantymoel	36	14	7	15	98	125	35
Caerau Athletic	36	15	3	18	90	102	33
Haverfordwest Athletic	36	10	6	20	89	115	26
Llanelly	36	11	3	22	70	99	25
Treharris Athletic	36	7	6	23	74	141	20
Newport County II	36	8	3	25	72	121	19
Cardiff Corinthians	36	8	2	26	60	119	18
Garw Welfare	36	7	4	25	64	187	18

Division 2 – Western Section

Brynna United	28	18	8	2	101	47	44
Mid-Rhondda FC	28	20	3	5	100	34	43
Ton Pentre	28	18	5	5	128	56	41
Briton Ferry Athletic	28	18	5	5	71	31	41
Onllwyn Welfare	28	16	4	8	72	53	36
Blaenrhondda	28	13	7	8	66	50	33
Mardy Athletic	28	11	8	9	56	57	30
Lewistown FC	28	10	6	12	50	56	26
Blaengarw Town	28	10	6	12	50	62	26
Dyffryn & Cynon	28	9	4	15	57	73	22
Caerau Athletic Reserves	28	9	4	15	42	78	22
Guest KB	28	5	4	19	42	87	14
Cwmavon Welfare	28	5	4	19	47	102	14
Nantymoel Corinthians	28	1	4	23	19	117	6

Glyncorrwg also played in Division 2 – Western Section during this season, but their record was omitted from the published table. A complete table has not yet been located.

Division 2 – Eastern Section

Lovells Athletic Reserves	28	21	5	2	119	26	47
Tynte Rovers	28	20	6	2	102	24	46
Bargoed United	28	17	8	3	87	40	42
New Tredegar Town	28	16	7	5	84	35	39
Abercynon Athletic	28	16	6	6	93	53	38
Penrhiwceiber	28	16	6	6	78	43	38
Cilfynydd Welfare	28	16	2	10	83	66	34
Llanbradach	28	13	3	12	93	74	30
Aberbargoed Rangers	28	8	7	14	57	71	23
Ynysybwl Athletic	28	10	2	16	69	75	22
Aberaman Athletic Reserves	28	9	1	18	55	86	19
Maesycwmmer	28	7	3	18	38	94	17
Trethomas	28	3	4	21	30	136	10
Ystrad Mynach	28	3	3	22	29	93	9
Aberbargoed Town	28	3	3	22	26	104	9

WELSH LEAGUE SOUTH 1946-47
Division 1

Lovells Athletic	38	26	8	4	135	36	60
Newport County II	38	22	6	10	126	78	50
Troedyrhiw	38	21	7	10	101	71	49
Cardiff City II	38	22	5	11	98	73	49
Gwynfi Welfare	38	20	5	13	77	67	45
Merthyr Town	38	20	4	14	90	67	44
Barry Town	38	19	5	14	79	61	43
Llanelly	38	17	8	13	92	87	42
Milford United	38	17	7	14	101	79	41
Ton Pentre	38	17	6	15	89	93	40
Caerau Athletic	38	16	5	17	104	92	37
Tredomen Works	38	16	5	17	71	98	37
Ebbw Vale	38	13	10	15	81	91	36
Swansea Town II	38	15	6	17	97	116	36
Treharris Athletic	38	13	7	18	90	101	33
Aberaman Athletic	38	11	10	17	87	116	32
Haverfordwest Athletic	38	9	9	20	75	104	27
Cardiff Corinthians	38	10	5	23	66	104	25
Nantymoel	38	8	4	26	67	127	20
Garw Welfare	38	4	6	28	55	132	14

Division 2 – Eastern Section

Penrhiwceiber	34	33	1	0	126	25	67
Tynte Rovers	34	21	4	9	93	53	46
Lovells Athletic Reserves	33	22	1	10	102	49	45
Aberbargoed Town	33	21	2	10	94	56	44
Bargoed United	34	20	4	10	103	76	44
Cwmffrwdoer	34	18	3	13	68	71	39
Abercynon Athletic	34	17	4	13	83	67	38
New Tredegar Town	34	17	3	14	101	71	37
Senghenydd Town	32	16	2	14	79	71	34
Tredegar Pals	34	15	3	16	81	97	33
Ystrad Mynach	34	14	4	16	66	68	32
Abergavenny	34	14	4	16	67	73	32
Blaina WS	34	10	6	18	67	83	26
Trethomas	34	11	4	19	77	101	26
Nelson Welfare	34	9	6	19	65	78	24
Llanbradach	34	8	0	26	35	94	16
Ynysybwl Athletic	34	8	0	26	51	102	14
Clifynydd Welfare	30	3	1	26	32	127	7

Not all fixtures were completed.
Ynysybwl Athletic had 2 points deducted.

Division 2 – Western Section

Briton Ferry Athletic	34	26	5	3	145	43	57
Pembroke Borough	34	26	4	4	143	52	56
Blaenrhondda	34	23	8	4	117	52	52
Caerau Athletic Reserves	34	19	5	10	89	56	43
Guest KB	33	15	8	10	96	65	38
Blaengarw Town	33	16	6	11	69	74	38
Seven Sisters FC	33	16	5	12	88	92	37
Mardy Athletic	34	14	7	13	75	75	35
Onllwyn Welfare	33	14	5	14	71	79	33
Cwmavon Welfare	34	12	7	15	69	67	31
Mid-Rhondda FC	34	12	5	17	62	80	29
Glyncorrwg	32	10	7	15	53	62	27
Lewistown FC	34	11	4	19	60	79	26
Ton Boys Club	33	9	6	18	64	96	24
Brynna United	33	9	5	19	57	93	23
Dyffryn & Cynon	33	7	7	19	55	109	21
Llanharan	26	5	5	16	42	66	15
Garw Valley	33	6	2	25	37	109	14

Not all fixtures were completed.

WELSH LEAGUE SOUTH 1947-48
Division 1

Lovells Athletic	38	25	8	5	116	35	58
Troedyrhiw	38	26	6	6	107	51	58
Newport County II	38	23	3	12	115	65	49
Caerau Athletic	38	20	6	12	94	77	46
Ton Pentre	38	20	6	12	110	100	46
Merthyr Town	38	21	3	14	88	50	45
Llanelly	38	21	3	14	101	69	45
Treharris Athletic	38	19	5	14	101	90	43
Ebbw Vale	38	18	6	14	72	69	41
Milford United	38	17	7	14	104	90	41
Haverfordwest Athletic	38	16	5	17	64	66	37
Barry Town	38	15	7	16	74	82	37
Gwynfi Welfare	38	14	7	17	69	73	35
Swansea Town II	38	14	3	21	69	89	31
Penrhiwceiber	38	13	5	20	71	99	31
Briton Ferry Athletic	38	13	4	21	67	91	30
Cardiff City II	38	12	6	20	73	101	30
Aberaman Athletic	38	9	6	23	63	104	24
Cardiff Corinthians	38	5	6	27	40	114	16
Tredomen Works	38	6	4	28	43	131	16

Division 2 – Eastern Section

Bargoed United	34	27	3	4	161	60	57
Abercynon Athletic	34	24	4	6	159	53	52
New Tredegar Town	34	23	4	7	106	56	50
Cwmbran Town	34	23	3	8	119	78	49
Pontllanfraith	34	20	6	8	92	68	46
Aberbargoed Town	34	20	5	9	103	60	45
Senghenydd Town	34	17	5	12	90	74	39
Aberdare Town	34	16	6	12	75	69	38
Nelson Welfare	34	15	5	14	67	63	35
Cwm Welfare	34	15	4	15	77	70	34
Abergavenny	34	11	8	15	79	85	30
Cwmffrwdoer	34	13	3	18	65	83	29
Tredegar Pals	34	11	7	16	78	109	29
Tynte Rovers	34	8	7	19	58	95	23
Ystrad Mynach	34	7	6	21	53	86	20
Blaina WS	34	7	4	23	70	116	18
Llanbradach	34	3	7	24	44	109	13
Trethomas	34	2	1	31	45	157	5

Division 2 – Western Section

Pembroke Borough	32	26	3	3	146	34	55
Blaenrhondda	32	26	2	4	101	37	54
Nantymoel	32	23	4	5	122	47	50
Ton Boys Club	32	21	5	6	87	48	47
Mardy Athletic	32	17	4	11	80	56	38
Garw Welfare	32	17	4	11	72	57	38
Port Talbot Athletic	32	15	4	13	74	66	34
Cwmavon Welfare	32	14	3	15	78	86	31
Onllwyn Welfare	32	12	4	16	50	82	28
Seven Sisters FC	32	11	5	16	70	105	27
Glyncorrwg	32	11	2	19	57	83	26
Bridgend Town	32	11	4	17	74	91	26
Lewistown FC	32	12	1	19	62	79	25
Mid-Rhondda FC	32	9	7	16	67	93	25
Brynna United	32	9	2	21	44	113	20
Caerau Athletic Reserves	32	8	2	22	59	90	18
Morris Motors FC	32	5	2	25	55	115	12

WELSH LEAGUE SOUTH 1948-49

Division 1

Merthyr Town	36	26	5	5	108	37	57
Milford United	36	20	5	11	90	66	45
Haverfordwest Athletic	36	20	4	12	97	69	44
Llanelly	36	18	6	12	69	54	42
Newport County II	36	17	6	13	82	69	40
Cardiff City II	36	15	8	13	87	67	38
Treharris Athletic	36	16	6	14	89	76	38
Lovells Athletic	36	15	7	14	78	59	37
Bargoed United	36	13	11	13	82	76	37
Pembroke Borough	36	13	8	15	72	82	34
Swansea Town II	36	16	2	18	68	80	34
Troedyrhiw	36	12	9	15	73	74	33
Penrhiwceiber	36	14	5	17	67	79	33
Ton Pentre	36	12	7	17	65	77	31
Gwynfi Welfare	36	12	7	17	55	84	31
Caerau Athletic	36	13	4	19	66	87	30
Aberaman Athletic	36	10	9	17	61	105	29
Barry Town	36	11	4	21	69	101	26
Briton Ferry Athletic	36	10	5	21	56	82	25

Division 2 – Eastern Section

Senghenydd Town	38	26	5	7	125	48	57
Tredomen Works	38	26	3	9	106	53	55
Abergavenny	38	22	9	7	136	76	53
Nelson Welfare	38	23	7	8	104	69	53
Aberdare Town	38	22	6	10	101	59	50
New Tredegar Town	38	20	6	12	101	64	46
Blaina WS	38	18	10	10	81	81	46
RTB Panteg	38	19	7	12	117	75	45
Aberbargoed Town	38	18	9	11	93	82	45
Abercynon Athletic	38	17	7	14	104	84	41
Cwmbran Town	38	18	5	15	79	69	41
Pontllanfraith	38	17	7	14	100	87	39
Rhymney	38	12	7	19	87	79	31
Ystrad Mynach	38	13	4	21	82	108	30
Cwm Welfare	38	11	5	22	96	121	27
Tredegar Pals	38	11	5	22	74	116	27
Cwmffrwdoer	38	9	7	22	59	107	25
Tynte Rovers	38	9	7	22	81	124	25
Abertillery	38	8	0	30	63	144	16
Llanbradach	38	2	2	34	31	166	6

Division 2 – Western Section

Cwm-parc	34	24	7	3	128	48	55
Llanelly Reserves	34	23	3	8	127	67	49
Ton Boys Club	34	19	6	9	108	85	44
Cardiff Corinthians	34	20	6	12	98	62	42
Brynna United	34	18	6	10	121	70	42
Pontardawe	34	15	9	10	89	67	39
Port Talbot Athletic	34	15	8	11	70	65	38
Blaenrhondda	34	15	5	14	77	72	35
Mardy Welfare	34	14	7	13	90	89	35
Seven Sisters FC	34	15	4	15	82	82	34
Grovesend Welfare	34	15	5	15	81	89	33
Garw Welfare	34	15	3	16	62	80	33
Nantymoel	34	12	6	16	86	97	30
Cwmavon Welfare	34	12	6	16	75	93	30
Caerau Athletic Reserves	34	9	6	19	85	108	24
Onllwyn Welfare	34	9	5	20	65	106	23
Glyncorrwg	34	6	4	24	49	136	16
Mid-Rhondda FC	34	3	3	28	41	128	9

WELSH LEAGUE SOUTH 1949-50

Division 1

Merthyr Tydvil AFC	38	28	5	5	113	49	61
Treharris Athletic	38	23	8	7	108	66	53
Pembroke Borough	38	23	9	6	87	64	52
Caerau Athletic	38	24	12	2	118	75	50
Llanelly AFC	38	22	11	5	114	45	49
Ebbw Vale AFC	38	17	10	11	89	73	45
Haverfordwest AFC	38	16	12	10	82	70	42
Milford United	38	16	14	8	85	65	40
Swansea Town Reserves	38	17	15	6	77	71	40
Newport County Reserves	38	15	15	8	77	67	38
Lovells Athletic	38	16	16	6	73	69	38
Senghenydd Town	38	14	15	9	60	73	37
Ton Pentre AFC	38	14	17	7	77	80	35
Bargoed United	38	13	16	9	74	87	35
Gwynfi Welfare	38	13	18	7	55	78	33
Troedyrhiw	38	11	19	8	64	95	30
Cardiff City Reserves	38	12	22	4	63	74	28
Penrhiwceiber	38	8	25	5	42	84	21
Cwmparc	38	7	24	7	55	136	21
Aberaman Athletic	38	4	30	4	46	134	12

Division 2 – Eastern Section

Nelson Welfare	36	24	3	9	138	54	57
Girlings FC (Cwmbran)	36	23	7	6	128	73	52
Pontllanfraith	36	22	7	7	128	57	51
Abergavenny Thursdays	36	22	7	7	112	67	51
Rhymney Town	36	22	8	6	135	67	50
Abercynon Athletic	36	21	11	4	99	70	46
Ystrad Mynach	36	18	10	8	84	61	44
Tredegar Town	36	17	10	9	121	68	43
Cardiff Corinthians	36	18	12	6	83	50	42
Blaina FC	36	18	12	6	75	59	42
RTB Panteg	36	15	11	10	80	63	40
Brecon Corinthians	36	13	17	6	100	93	32
Tredomen Works	36	13	18	5	76	96	31
Cwm Welfare	36	10	19	7	79	124	27
Tynte Rovers	36	7	24	5	57	128	19
Aberbargoed	36	5	24	7	44	153	17
Cwmffrwdoer	36	4	26	6	40	122	14
New Tredegar Town	36	4	27	5	54	127	13
Llanbradach AFC	36	4	27	5	52	136	13

Division 2 – Western Section

Llanelly AFC	38	31	4	3	184	64	65
Ton Boys Club	38	27	7	4	145	68	58
Barry Town	38	21	9	8	88	55	50
Neath Athletic	38	21	10	7	128	82	49
Nantymoel Athletic	38	20	9	8	84	55	48
Godrergraig	38	19	11	8	106	69	46
Pontardawe Athletic	38	16	15	7	101	81	39
Brynna United	38	16	16	6	97	93	38
Grovesend Welfare	38	13	14	11	73	79	37
Seven Sisters	38	15	16	7	90	95	37
Bettws FC (Ammanford)	38	13	14	11	69	86	37
Blaenrhondda	38	16	17	5	89	102	37
Port Talbot Athletic	38	14	17	7	79	109	35
Briton Ferry Athletic	38	14	18	6	83	73	34
Garw Welfare	38	11	19	8	74	108	30
Glyncorrwg	38	11	20	7	77	110	29
Mardy Athletic	38	11	23	4	82	112	26
Cwmavon AFC	38	7	19	12	74	121	26
Lewistown AFC	38	9	22	7	61	131	25
Mid-Rhondda	38	7	28	3	53	139	17

WELSH LEAGUE SOUTH 1950-51

Division 1

Team	P	W	D	L	F	A	Pts
Swansea Town Reserves	38	25	6	7	103	53	56
Merthyr Tydfil AFC	38	24	4	10	140	73	52
Newport County Reserves	38	21	7	10	111	61	49
Caerau Athletic	38	21	7	10	120	90	49
Pembroke Borough	38	19	7	12	104	76	45
Milford United	38	20	5	13	103	78	45
Ebbw Vale AFC	38	20	4	14	107	80	44
Cardiff City Reserves	38	20	4	14	85	64	44
Haverfordwest AFC	38	18	7	13	86	65	43
Lovells Athletic	38	18	4	16	77	65	40
Treharris Athletic	38	14	10	14	88	89	38
Troedyrhiw	38	16	5	17	68	82	37
Senghenydd Town	38	13	9	16	70	68	35
Llanelly AFC	38	14	5	19	76	102	33
Ton Pentre AFC	38	13	6	19	63	79	32
Nelson Welfare	38	12	7	19	64	104	31
Bargoed United	38	11	3	24	67	99	25
Gwynfi Welfare	38	11	3	24	75	127	25
Penrhiwceiber	38	11	1	26	54	108	23
Ton Corinthians	38	6	4	28	48	144	16

Division 2 – Western Section

Team	P	W	D	L	F	A	Pts
Cwmparc	38	30	2	6	129	55	62
Seven Sisters	38	29	0	9	153	54	58
Port Talbot Athletic	38	22	6	10	96	59	50
Briton Ferry Athletic	38	18	11	9	83	59	47
Garthmor	38	20	7	11	77	61	47
Godrergraig	38	19	6	13	111	90	44
Bettws FC (Ammanford)	38	16	9	13	76	65	41
Nantymoel Athletic	38	18	5	15	93	81	41
Barry Town	38	16	7	15	91	68	39
N.O.R. (Neath)	38	18	3	17	94	86	39
Mardy Athletic	38	15	7	16	83	107	37
Clydach United	38	16	4	18	83	93	36
Pontardawe Athletic	38	15	5	18	90	90	35
Glyncorrwg	38	15	1	22	94	97	31
Blaenrhondda	38	9	11	18	55	87	29
Grovesend Welfare	38	12	4	22	65	103	28
Cwmavon AFC	38	11	4	23	64	99	26
Lewistown AFC	38	10	6	22	69	114	26
Garw Welfare	38	8	10	20	60	102	26
Brynna United	38	6	6	26	60	144	18

Division 2 – Eastern Section

Team	P	W	D	L	F	A	Pts
Abergavenny Thursdays	34	30	3	1	148	32	63
Tredomen Works	34	26	1	7	141	63	53
Tredegar Town	34	21	6	7	118	56	48
Pontllanfraith	34	20	7	7	130	62	47
Cardiff Corinthians	34	19	7	8	85	44	45
Ystrad Mynach	34	18	7	9	86	61	43
Rhymney Town	34	13	12	9	94	60	38
Girlings FC (Cwmbran)	34	15	8	11	101	69	38
Brecon Corinthians	34	15	7	12	88	87	37
Blaina FC	34	16	3	15	85	76	35
Aberaman Athletic	34	12	7	15	80	92	31
RTB Panteg	34	10	7	17	63	80	27
Tynte Rovers	34	10	4	20	65	101	24
Abercynon Athletic	34	8	7	19	67	101	23
New Tredegar Town	34	4	9	21	40	95	17
Aberdare	34	8	1	25	45	136	17
Cwm Welfare	34	5	4	25	74	164	14
Llanbradach AFC	34	5	2	27	50	176	12

WELSH LEAGUE SOUTH 1951-52

Division 1

Team	P	W	D	L	F	A	Pts
Merthyr Tydfil AFC	36	26	4	6	118	63	56
Newport County Reserves	36	22	7	7	99	81	51
Caerau Athletic	36	21	4	11	114	86	46
Cardiff City Reserves	36	18	8	10	72	55	44
Lovells Athletic	36	17	6	13	86	61	40
Pembroke Borough	36	18	4	14	117	83	40
Ebbw Vale AFC	36	15	8	13	94	76	38
Ton Pentre AFC	36	16	6	14	81	74	38
Abergavenny Thursdays	36	15	8	13	90	83	38
Bargoed United	36	15	6	15	72	80	36
Milford United	36	16	3	17	87	88	35
Cwmparc	36	13	7	15	66	71	35
Swansea Town Reserves	36	12	8	16	72	75	32
Haverfordwest AFC	36	13	6	17	85	98	32
Treharris Athletic	36	10	9	17	77	92	29
Senghenydd Town	36	7	11	18	63	78	25
Llanelly AFC	36	11	3	22	68	133	25
Troedyrhiw	36	10	4	22	75	106	24
Nelson Welfare	36	7	6	23	57	97	20

Division 2 – Eastern Section

Team	P	W	D	L	F	A	Pts
Barry Town	36	26	7	3	150	53	59
Rhymney Town	36	27	2	5	143	49	58
Cardiff Corinthians	36	24	6	6	114	42	54
Aberaman Athletic	36	23	4	9	113	57	50
Blaina FC	36	22	5	9	117	69	49
Girlings FC (Cwmbran)	36	JO	7	10	108	80	45
Pontllanfraith	36	20	5	11	108	82	45
RTB Panteg	36	14	11	11	93	78	39
Risca United	36	14	9	13	76	76	37
Tredegar Town	36	14	8	14	102	88	36
Penrhiwceiber	36	15	6	15	77	76	36
Abercynon Athletic	36	12	6	18	74	95	30
Ystrad Mynach	36	10	7	19	74	107	27
Tredomen Works	36	9	8	19	86	111	26
Brecon Corinthians	36	11	4	21	78	112	26
Porth Welfare	36	9	7	20	86	115	25
Aberdare	36	5	10	21	62	115	20
Tynte Rovers	36	7	6	23	67	130	20
Llanbradach AFC	36	1	0	35	41	226	2

Division 2 – Western Section

Team	P	W	D	L	F	A	Pts
Aberystwyth Town	32	24	2	6	126	57	50
Morriston Town	32	20	5	7	85	53	45
Briton Ferry Athletic	32	20	5	7	89	68	45
Seven Sisters	32	20	4	8	112	73	44
Clydach United	32	16	6	10	87	68	38
Port Talbot Athletic	32	17	3	12	79	63	37
Neath Athletic	32	14	4	14	59	61	32
Godrergraig	32	14	4	14	64	79	32
Blaenrhondda	32	14	3	15	71	66	31
Grovesend Welfare	32	12	6	14	74	78	30
Pontardawe Athletic	32	12	5	15	78	85	29
N.O.R. (Neath)	32	13	2	17	82	72	28
Bettws FC (Ammanford)	32	10	5	17	72	105	25
Garw Welfare	32	7	10	15	64	77	24
Lewistown AFC	32	9	6	17	62	79	24
Nantymoel Athletic	32	5	8	19	60	113	18
Cwmavon AFC	32	3	6	23	52	110	12

WELSH LEAGUE SOUTH 1952-53

Division 1

Ebbw Vale & Cwm	38	30	5	3	126	36	65
Pembroke Borough	38	21	4	13	93	91	46
Swansea Town II	38	18	9	11	110	84	45
Treharris Athletic	38	20	5	13	95	77	45
Milford United	38	17	9	12	89	67	43
Cwmparc	38	19	3	16	93	84	41
Llanelly	38	18	4	16	99	75	40
TonPentre	38	18	3	17	80	84	39
Aberystwyth Town	38	16	6	16	94	88	38
Lovells Athletic	38	16	5	17	82	75	37
Cardiff City II	38	16	5	17	79	86	37
Newport County II	38	15	5	18	101	77	35
Abergavenny	38	14	7	17	88	102	35
Caerau Athletic	38	15	4	19	75	102	34
Barry Town	38	14	4	20	79	91	32
Merthyr Tydfil	38	12	7	19	78	101	31
Haverfordwest FC	38	14	3	21	85	119	31
Gwynfi Welfare	38	12	7	19	82	118	31
Senghenydd Town	38	11	8	19	72	97	30
Bargoed United	38	10	5	23	69	111	25

Division 2 – Eastern Section

Pontllanfraith	36	30	4	2	157	43	64
Nelson	36	29	4	3	158	55	62
Troedyrhiw	36	24	5	7	108	65	53
Tynte Rovers	36	21	9	6	124	77	51
Tredegar Town	36	20	6	10	120	74	46
Rhymney Town	36	19	6	11	125	79	44
RTB Panteg	36	18	7	11	110	93	43
Blaina	36	18	5	13	98	62	41
Risca United	36	17	5	14	94	83	39
Cardiff Corinthians	36	18	2	16	99	69	38
Ystrad Mynach	36	13	5	18	73	82	31
Abercynon	36	13	4	19	81	110	30
Aberaman	36	12	5	19	88	113	29
Brecon Cornthians	36	11	7	18	70	97	29
Girlings FC Cwmbran	36	11	4	21	77	125	26
Tredomen	36	7	2	27	72	130	16
Porth Welfare	36	6	3	27	65	133	15
Llanbradach	36	5	4	27	49	167	14
Penrhiwceiber	36	5	3	28	43	138	13

Division 2 – Western Section

Tonyrefail	32	21	7	4	152	61	49
Atlas Sports Swansea	32	20	6	6	107	44	46
Morriston Town	32	19	6	7	102	61	44
Garw Welfare	32	21	2	9	115	78	44
Clydach United	32	19	4	9	101	64	42
Bettws Ammanford	32	15	6	11	90	78	36
Godrergraig	32	17	2	13	76	66	36
Blaenrhondda	32	16	3	13	96	89	35
Grovesend Welfare	32	14	4	14	68	63	32
Lewistown	32	13	6	13	99	90	32
Neath Athletic	32	11	6	15	72	X	28
Seven Sisters	32	12	3	17	68	X	27
Cwmavon	32	9	4	19	62	97	22
Briton Ferry Athletic	32	7	5	20	53	94	19
Nantymoel Athletic	32	6	6	20	47	113	18
Pontardawe	32	7	3	22	47	97	17
NOR Neath	32	6	5	21	57	154	17

WELSH LEAGUE SOUTH 1953-54

Division 1

Pembroke Borough	38	25	3	10	117	90	53
Cardiff City	38	20	5	13	86	65	45
Aberystwyth Town	38	18	9	11	104	87	45
Treharris Athletic	38	19	7	12	105	88	45
Lovells Athletic	38	16	11	11	97	71	43
Milford United	38	15	12	11	68	45	42
Ebbw Vale & Cwm	38	16	10	12	93	77	42
Swansea Town	38	17	6	15	94	85	41
Tonyrefail Welfare	38	17	6	15	90	97	40
Barry Town	38	17	5	16	71	95	39
Llanelly	38	16	5	17	94	89	37
Abergavenny	38	16	3	19	94	93	35
Caerau Athletic	38	14	6	18	100	105	34
Newport County	38	15	3	20	87	82	33
Merthyr Tydfil	38	13	7	18	91	98	33
Pontllanfraith	38	15	3	20	98	110	33
Ton Pentre	38	12	8	18	76	93	32
Cwmparc	38	13	5	20	82	95	31
Haverfordwest Athletic	38	11	9	18	86	121	32
Gwynfi Welfare	38	10	7	21	68	115	27

Division 2 – Eastern Section

Nelson	38	31	5	2	164	50	67
Troedyrhiw	38	30	3	5	137	51	63
Cardiff Cornea	38	20	11	7	132	70	51
Brecon Corinthians	38	20	8	10	117	74	48
Tredegar Town	38	20	6	12	111	83	46
Girlings Cwmbran	38	18	9	11	108	87	45
New Tredegar	38	18	7	13	83	78	43
Tynte Rovers	38	18	5	15	93	80	41
Tredomen Works	38	18	5	15	98	92	41
Abercynon Athletic	38	17	6	15	81	88	41
RTB Panteg	38	18	3	17	117	97	39
Rhymney Town	38	15	9	14	119	105	39
Risca United	38	14	8	16	95	111	36
Bargoed United	38	12	8	18	79	99	32
Senghennydd Town	38	11	7	20	70	107	29
Aberaman Athletic	38	11	5	22	91	113	27
Llanbradach	38	7	5	26	69	163	20
Blaina	38	7	5	26	86	127	19
Ystrad Mynach	38	7	4	27	72	152	18
Penrhiwceiber	38	5	6	27	51	143	16

Division 2 – Western Section

Atlas Sports (Swansea)	36	27	6	3	112	48	60
Port Talbot Athletic	36	24	7	5	111	60	55
Blaenrbondda AFC	36	23	4	9	131	74	50
Morriston Town	36	21	7	8	119	66	49
Clydach United	36	20	7	9	98	59	47
Betws (Amananford)	36	18	5	13	89	73	41
Nantymoel Athletic	36	16	6	14	106	88	38
Grovesend Welfare	36	16	5	15	74	77	37
Garw Welfare	36	12	9	15	67	87	33
Briton Ferry Athletic	36	14	4	18	70	X	32
Lewistown	36	12	7	17	74	X	31
Garw Athletic	36	14	2	20	75	83	30
Seven Sisters	36	11	6	19	64	110	28
Godrergraig	36	11	4	21	61	84	26
Neath Athletic	36	11	4	21	76	109	26
Porth Welfare	36	11	4	21	75	114	26
Pontardawe Athletic	36	9	7	20	75	97	26
Cwmavon	36	9	7	20	65	99	25
NOR Neath	36	9	7	20	68	104	25

The goals against figures are not recorded for Briton Ferry Athletic and Lewistown.

WELSH LEAGUE SOUTH 1954-55

Division 1

Team	P	W	D	L	F	A	Pts
Newport County Reserves	38	23	7	8	98	52	53
Abergavenny Thursdays	38	24	1	13	105	59	49
Cardiff City Reserves	38	20	9	9	95	62	49
Aberystwyth Town	38	22	5	11	101	81	49
Pembroke Borough	38	23	1	14	117	84	47
Treharris Athletic	38	20	4	14	93	77	44
Lovells Athletic	38	17	7	14	90	70	41
Pontllanfraith	38	17	6	15	91	86	40
Ebbw Vale AFC	38	17	5	16	82	74	39
Barry Town	38	16	6	16	88	85	38
Swansea Town Reserves	38	16	6	16	86	82	38
Merthyr Tydfil AFC	38	18	1	19	89	80	37
Fforestfach	38	16	4	18	88	86	36
Ton Pentre AFC	38	15	4	19	88	92	34
Milford United	38	15	4	19	81	95	34
Caerau Athletic	38	14	6	18	99	122	34
Llanelly AFC	38	11	9	18	76	84	31
Tonyrefail Welfare	38	12	4	22	91	150	28
Cwmparc	38	9	5	24	68	121	23
Nelson Welfare	38	7	2	29	48	132	16

Division 2 – Eastern Section

Team	P	W	D	L	F	A	Pts
Brecon Corinthians	36	31	0	5	196	59	62
Troedyrhiw	36	31	0	5	143	47	62
Rhymney Town	36	26	4	6	124	59	56
Tredomen Works	36	23	6	7	122	73	52
Aberaman Athletic	36	20	5	11	100	69	45
Cardiff Corinthians	36	17	9	10	111	79	43
Abercynon Athletic	30	19	3	14	121	93	41
Chepstow Town	36	16	7	13	99	82	39
Risca United	36	16	7	13	82	89	39
RTB Panteg	36	15	5	16	101	88	35
Senghenydd Town	36	14	7	15	85	93	35
Tredegar Town	36	13	3	20	94	115	29
New Tredegar Town	36	10	9	17	78	114	29
Tynte Rovers	36	11	4	21	64	103	26
Girlings FC (Cwmbran)	36	11	3	22	65	104	25
Porth Welfare	36	9	4	23	86	140	22
Llanbradach AFC	36	7	5	24	64	138	19
Bargoed United	36	7	2	27	59	144	16
Blaina FC	36	2	5	29	38	143	9

Division 2 – Western Section

Team	P	W	D	L	F	A	Pts
Gwynfi Welfare	38	33	2	3	197	38	68
Haverfordwest AFC	38	33	2	3	163	36	68
Carmarthen Town	38	30	5	3	144	42	65
Port Talbot Athletic	38	30	3	5	133	67	63
Nantymoel Athletic	38	24	3	11	130	100	51
Bettws FC (Ammanford)	38	17	4	17	95	99	38
Lewistown AFC	38	18	0	20	82	95	36
Seven Sisters	38	15	4	19	110	124	34
Garw Athletic	38	14	6	18	88	101	34
Grovesend Welfare	38	15	4	19	75	88	34
Blaenrhondda	38	14	5	19	77	97	33
Morriston Town	38	12	7	19	72	99	31
Clydach United	38	13	4	21	86	124	30
Godrergraig	38	12	6	20	66	122	30
Neath Athletic	38	12	3	23	97	128	27
Briton Ferry Athletic	38	10	7	21	64	97	27
N.O.R. (Neath)	38	11	4	23	64	100	26
Pontardawe Athletic	38	10	5	23	54	122	25
Glyncorrwg	38	7	7	24	69	118	21
Garw Welfare	38	7	5	26	70	139	19

WELSH LEAGUE SOUTH 1955-56

Division 1

Team	P	W	D	L	F	A	Pts
Pembroke Borough	38	25	6	7	124	56	56
Aberystwyth Town	38	24	7	7	101	58	55
Abergavenny Thursdays	38	23	5	10	107	50	51
Pontllanfraith	38	24	3	11	113	88	51
Newport County Reserves	38	21	8	9	108	61	50
Ebbw Vale AFC	38	19	10	9	106	75	48
Treharris Athletic	38	22	2	14	113	81	46
Cardiff City Reserves	38	16	9	13	117	77	41
Milford United	38	17	5	16	106	94	39
Swansea Town Reserves	38	16	5	17	89	88	37
Ton Pentre AFC	38	16	5	17	112	112	37
Lovells Athletic	38	14	8	16	84	97	36
Gwynfi Welfare	38	13	9	16	84	88	35
Brecon Corinthians	38	14	7	17	94	102	35
Caerau Athletic	38	13	7	18	81	108	33
Barry Town	38	12	6	20	80	106	30
Merthyr Tydfil AFC	38	10	9	19	83	115	29
Llanelly AFC	38	8	7	23	67	99	23
Fforestfach	38	8	6	24	65	133	22
Tonyrefail Welfare	38	2	2	34	42	188	6

Division 2 – Eastern Section

Team	P	W	D	L	F	A	Pts
Cwmparc	34	26	6	2	164	54	58
Tredomen Works	34	23	4	7	105	74	50
Senghenydd Town	34	20	5	9	102	63	45
Nelson Welfare	34	16	10	8	112	74	42
Troedyrhiw	34	15	10	9	75	59	40
Cardiff Corinthians	34	14	9	11	100	72	37
Abercynon Athletic	34	15	7	12	105	79	37
Rhymney Town	34	15	6	13	96	95	36
Porth Welfare	34	15	6	13	86	86	36
Aberaman Athletic	34	15	6	13	86	87	36
Blaenrhondda	34	13	9	12	79	90	35
Risca United	34	13	7	14	76	78	33
RTB Panteg	34	11	7	16	77	93	29
New Tredegar Town	34	10	6	18	77	121	26
Chepstow Town	34	10	5	19	76	107	25
Girlings FC (Cwmbran)	34	6	8	20	52	100	20
Llanbradach AFC	34	5	5	24	67	136	15
Blaina FC	34	3	6	25	50	117	12

Division 2 – Western Section

Team	P	W	D	L	F	A	Pts
Haverfordwest AFC	32	27	3	2	146	25	57
Carmarthen Town	32	26	4	2	122	35	56
Clydach United	32	19	5	8	83	56	43
Lewistown AFC	32	17	6	9	88	61	40
N.O.R. (Neath)	32	18	4	10	79	56	40
Port Talbot Athletic	32	17	3	12	93	67	37
Seven Sisters	32	13	6	13	80	59	32
Briton Ferry Athletic	32	11	8	13	69	71	30
Neath Athletic	32	14	2	16	71	82	30
Glyncorrwg	32	13	3	16	71	74	29
Garw Athletic	32	13	3	16	68	87	29
Nantymoel Athletic	32	13	3	16	68	111	29
Grovesend Welfare	32	10	3	19	53	78	23
Pontardawe Athletic	32	8	5	19	53	97	21
Bettws FC (Ammanford)	32	5	7	20	61	106	17
Morriston Town	32	7	3	22	48	114	17
Garw Welfare	32	4	6	22	32	106	14

WELSH LEAGUE SOUTH 1956-57

Division 1

	P	W	D	L	F	A	Pts
Haverfordwest County	38	22	9	7	97	51	53
Pembroke Borough	38	22	5	11	123	74	49
Abergavenny Thursdays	38	20	9	9	102	73	49
Ebbw Vale AFC	38	19	7	12	110	89	45
Newport County Reserves	38	20	5	13	116	94	45
Milford United	38	18	6	14	97	87	42
Ton Pentre AFC	38	18	6	14	105	97	42
Caerau Athletic	38	17	8	13	93	103	42
Treharris Athletic	38	17	5	16	102	90	39
Aberystwyth Town	38	15	8	15	81	84	38
Pontllanfraith	38	15	6	17	88	92	36
Swansea Town Reserves	38	13	8	17	100	85	34
Lovells Athletic	38	13	8	17	75	87	34
Cardiff City Reserves	38	13	7	18	81	93	33
Gwynfi Welfare	38	14	5	19	82	116	33
Brecon Corinthians	38	12	7	19	92	107	31
Cwmparc	38	9	13	16	80	108	31
Merthyr Tydfil AFC	38	10	10	18	83	111	30
Barry Town	38	12	4	22	69	95	28
Llanelly AFC	38	10	6	22	65	105	26

Division 2 – Eastern Section

	P	W	D	L	F	A	Pts
Cardiff Corinthians	34	28	2	4	138	42	58
Ferndale Athletic	34	26	3	5	142	66	55
Rhymney Town	34	19	8	7	120	69	46
Tredomen Works	34	20	5	9	121	80	45
Risca United	34	17	10	7	82	51	44
Nelson Welfare	34	18	5	11	111	81	41
Tonyrefail Welfare	34	18	4	12	91	79	40
Abercynon Athletic	34	14	9	11	111	92	37
Troedyrhiw	34	16	4	14	84	74	36
Girlings FC (Cwmbran)	34	15	5	14	74	88	35
Senghenydd Town	34	16	2	16	87	92	34
Aberaman Athletic	34	11	8	15	69	90	30
Chepstow Town	34	12	4	18	81	107	28
RTB Panteg	34	10	5	19	77	95	25
Porth Welfare	34	7	8	19	69	101	22
Blaina FC	34	6	5	23	59	107	17
Llanbradach AFC	34	4	2	28	56	152	10
New Tredegar Town	34	1	7	26	57	163	9

Division 2 – Western Section

	P	W	D	L	F	A	Pts
Port Talbot Athletic	32	24	6	2	120	44	54
Carmarthen Town	32	23	5	4	113	41	51
Fforestfach	32	22	3	7	119	59	47
Clydach United	22	18	5	9	95	59	41
Lewistown AFC	32	19	0	13	90	79	38
BP Llandarcy	32	15	7	10	82	62	37
Garw Athletic	32	17	3	12	71	58	37
Blaenrhondda	32	15	6	11	75	73	36
Bettws FC (Ammanford)	32	14	6	12	72	54	34
Nantymoel Athletic	32	14	5	13	76	82	33
Neath Athletic	32	10	3	19	69	87	23
Grovesend Welfare	32	10	2	20	62	94	22
Pontardawe Athletic	32	9	3	20	55	88	21
Seven Sisters	32	9	1	22	71	101	19
Glyncorrwg	32	8	2	22	52	122	18
Briton Ferry Athletic	32	7	3	22	61	96	17
Morriston Town	32	7	2	23	43	127	16

WELSH LEAGUE SOUTH 1957-58

Division 1

	P	W	D	L	F	A	Pts
Ton Pentre AFC	38	22	6	10	110	80	50
Newport County Reserves	38	19	11	8	110	56	49
Cardiff City Reserves	38	21	7	10	119	73	49
Brecon Corinthians	38	23	3	12	104	75	49
Pontllanfraith	38	21	4	13	107	90	46
Swansea Town Reserves	38	19	5	14	107	86	43
Pembroke Borough	38	17	7	14	89	63	41
Haverfordwest County	38	17	7	14	77	53	41
Caerau Athletic	38	17	6	15	96	98	40
Merthyr Tydfil AFC	38	15	9	14	100	96	39
Abergavenny Thursdays	38	16	7	15	95	92	39
Gwynfi Welfare	38	16	5	17	87	85	37
Milford United	38	13	8	17	78	86	34
Ebbw Vale AFC	38	15	4	19	78	88	34
Aberystwyth Town	38	14	5	19	76	98	33
Lovells Athletic	38	12	7	19	69	90	31
Port Talbot Athletic	38	14	3	21	62	94	31
Treharris Athletic	38	12	7	19	72	112	31
Cardiff Corinthians	38	10	7	21	76	109	27
Cwmparc	38	6	4	28	64	152	16

Division 2 – Eastern Section

	P	W	D	L	F	A	Pts
Barry Town	32	25	4	3	111	44	54
Abercynon Athletic	32	22	5	5	108	64	49
Rhymney Town	32	19	5	8	110	66	43
Ferndale Athletic	32	20	2	10	105	78	42
Girlings FC (Cwmbran)	32	17	5	10	101	78	39
Troedyrhiw	32	16	5	11	87	57	37
Senghenydd Town	32	15	7	10	99	76	37
Blaina FC	32	14	3	15	71	99	31
Aberaman Athletic	32	11	7	14	61	64	29
New Tredegar Town	32	11	6	15	61	78	28
Tredomen Works	32	9	8	15	80	94	26
Risca United	32	11	4	17	57	73	26
Tonyrefail Welfare	32	9	7	16	72	96	25
Nelson Welfare	32	7	10	15	62	90	24
Porth Welfare	32	9	4	19	66	107	22
Chepstow Town	32	7	4	21	69	105	18
RTB Panteg	32	4	6	22	44	95	14

Division 2 – Western Section

	P	W	D	L	F	A	Pts
Llanelly AFC	38	31	4	3	160	53	66
Bettws FC (Ammanford)	38	27	7	4	130	56	61
Carmarthen Town	38	27	5	6	142	47	59
Briton Ferry Athletic	38	25	6	7	113	53	56
Fforestfach	38	25	5	8	113	63	55
Clydach United	38	23	5	10	114	71	51
Nantymoel Athletic	38	20	4	14	100	59	44
Blaenrhondda	38	18	7	13	103	89	43
Pontardawe Athletic	38	18	3	17	98	105	39
BP Llandarcy	38	16	3	19	82	85	35
Grovesend Welfare	38	14	5	19	74	113	33
Glyn-Neath Welfare	38	12	7	19	58	77	31
Garw Athletic	38	12	6	20	73	116	30
3M Gorseinon	38	13	2	23	66	93	28
Seven Sisters	38	9	8	21	79	107	26
Lewistown AFC	38	8	8	22	88	120	24
Glyncorrwg	38	9	6	23	75	120	24
Cwmavon AFC	38	9	4	25	77	147	22
Neath Athletic	38	8	6	24	64	132	22
Morriston Town	38	5	1	32	54	157	11

WELSH LEAGUE SOUTH 1958-59

Division 1

Abergavenny Thursdays	36	28	4	4	112	37	60
Cardiff City Reserves	36	19	7	10	90	68	45
Swansea Town Reserves	36	21	3	12	98	85	45
Haverfordwest County	36	19	6	11	85	76	44
Newport County Reserves	36	18	7	11	99	69	43
Merthyr Tydfil AFC	36	17	7	12	87	63	41
Milford United	36	17	7	12	85	84	41
Llanelly AFC	36	16	7	13	82	65	39
Caerau Athletic	36	18	3	15	82	66	39
Pembroke Borough	36	16	5	15	89	82	37
Ton Pentre AFC	36	14	8	14	97	83	36
Gwynfi Welfare	36	13	10	13	87	84	36
Lovells Athletic	36	12	10	14	71	86	34
Brecon Corinthians	36	11	7	18	75	87	29
Treharris Athletic	36	10	8	18	94	118	28
Aberystwyth Town	36	11	3	22	81	103	25
Barry Town	36	9	6	21	64	98	24
Ebbw Vale AFC	36	8	6	22	70	109	22
Port Talbot Athletic	36	7	2	27	55	140	16

Division 2 – Eastern Section

Tredomen Works	34	26	4	4	155	60	56
Cardiff Corinthians	34	22	7	5	138	51	51
Blaina FC	34	21	6	7	126	60	48
Abercynon Athletic	34	22	3	9	126	99	47
Porth Welfare	34	18	7	9	96	76	43
Ferndale Athletic	34	19	2	13	114	92	40
Rhymney Town	34	15	6	13	111	95	36
Troedyrhiw	34	16	4	14	76	79	36
Girlings FC (Cwmbran)	34	14	5	15	87	80	33
Senghenydd Town	34	15	3	16	89	82	33
Tonyrefail Welfare	34	12	7	15	93	105	31
Aberaman Athletic	34	11	5	18	79	114	27
Risca United	34	10	6	18	68	99	26
Chepstow Town	34	9	6	19	63	107	24
RTB Panteg	34	8	6	20	80	128	22
Tynte Rovers	34	8	5	21	62	131	21
Nelson Welfare	34	6	8	20	59	112	20
New Tredegar Town	34	7	4	23	89	137	18

Division 2 – Western Section

Bettws FC (Ammanford)	36	27	4	5	144	60	58
Carmarthen Town	36	25	2	9	128	51	52
Clydach United	36	23	6	7	106	46	52
Pontardawe Athletic	36	23	4	9	133	73	50
Fforestfach	36	23	2	11	98	57	48
Cwmparc	36	18	7	11	88	67	43
3M Gorseinon	36	17	6	13	101	76	40
Nantymoel Athletic	36	16	8	12	87	70	40
Glyn-Neath Welfare	36	14	7	15	84	85	35
Blaenrhondda	36	14	6	16	106	116	34
Briton Ferry Athletic	36	14	3	19	87	104	31
Morriston Town	36	13	4	19	83	119	30
Seven Sisters	36	12	5	19	81	118	29
Glyncorrwg	36	12	5	19	72	112	29
Lewistown AFC	36	12	3	21	83	108	27
Garw	36	10	7	19	75	98	27
Grovesend Welfare	36	7	7	22	65	92	21
Cwmavon AFC	36	9	2	25	84	163	20
Neath Athletic	36	7	4	25	66	156	18

WELSH LEAGUE SOUTH 1959-60

Division 1

Abergavenny Thursdays	38	30	5	3	126	39	65
Llanelly AFC	38	28	4	6	130	48	60
Ton Pentre AFC	38	24	9	5	135	68	57
Newport County Reserves	38	24	5	9	122	50	53
Swansea Town Reserves	38	21	11	6	99	65	53
Caerau Athletic	38	20	5	13	107	75	45
Cardiff City Reserves	38	15	11	12	111	79	41
Gwynfi Welfare	38	15	9	14	69	67	39
Aberystwyth Town	38	16	7	15	90	92	39
Lovells Athletic	38	14	6	18	97	86	34
Brecon Corinthians	38	14	6	18	92	112	34
Milford United	38	13	7	18	80	93	33
Pontllanfraith	38	13	7	18	79	102	33
Haverfordwest County	38	12	8	18	63	99	32
Merthyr Tydfil AFC	38	11	9	18	75	85	31
Bettws FC (Ammanford)	38	12	7	19	73	111	31
Pembroke Borough	38	11	6	21	86	107	28
Barry Town	38	9	7	22	54	107	25
Treharris Athletic	38	6	3	29	68	163	15
Tredomen Works	38	5	2	31	58	166	12

Division 2 – Eastern Section

Cardiff Corinthians	32	26	3	3	123	47	55
Ebbw Vale AFC	32	23	5	4	128	40	51
Ferndale Athletic	32	23	4	5	123	64	50
Cwmparc	32	17	8	7	85	65	42
Rhymney Town	32	17	5	10	110	84	39
Troedyrhiw	32	13	8	11	92	79	34
Tynte Rovers	32	15	4	13	79	71	34
Aberaman Athletic	32	14	5	13	91	98	33
Abercynon Athletic	32	13	5	14	91	107	31
Chepstow Town	32	11	7	14	79	97	29
Blaina FC	32	12	4	16	77	91	28
Senghenydd Town	32	11	6	15	64	91	28
New Tredegar Town	32	10	3	19	76	97	23
Risca United	32	7	6	19	67	102	20
Tonyrefail Welfare	32	8	4	20	67	118	20
Porth Welfare	32	7	4	21	57	96	18
RTB Panteg	32	2	5	25	46	108	9

Division 2 – Western Section

Carmarthen Town	34	25	5	4	133	47	55
Clydach United	34	24	5	5	109	47	53
Pontardawe Athletic	34	24	4	6	124	48	52
Glyncorrwg	34	20	3	11	95	69	43
Briton Ferry Athletic	34	18	5	11	93	67	41
Port Talbot Athletic	34	18	4	12	72	59	40
Lewistown AFC	34	15	8	11	103	82	38
Bridgend Town	34	11	9	14	94	88	31
Fforestfach	34	11	9	14	60	61	31
Nantymoel Athletic	34	11	8	15	74	86	30
Cwmavon AFC	34	13	4	17	70	98	30
Blaenrhondda	34	11	8	15	60	96	30
Garw	34	10	6	17	71	93	28
Neath Athletic	34	10	5	19	58	98	25
3M Gorseinon	34	8	8	18	72	84	24
Seven Sisters	34	7	10	17	63	75	24
Morriston Town	34	9	3	22	61	144	21
Glyn-Neath Welfare	34	6	4	24	50	120	16

WELSH LEAGUE SOUTH 1960-61
Division 1

Ton Pentre AFC	38	27	6	5	137	34	60
Cardiff City Reserves	38	23	9	6	99	50	55
Abergavenny Thursdays	38	24	4	10	107	52	52
Llanelly AFC	38	23	5	10	79	52	51
Haverfordwest County	38	21	8	9	76	46	50
Newport County Reserves	38	21	6	11	101	62	48
Swansea Town Reserves	38	19	4	15	104	78	42
Pembroke Borough	38	18	6	14	80	70	42
Lovells Athletic	38	16	8	14	95	73	40
Brecon Corinthians	38	17	5	16	61	65	39
Caerau Athletic	38	16	6	16	80	90	38
Pontlanfraith	38	16	4	18	78	90	36
Gwynfi Welfare	38	16	4	18	75	100	36
Merthyr Tydfil AFC	38	14	7	17	71	84	35
Aberystwyth Town	38	14	5	19	63	81	33
Cardiff Corinthians	38	12	2	24	64	110	26
Barry Town	38	10	5	23	70	116	25
Milford United	38	8	6	24	63	108	22
Ammanford Town	38	6	4	28	56	113	16
Carmarthen Town	38	5	4	29	48	133	14

Division 2 – Western Section

Pontardawe Athletic	32	28	2	2	112	33	58
Clydach United	32	27	1	4	134	30	55
3M Gorseinon	32	23	4	5	104	43	50
Port Talbot Athletic	32	20	5	7	92	54	45
Glyncorrwg	32	19	2	11	93	75	40
Bridgend Town	32	15	6	11	82	67	36
Briton Ferry Athletic	32	14	5	13	91	75	33
Cwmavon AFC	32	14	4	14	82	97	32
Seven Sisters	32	14	3	15	84	96	31
Nantymoel	32	10	6	16	59	89	26
Morriston Town	32	8	8	16	69	85	24
Blaenrhondda	32	9	3	20	68	124	21
Lewistown	32	8	4	20	66	95	20
Glyn-Neath	32	6	7	19	60	91	19
Fforestfach	32	8	3	21	42	75	19
Garw	32	9	0	23	61	124	18
Neath	32	7	3	22	48	94	17

Division 2 – Eastern Section

Ebbw Vale AFC	34	30	2	2	174	43	62
Tynte Rovers	34	29	2	3	132	45	60
Ferndale Athletic	34	25	5	4	134	63	55
Abercynon Athletic	34	20	4	10	114	79	44
Cwmparc	34	18	3	13	107	86	39
Treharris Athletic	34	16	6	12	113	90	38
Aberaman Athletic	34	18	2	14	107	102	38
Tonyrefail Welfare	34	14	8	12	120	117	36
Troedyrhiw	34	14	5	15	73	86	33
Blaina FC	34	14	4	16	78	93	32
Senghenydd Town	34	14	3	17	83	90	31
Rhymney	34	11	4	19	93	116	26
Tredomen Works	34	10	6	18	82	108	26
RTB Panteg	34	10	5	19	68	104	25
Chepstow Town	34	10	4	20	85	123	24
Risca United	34	7	2	25	64	127	16
Porth	34	6	2	26	61	134	14
New Tredegar Town	34	4	5	25	55	137	13

WELSH LEAGUE SOUTH 1961-62
Division 1

Swansea Town Reserves	38	27	6	5	123	44	60
Cardiff City Reserves	38	23	10	5	105	51	56
Ton Pentre AFC	38	22	6	10	99	59	50
Abergavenny Thursdays	38	20	6	12	67	46	46
Llanelly AFC	38	19	7	12	93	66	45
Newport County Reserves	38	19	7	12	79	62	45
Haverfordwest County	38	18	7	13	79	57	43
Pembroke Borough	38	19	5	14	82	83	43
Lovells Athletic	38	18	6	14	83	71	42
Brecon Corinthians	38	17	2	19	86	90	36
Aberystwyth Town	38	12	11	15	70	70	35
Cardiff Corinthians	38	14	6	18	82	88	34
Barry Town	38	14	5	19	67	84	33
Gwynfi Welfare	38	13	6	19	69	86	32
Pontlanfraith	38	12	7	19	56	80	31
Ebbw Vale AFC	38	9	9	20	61	94	27
Caerau Athletic	38	10	7	21	53	95	27
Merthyr Tydfil AFC	38	9	8	21	56	86	26
Pontardawe Athletic	38	10	6	22	58	107	26
Milford United	38	7	9	22	37	86	23

Division 2 – Eastern Section

Ferndale Athletic	30	24	4	2	131	52	52
Tynte Rovers	30	20	2	8	94	51	42
Treharris Athletic	30	18	6	6	96	59	42
Tonyrefail Welfare	30	15	5	10	102	81	35
Tredomen Works	30	14	4	12	88	82	32
Abercynon Athletic	30	12	7	11	100	87	31
Troedyrhiw	30	13	5	12	69	68	31
Aberaman Athletic	30	14	2	14	92	81	30
RTB Panteg	30	11	7	12	70	63	29
Cwmparc	30	12	4	14	96	99	28
Glyn-Neath	30	13	1	16	68	93	27
Senghenydd Town	30	12	1	17	74	85	25
Rhymney	30	10	3	17	69	100	23
Chepstow Town	30	7	7	16	64	107	21
New Tredegar Town	30	7	2	21	58	109	16
Blaina FC	30	6	4	20	59	113	16

Division 2 – Western Section

Port Talbot Athletic	30	21	4	5	107	27	46
Carmarthen Town	30	20	5	5	71	42	45
Bridgend Town	30	21	2	7	88	55	44
Clydach United	30	19	3	8	107	55	41
Ammanford Town	30	19	3	8	92	49	41
Neath	30	16	4	10	77	59	36
Seven Sisters	30	16	2	12	78	58	34
3M Gorseinon	30	13	7	10	70	67	33
Morriston Town	30	11	3	16	53	84	25
Cwmavon AFC	30	9	5	16	58	83	23
Fforestfach	30	6	10	14	42	66	22
Nantymoel	30	9	3	18	41	77	21
Glyncorrwg	30	6	8	16	54	86	20
Lewistown	30	8	4	18	47	79	20
Blaenrhondda	30	6	7	17	54	85	19
Garw	30	3	4	23	36	103	10

WELSH LEAGUE SOUTH 1962-63

Division 1

	P	W	D	L	F	A	Pts
Swansea Town Reserves	38	33	2	3	124	30	68
Abergavenny Thursdays	38	28	5	5	126	52	61
Ton Pentre AFC	38	21	7	10	90	63	49
Lovells Athletic	38	21	6	11	76	69	48
Brecon Corinthians	38	20	4	14	86	74	44
Cardiff City Reserves	38	18	7	13	61	53	43
Newport County Reserves	38	18	6	14	85	72	42
Pembroke Borough	38	18	6	14	84	81	42
Merthyr Tydfil AFC	38	17	5	16	72	67	39
Aberystwyth Town	38	14	10	14	71	56	38
Llanelly AFC	38	13	8	17	68	61	34
Ferndale Athletic	38	13	7	18	67	84	33
Cardiff Corinthians	38	13	7	18	74	93	33
Haverfordwest County	38	11	9	18	63	73	31
Gwynfi Welfare	38	11	9	18	79	105	31
Pontllanfraith	38	12	6	20	43	71	30
Caerau Athletic	38	11	7	20	63	83	29
Ebbw Vale AFC	38	12	5	21	53	86	29
Barry Town	38	6	10	22	47	73	22
Port Talbot Athletic	38	3	8	27	40	126	14

Division 2 – Western Section

	P	W	D	L	F	A	Pts
Milford United	30	25	2	3	126	23	52
Pontardawe Athletic	30	23	2	5	111	55	48
Clydach United	30	20	4	6	110	53	44
Carmarthen Town	30	20	2	8	91	46	42
Seven Sisters	:30	16	3	11	93	70	35
Ammanford Town	30	14	2	14	99	84	30
Cwmavon AFC	30	12	6	12	76	84	30
Briton Ferry Athletic	30	12	5	13	66	56	29
Neath	30	13	2	15	90	80	28
Glyncorrwg	30	11	4	15	55	78	26
Garw	30	11	3	16	51	98	25
3M Gorseinon	30	9	6	15	54	79	24
Lewistown	30	10	2	18	62	113	22
Morriston Town	30	8	5	17	61	101	21
Fforestfach	30	5	2	23	32	84	12
Nantymoel	30	5	2	23	37	110	12

Division 2 – Eastern Section

	P	W	D	L	F	A	Pts
Bridgend Town	30	24	6	0	105	27	54
Tynte Rovers	30	22	5	3	95	42	49
Tredomen Works	30	17	7	6	91	52	41
Aberaman Athletic	30	20	0	10	122	58	40
RTB Panteg	30	17	6	7	73	52	40
Troedyrhiw	30	18	2	10	88	71	38
Tonyrefail Welfare	30	14	7	9	100	85	35
Treharris Athletic	30	14	5	11	76	72	33
Blaenrhondda	30	12	5	13	79	87	29
Abercynon Athletic	30	13	3	14	77	103	29
Senghenydd Town	30	7	6	17	66	86	20
Blaina FC	30	7	5	18	69	94	19
Chepstow Town	30	8	2	20	61	109	18
Cwmparc	30	5	3	22	44	91	13
Glyn-Neath	30	5	1	24	50	99	11
New Tredegar Town	30	3	5	22	45	113	11

WELSH LEAGUE SOUTH 1963-64

Division 1

	P	W	D	L	F	A	Pts
Swansea Town Reserves	34	23	10	1	110	36	56
Abergavenny Thursdays	34	22	7	5	107	42	51
Haverfordwest County	34	23	5	6	89	45	51
Ton Pentre AFC	34	22	5	7	87	41	49
Llanelli AFC	34	19	5	10	75	41	43
Brecon Corinthians	34	19	4	11	74	54	42
Newport County Reserves	34	14	8	12	71	62	36
Lovells Athletic	34	13	8	13	69	62	34
Caerau Athletic	34	13	7	14	51	48	33
Merthyr Tydfil AFC	34	14	4	16	70	77	32
Gwynfi Welfare	34	12	8	14	69	86	32
Pembroke Borough	34	12	4	18	61	90	28
Ferndale Athletic	34	9	8	17	55	87	26
Bridgend Town	34	9	6	19	59	99	24
Cardiff City Reserves	34	8	7	19	38	73	23
Milford United	34	9	4	21	49	84	22
Ebbw Vale AFC	34	6	6	22	47	91	18
Cardiff Corinthians	34	2	8	24	44	107	12

Division 2 – Eastern Section

	P	W	D	L	F	A	Pts
South Wales Switchgear	30	25	1	4	108	44	51
Tynte Rovers	30	21	3	6	87	51	45
Aberaman Athletic	30	18	5	7	132	63	41
Tonyrefail Welfare	30	18	4	8	98	59	40
Tredomen Works	30	16	4	10	100	71	36
Barry Town	30	15	4	11	78	48	34
Troedyrhiw	30	12	5	13	75	83	29
Semtex	30	13	1	16	69	74	27
RTB Panteg	30	10	6	14	63	86	26
Aber Valley	30	10	5	15	68	88	25
Chepstow Town	30	10	4	16	71	87	44
Treharris Athletic	30	9	4	17	66	102	22
New Tredegar Town	30	9	4	17	64	103	22
Abercynon Athletic	30	8	5	17	62	92	21
Blaenrhondda	30	9	2	19	44	91	20
Blaina West Side	30	5	7	18	50	93	17

Division 2 – Western Section

	P	W	D	L	F	A	Pts
Clydach United	26	17	7	2	77	27	41
Carmarthen Town	26	16	8	2	78	26	40
Briton Ferry Athletic	26	14	8	4	65	31	36
Neath Athletic	26	15	6	5	93	46	36
Pontardawe Athletic	26	16	3	7	73	38	35
Port Talbot Athletic	26	14	4	8	74	38	32
Glyncorrwg United	26	12	5	9	73	62	29
Seven Sisters	26	11	5	10	59	56	27
Ammanford Town	26	8	4	14	51	63	20
Maesteg Park Athletic	26	7	5	14	73	84	19
Morriston Town	26	7	3	16	39	69	17
Garw Athletic	26	5	4	17	47	85	14
Lewistown Welfare	26	5	2	19	35	94	12
Nantymoel Athletic	26	2	2	22	18	136	6

WELSH LEAGUE SOUTH 1964-65

Premier Division

Swansea Town Reserves	30	21	6	3	88	27	48
Abergavenny Thursdays	30	19	4	7	97	48	42
Llanelly AFC	30	16	7	7	61	38	39
Haverfordwest County	30	15	7	8	60	44	37
Merthyr Tydfil AFC	30	14	4	12	63	60	32
Ton Pentre AFC	30	12	8	10	59	59	32
Caerau Athletic	30	11	10	9	32	34	32
Cardiff City Reserves	30	10	10	10	51	54	30
Pembroke Borough	30	11	7	12	57	62	29
Bridgend Town	30	11	6	13	48	57	28
Lovells Athletic	30	9	7	14	49	51	25
Newport County Reserves	30	11	3	16	49	59	25
Ferndale Athletic	30	8	9	13	52	67	25
Gwynfi Welfare	30	6	11	13	46	68	23
Brecon Corinthians	30	8	7	15	39	72	23
Milford United	30	2	6	22	27	78	10

Division 1

Ebbw Vale AFC	30	27	0	3	113	37	54
South Wales Switchgear	30	26	1	3	96	23	53
Tynte Rovers	30	17	5	8	104	57	39
Tredomen Works	30	15	4	11	74	62	34
Barry Town	30	11	10	9	70	62	32
Port Talbot Athletic	30	11	9	10	57	64	31
Carmarthen Town	30	10	8	12	67	69	28
Pontardawe Athletic	30	12	3	15	64	73	27
Cardiff Corinthians	30	11	4	15	68	62	26
Neath Athletic	30	10	5	15	70	67	25
Tonyrefail Welfare	30	10	5	15	50	62	25
Aberaman Athletic	30	8	8	14	64	95	24
Clydach United	30	10	2	18	45	72	22
Seven Sisters	30	9	4	17	58	93	22
Troedyrhiw	30	8	3	19	59	99	19
Briton Ferry Athletic	30	7	5	18	56	118	19

Division 2

Chepstow Town	30	24	2	4	107	40	50
Ammanford Town	30	23	3	4	92	35	49
Treharris Athletic	30	19	5	6	90	48	43
Abercynon Athletic	30	16	3	11	73	61	35
Semtex	30	15	4	11	80	61	34
Maesteg Park Athletic	30	13	7	10	86	71	33
Aber Valley	30	13	4	13	90	67	30
RTB Panteg	30	11	6	13	67	70	28
Garw Athletic	30	11	6	13	58	62	28
New Tredegar Town	30	11	4	15	55	73	26
Morriston Town	30	9	7	14	69	83	25
Glyncorrwg Athletic	29	9	5	15	56	72	23
Blaina West Side	29	8	5	16	56	83	21
Blaenrhondda	30	9	3	18	55	84	21
Lewistown	30	8	4	18	51	88	20
Nantymoel Athletic	30	4	4	22	38	124	12

Youth Division

Swansea Town Reserves	18	17	0	1	94	14	34
Cardiff City Reserves	18	16	0	2	87	12	32
Ammanford Town	18	11	2	5	52	30	24
Merthyr Tydfil AFC	18	9	1	8	64	44	19
Aberaman Athletic	18	8	1	9	46	65	17
Cardiff Corinthians	18	6	2	10	39	60	14
Newport County Reserves	18	5	3	10	42	52	13
Caerau Athletic	18	5	1	12	29	69	11
Llanelly AFC	18	4	2	12	34	55	10
Port Talbot Athletic	18	3	0	15	16	103	6

WELSH LEAGUE SOUTH 1965-66

Premier Division

Lovells Athletic	30	24	5	1	80	23	53
Newport County Reserves	30	21	2	7	71	39	44
Swansea Town Reserves	30	16	7	7	72	46	39
Abergavenny Thursdays	30	16	6	8	80	45	38
South Wales Switchgear	30	15	6	9	65	47	36
Ton Pentre AFC	30	14	8	8	59	49	36
Ebbw Vale AFC	30	12	5	13	58	52	29
Llanelli AFC	30	13	3	14	48	45	29
Bridgend Town	30	11	7	12	50	62	29
Cardiff City Reserves	30	9	8	13	45	49	26
Haverfordwest County	30	9	7	14	62	56	25
Merthyr Tydfil AFC	30	9	7	14	SI	56	25
Ferndale Athletic	30	10	1	19	50	88	21
Pembroke Borough	30	8	2	20	54	91	18
Caerau Athletic	30	6	4	20	40	78	16
Gwynfi Welfare	30	7	2	21	47	106	16

Division 1

Ammanford Town	30	24	5	1	85	32	53
Tredomen Works	30	21	4	5	94	35	46
Tynte Rovers	30	20	4	6	101	49	44
Brecon Corinthians	30	19	3	8	72	47	41
Cardiff Corinthians	30	18	4	8	84	52	40
Tonyrefail Welfare	30	14	4	12	71	46	32
Carmarthen Town	30	10	9	11	74	69	29
Chepstow Town	30	11	7	12	67	71	29
Clydach United	30	10	6	14	49	64	26
Barry Town	30	9	5	16	45	63	23
Milford United	30	10	3	17	52	73	23
Neath Athletic	30	9	4	17	64	83	22
Port Talbot Athletic	30	9	4	17	37	67	22
Pontardawe Athletic	30	7	7	16	57	96	21
Seven Sisters	30	7	2	21	52	93	16
Aberaman Athletic	30	3	7	20	54	118	13

Division 2

Caerleon	30	25	4	1	111	25	54
Treharris Athletic	30	21	6	3	99	42	48
Aber Valley	30	19	5	6	88	51	43
Abercynon Athletic	30	14	8	8	72	61	36
Velindre	30	14	7	9	69	57	35
Semtex	30	15	5	12	74	55	33
Briton Ferry Athletic	30	13	6	11	78	63	32
RTB Panteg	30	12	7	11	64	64	31
Blaenrhondda	30	12	4	14	70	66	28
Garw Athletic	30	12	3	15	58	82	27
New Tredegar Town	30	11	4	15	53	82	26
Morriston Town	30	9	7	14	62	72	25
Glyncorrwg Athletic	30	10	4	16	72	90	24
Blaina West Side	30	8	4	18	54	73	20
Maesteg Park Athletic	30	5	5	20	62	99	15
Lewistown	30	1	1	28	21	131	3

Youth Division

Swansea Town Reserves	12	11	1	0	38	10	23
Cardiff City Reserves	12	9	1	2	49	16	19
Newport County Reserves	12	6	1	5	33	32	13
Cardiff Corinthians	12	5	1	6	33	35	11
Caerau Athletic	12	3	1	8	21	44	7
Port Talbot Athletic	12	2	2	8	21	39	6
Clydach United	12	2	1	9	23	42	5

WELSH LEAGUE SOUTH 1966-67

Premier Division

	P	W	D	L	F	A	Pts
Cardiff City Reserves	30	20	4	6	88	34	44
Ammanford Town	30	17	6	7	70	44	40
Abergavenny Thursdays	30	17	5	8	55	47	39
Swansea Town Reserves	30	15	7	8	55	51	37
Newport County Reserves	30	13	8	9	64	39	34
Ton Pentre AFC	30	14	5	11	51	37	33
Lovells Athletic	30	14	5	11	68	53	33
Llanelli AFC	30	13	6	11	49	44	32
Bridgend Town	30	11	8	11	45	41	30
Haverfordwest County	30	12	4	14	50	63	28
Ferndale Athletic	30	8	9	13	49	84	25
Ebbw Vale AFC	30	6	12	12	51	61	24
South Wales Switchgear	30	8	8	14	44	54	24
Merthyr Tydfil AFC	30	9	6	15	53	72	24
Tredomen Works	30	8	2	20	47	73	18
Pembroke Borough	30	5	5	20	40	82	15

Division 1

	P	W	D	L	F	A	Pts
Tonyrefail Welfare	30	21	3	6	92	34	45
Neath	30	20	3	7	92	44	43
Carmarthen Town	30	17	6	7	84	50	40
Tynte Rovers	30	16	6	8	71	42	38
Caerleon	30	16	6	8	60	43	38
Treharris Athletic	30	14	5	11	78	61	33
Barry Town	30	14	3	13	65	62	31
Brecon Corinthians	30	14	1	15	65	55	29
Cardiff Corinthians	30	12	4	14	56	51	28
Caerau Athletic	30	10	5	15	51	75	25
Milford United	30	9	7	14	55	88	25
Port Talbot Athletic	30	10	5	15	50	80	25
Chepstow Town	30	8	8	14	39	63	24
Clydach United	30	10	4	16	39	65	24
Pontardawe Athletic	30	8	4	18	61	91	20
Gwynfi Welfare	30	4	4	22	30	83	12

Division 2

	P	W	D	L	F	A	Pts
Swansea University	32	24	1	7	119	51	49
Velindre	32	19	6	7	92	50	44
Aber Valley	32	20	3	9	112	77	43
Briton Ferry Athletic	32	18	7	7	80	55	43
RTB Panteg	32	20	3	9	69	51	43
Morriston Town	32	18	6	8	88	47	42
Abercynon Athletic	32	14	8	10	89	78	36
Semtex	32	14	6	12	62	57	34
Maesteg Park	32	14	4	14	84	82	32
Blaina FC	32	13	3	16	72	72	29
Garw	32	13	2	17	67	75	28
Glyncorrwg	32	11	4	17	58	77	26
Aberaman Athletic	32	11	3	18	62	81	25
Blaenrhondda	32	10	4	18	63	93	24
Seven Sisters	32	9	5	18	64	94	23
New Tredegar Town	32	5	6	21	55	95	16
Lewistown	32	3	1	28	39	140	7

Youth Division

	P	W	D	L	F	A	Pts
Swansea Town Reserves	10	8	2	0	47	12	18
Newport County Reserves	10	7	2	1	24	8	16
Cardiff City Reserves	10	6	1	3	45	18	13
Port Talbot Athletic	10	4	1	5	18	19	9
Tredomen Works	10	1	1	8	5	54	3
Aberaman Athletic	10	0	1	9	7	35	1
Youth Cup Cardiff City Reserves	10	8	1	1	41	10	17
Swansea Town Reserves	10	6	1	3	38	11	13
Newport County Reserves	10	5	3	2	27	12	13
Port Talbot Athletic	10	4	1	5	23	30	9
Aberaman Athletic	10	2	1	7	13	33	5
Tredomen Works	10	1	1	8	7	52	3

WELSH LEAGUE SOUTH 1967-68

Premier Division

	P	W	D	L	F	A	Pts
Cardiff City Reserves	34	25	6	3	136	45	56
Ammanford Town	34	25	5	4	85	37	55
Bridgend Town	34	19	8	7	69	46	46
Swansea Town Reserves	34	20	3	11	97	71	43
Abergavenny Thursdays	34	15	10	9	57	48	40
Llanelli AFC	34	15	8	11	54	44	38
Pembroke Borough	34	12	10	12	53	51	34
Lovells Athletic	34	11	12	11	60	63	34
South Wales Switchgear	34	14	6	14	51	62	34
Ton Pentre AFC	34	13	7	14	49	57	33
Ferndale Athletic	34	12	7	15	68	74	31
Newport County Reserves	34	10	10	14	51	54	30
Haverfordwest County	34	12	5	17	60	79	29
Tredomen Works	34	9	8	17	48	72	26
Merthyr Tydfil AFC	34	9	6	19	40	63	24
Ebbw Vale AFC	34	9	6	19	38	69	24
Neath	34	9	5	20	53	93	23
Tonyrefail Welfare	34	4	4	26	38	79	12

Division 1

	P	W	D	L	F	A	Pts
Caerleon	32	22	7	3	99	33	51
Swansea University	32	21	7	4	76	42	49
Treharris Athletic	32	16	10	6	73	57	42
Clydach United	32	17	5	10	77	72	39
Cardiff Corinthians	32	16	6	10	80	53	38
Barry Town	32	13	6	13	47	42	32
Gwynfi Welfare	32	12	8	12	52	67	32
Tynte Rovers	32	12	7	13	65	71	31
Briton Ferry Athletic	32	10	10	12	67	62	30
Carmarthen Town	32	11	8	13	57	54	30
Caerau Athletic	32	9	11	12	62	68	29
Port Talbot Athletic	32	13	3	16	44	57	29
Pontardawe Athletic	32	11	6	15	60	73	28
Milford United	32	8	8	16	55	64	24
Velindre	32	9	5	18	61	76	23
Chepstow Town	32	9	5	18	45	70	23
Aber Valley	32	5	4	23	49	108	14

Division 2

	P	W	D	L	F	A	Pts
Cwmbran Town	32	26	2	4	156	42	54
RTB Panteg	32	22	5	5	78	36	49
Croesyceiliog	32	22	3	7	107	47	47
Ynysybwl	32	22	1	9	109	59	45
Morriston Town	32	18	9	5	82	49	45
Aberaman Athletic	32	19	4	9	101	48	42
Semtex	32	13	8	11	65	60	34
Tondu Robins	32	16	1	15	73	84	33
Seven Sisters	32	14	3	15	68	99	31
Maesteg Park	32	13	4	15	73	80	30
Garw	32	13	1	18	58	79	27
Glyncorrwg	32	10	4	18	48	77	24
Abercynon Athletic	32	9	3	20	65	96	21
Blaenrhondda	32	7	7	18	56	87	21
Lewistown	32	7	5	20	52	123	19
Blaina FC	32	7	4	21	49	85	18
New Tredegar Town	32	1	2	29	42	131	4

Youth Division

	P	W	D	L	F	A	Pts
Cardiff City Reserves	8	5	3	0	38	9	13
Swansea Town Reserves	8	4	3	1	21	10	11
Newport County Reserves	8	1	5	2	15	16	7
Cardiff Corinthians	8	1	3	4	10	19	5
Gwynfi Welfare	8	1	2	5	9	39	4

WELSH LEAGUE SOUTH 1968-69

Premier Division

Team	P	W	D	L	F	A	Pts
Bridgend Town	34	25	5	4	87	30	55
Pembroke Borough	34	19	12	3	66	31	50
Haverfordwest County	34	19	9	6	78	41	47
Lovells Athletic	34	17	11	6	80	45	45
Abergavenny Thursdays	34	16	9	9	67	53	41
South Wales Switchgear	34	15	10	9	62	58	40
Ton Pentre AFC	34	15	8	11	54	46	38
Swansea Town Reserves	34	12	10	12	58	41	34
Cardiff City Reserves	34	15	4	15	68	52	34
Caerleon	34	11	12	11	46	54	34
Ammanford Town	34	12	9	13	64	49	33
Newport County Reserves	34	12	9	13	57	57	33
Llanelli AFC	34	12	8	14	49	53	32
Ferndale Athletic	34	11	8	15	58	66	30
Merthyr Tydfil AFC	34	6	10	8	35	81	22
Ebbw Vale AFC	34	3	10	21	32	78	16
Tredomen Works	34	6	2	26	43	99	14
Swansea University	34	5	4	25	32	102	14

Division 1

Team	P	W	D	L	F	A	Pts
Caerau Athletic	34	22	6	6	101	57	50
Barry Town	34	21	7	6	87	43	49
Treharris Athletic	34	22	4	8	106	55	48
Tonyrefail Welfare	34	20	7	7	94	48	47
Port Talbot Athletic	34	15	14	5	64	41	44
Neath	34	17	9	8	74	51	43
Cwmbran Town	34	19	4	11	103	63	42
Cardiff Corinthians	34	14	5	15	68	68	33
Clydach United	34	13	7	14	68	75	33
Briton Ferry Athletic	34	14	4	16	71	68	32
RTB Panteg	34	12	7	15	48	46	31
Carmarthen Town	34	11	8	15	64	78	30
Tynte Rovers	34	12	4	18	65	84	28
Velindre	34	10	7	17	50	70	27
Chepstow Town	34	10	7	17	61	98	27
Pontardawe Athletic	34	6	9	19	55	94	21
Milford United	34	6	3	25	47	133	15
Gwynfi Welfare	34	3	6	25	44	98	12

Division 2

Team	P	W	D	L	F	A	Pts
Ynysybwl	34	28	4	2	111	29	60
Maesteg Park	34	25	7	2	111	41	57
Aberaman Athletic	34	27	2	5	133	46	56
Morriston Town	34	18	9	7	84	55	45
Cardiff University	34	19	4	11	80	48	42
Blaenrhondda	34	18	4	12	96	69	40
Croesyceiliog	34	17	5	12	78	51	39
Seven Sisters	34	16	4	14	83	56	36
Tondu Robins	34	14	8	12	56	58	36
Semtex	34	12	8	14	69	86	32
Lewistown	34	11	6	17	59	95	28
Blaenavon Blues	34	10	7	17	72	89	27
Pontyclun	34	9	7	18	51	74	25
Blaina West Side	34	10	4	20	75	89	24
Abercynon Athletic	34	7	9	18	49	92	23
Glyncorrwg	34	6	7	21	60	116	19
Garw	34	3	7	24	38	104	13
New Tredegar Town	34	4	2	28	31	138	10

WELSH LEAGUE SOUTH 1969-70

Premier Division

Team	P	W	D	L	F	A	Pts
Cardiff City Reserves	34	25	8	1	106	35	58
Haverfordwest County	34	20	8	6	80	40	48
Ton Pentre AFC	34	18	9	7	61	43	45
Llanelli AFC	34	19	6	9	64	37	44
Swansea City Reserves	34	17	8	9	68	49	42
Bridgend Town	34	16	9	9	79	42	41
Newport County Reserves	34	16	9	9	60	37	41
Ammanford Town	34	5	9	10	62	47	39
Abergavenny Thursdays	34	16	5	13	78	54	37
Caerleon	34	11	0	13	45	43	32
Pembroke Borough	34	0	11	13	61	61	31
Ebbw Vale AFC	34	8	14	11	43	54	30
Ferndale Athletic	34	8	12	14	46	57	28
South Wales Switchgear	34	10	6	18	48	60	26
Barry Town	34	9	7	18	48	70	25
Merthyr Tydfil AFC	34	7	7	20	33	78	21
Caerau Athletic	34	5	3	26	35	126	13
Tredomen Works	34	3	5	26	38	122	11

Division 1

Team	P	W	D	L	F	A	Pts
Swansea University	32	19	9	4	81	40	47
Cwmbran Town	32	21	5	6	61	39	47
Treharris Athletic	32	19	6	7	108	41	44
Neath	32	16	10	6	67	45	42
Maesteg Park	32	17	8	7	61	37	42
Cardiff Corinthians	32	16	8	8	61	41	40
Ynysybwl	32	15	9	8	76	54	39
Clydach United	32	15	5	12	68	54	35
Milford United	32	11	12	9	62	53	34
Briton Ferry Athletic	32	11	9	12	53	53	31
Tynte Rovers	32	11	8	13	60	74	30
Panteg	32	9	6	17	45	72	24
Tonyrefail Welfare	32	6	11	15	63	72	23
Port Talbot Athletic	32	7	5	20	49	72	19
Chepstow Town	32	7	4	21	38	117	18
Carmarthen Town	32	5	5	22	42	78	15
Pontardawe Athletic	32	4	6	22	46	96	14

Division 2

Team	P	W	D	L	F	A	Pts
Croesyceiliog	34	26	4	4	117	35	56
Aberaman Athletic	34	24	6	4	116	41	54
Morriston Town	34	24	4	6	110	45	52
Pontlottyn	34	20	8	6	113	62	48
Seven Sisters	34	17	10	7	93	59	44
Blaenrhondda	34	17	8	9	93	60	42
Pontyclun	34	18	6	10	65	44	42
Abercynon Athletic	34	18	5	11	89	65	41
Cardiff University	34	15	3	16	76	61	33
Newbridge	34	12	8	14	64	59	32
Blaenavon Blues	34	13	5	16	80	91	31
Tondu Robins	34	11	9	14	57	69	31
Blaina FC	34	12	5	17	73	90	29
Garw	34	10	5	19	58	100	25
New Tredegar Town	34	5	5	24	40	109	15
Glyncorrwg	34	4	6	24	57	132	14
Semtex	34	5	4	25	44	110	14
Lewistown	34	3	3	27	41	154	9

WELSH LEAGUE SOUTH 1970-71

Premier Division

Llanelli AFC	34	25	6	3	73	22	56
Haverfordwest County	34	24	6	4	86	35	54
Cardiff City Reserves	34	21	10	3	82	21	52
Bridgend Town	34	21	7	6	81	29	49
Ton Pentre AFC	34	15	13	6	47	24	43
Newport County Reserves	34	17	9	8	68	41	43
Ferndale Athletic	34	18	7	9	70	43	43
Abergavenny Thursdays	34	16	8	10	68	46	40
Ammanford Town	34	14	6	4	52	45	34
Caerleon	34	13	8	13	43	48	34
Swansea City Reserves	34	15	2	17	53	53	32
Merthyr Tydfil AFC	34	10	8	16	43	52	28
Ebbw Vale AFC	34	7	10	17	41	48	24
Cwmbran Town	34	6	10	18	52	72	22
Pembroke Borough	34	6	9	19	35	68	21
Swansea University	34	8	4	22	40	78	20
Barry Town	34	3	3	28	37	91	9
Caerau Athletic	34	2	4	28	28	183	8

Division 1

Cardiff Corinthians	34	26	6	2	104	34	58
Milford United	34	21	7	6	64	31	49
Briton Ferry Athletic	34	22	5	7	76	37	49
Tynte Rovers	34	19	8	7	91	56	46
Tonyrefail Welfare	34	20	4	10	87	51	44
Croesyceiliog	34	15	7	12	84	67	37
Aberaman Athletic	34	17	3	14	83	67	37
Carmarthen Town	34	13	9	12	70	68	35
Treharris Athletic	34	14	6	14	88	73	34
Maesteg Park	34	12	8	14	48	45	32
Ynysybwl	34	13	6	15	66	66	32
Panteg	34	12	5	17	69	71	29
Skewen Athletic	34	12	5	17	63	71	29
Tredomen Works	34	10	7	17	66	84	27
Pontardawe Athletic	34	11	4	19	59	97	26
Clydach United	34	9	7	18	39	69	25
Port Talbot Athletic	34	7	3	24	51	120	17
Morriston Town	34	1	4	29	36	137	6

Division 2

Cardiff University	30	21	7	2	94	31	49
Blaenrhondda	30	22	3	5	88	40	47
Blaina West Side	30	19	6	5	86	38	44
Pontlottyn	30	17	5	8	68	40	39
Pontyclun	30	16	6	8	63	31	38
Lewistown	30	10	12	8	40	32	32
Seven Sisters	30	13	5	12	72	61	31
Ystradgynlais	30	12	7	11	78	77	31
Tondu Robins	30	11	7	12	55	68	29
Trelewis	30	11	6	13	78	70	28
Newbridge	30	9	7	14	52	66	25
Abercynon Athletic	30	8	8	14	59	67	24
Blaenavon Blues	30	7	9	14	46	54	23
Garw	30	3	10	17	34	86	16
Semtex	30	5	3	22	32	90	13
New Tredegar Town	30	2	7	21	30	124	11

WELSH LEAGUE SOUTH 1971-72

Premier Division

Cardiff City Reserves	34	23	6	5	94	24	52
Newport County Reserves	34	22	5	7	72	40	49
Llanelli AFC	34	21	5	8	75	35	47
Haverfordwest County	34	18	7	9	55	41	43
Ton Pentre AFC	34	15	12	7	51	40	42
Pembroke Borough	34	13	12	9	63	48	38
Bridgend Town	34	15	6	13	52	42	36
Ferndale Athletic	34	12	12	10	59	50	36
Caerleon	34	13	7	14	45	43	33
Ammanford Town	34	13	7	14	57	59	33
Cardiff Corinthians	34	12	9	13	52	57	33
Swansea City Reserves	34	11	9	14	49	51	31
Merthyr Tydfil AFC	34	10	9	15	47	66	29
Abergavenny Thursdays	34	10	6	18	48	75	26
Ebbw Vale AFC	34	7	10	17	35	53	24
Cwmbran Town	34	8	7	19	40	77	23
Swansea University	34	5	9	20	37	72	19
Milford United	34	7	4	23	41	99	18

Division 1

Briton Ferry Athletic	34	25	6	3	119	35	56
Cardiff University	34	23	5	6	76	39	51
Tonyrefail Welfare	34	22	3	9	88	62	47
Tynte Rovers	34	17	10	7	77	50	44
Blaenrhondda	34	12	12	10	58	49	36
Ynysybwl	34	13	10	11	56	50	36
Maesteg Park	34	14	8	12	46	45	36
Treharris Athletic	34	15	5	14	76	61	35
Clydach United	34	14	7	13	65	64	35
Pontardawe Athletic	34	15	5	14	66	75	35
Carmarthen Town	34	14	4	16	61	70	32
Skewen Athletic	34	9	10	15	42	53	28
Barry Town	34	10	8	16	56	90	28
Panteg	34	11	5	18	52	67	27
Aberaman Athletic	34	10	6	18	54	69	26
Tredomen Works	34	9	7	18	63	83	25
Croesyceiliog	34	6	8	20	53	86	20
Caerau Athletic	34	4	7	23	38	98	15

Division 2

Sully	34	27	4	3	95	29	58
Lewistown	34	24	8	2	106	35	56
Afan Lido FC	34	25	5	4	111	35	55
Blaina West Side	34	23	4	7	94	46	50
BP Llandarcy	34	21	7	6	106	51	49
Pontlottyn	34	16	13	5	72	45	45
Blaenavon Blues	34	18	4	12	68	48	40
Ystradgynlais	34	16	1	17	74	76	33
Abercynon Athletic	34	13	5	16	90	90	31
Seven Sisters	34	11	6	17	54	79	28
Morriston Town	34	11	4	9	54	94	26
Garw	34	8	9	17	48	79	25
Pontyclun	34	8	8	18	51	67	24
Trelewis	34	8	6	20	75	101	22
Newbridge	34	9	2	23	52	106	20
Port Talbot Athletic	34	7	5	22	42	86	19
Tondu Robins	34	7	4	23	49	110	18
Semtex	34	4	5	25	41	105	13

WELSH LEAGUE SOUTH 1972-73

Premier Division

Team	P	W	D	L	F	A	Pts
Bridgend Town	34	25	5	4	91	33	55
Llanelli AFC	34	18	8	8	62	41	44
Ton Pentre AFC	34	17	9	8	74	39	43
Pembroke Borough	34	19	5	10	71	46	43
Cardiff City Reserves	28	19	4	5	87	35	42
Caerleon	34	15	8	11	68	60	38
Newport County Reserves	33	13	12	8	51	47	38
Ferndale Athletic	33	13	9	11	55	44	35
Ammanford Town	34	14	6	14	53	55	34
Cwmbran Town	33	13	5	15	51	56	31
Swansea City Reserves	34	11	9	14	43	63	31
Haverfordwest County	32	12	6	14	57	68	30
Cardiff Corinthians	34	9	11	14	59	56	29
Briton Ferry Athletic	34	8	10	16	55	66	26
Cardiff University	32	8	8	16	44	54	24
Merthyr Tydfil AFC	33	9	6	18	51	68	24
Ebbw Vale AFC	34	7	8	19	43	70	22
Abergavenny Thursdays	34	3	3	28	21	135	9

Division 1

Team	P	W	D	L	F	A	Pts
Lewistown	34	21	9	4	66	25	51
Maesteg Park	34	23	5	6	68	27	51
Carmarthen Town	34	21	6	7	76	40	48
Panteg	34	19	8	7	67	40	46
Treharris Athletic	34	19	6	9	53	40	44
Barry Town	34	16	8	10	61	41	40
Tonyrefail Welfare	34	17	3	14	77	62	37
Tynte Rovers	34	15	6	13	79	74	36
Sully	34	12	11	11	59	58	35
Aberaman Athletic	34	13	6	15	68	66	32
Clydach United	34	13	5	16	56	60	31
Blaenrhondda	34	9	10	15	57	54	28
Swansea University	34	10	6	18	50	67	26
Tredomen Works	34	9	5	20	47	70	23
Pontardawe Athletic	34	7	8	19	57	78	22
Ynysybwl	34	7	7	20	32	64	21
Skewen Athletic	34	8	5	21	35	85	21
Milford United	34	8	4	22	38	95	20

Division 2

Team	P	W	D	L	F	A	Pts
Pontllanfraith	36	31	1	4	156	38	63
Spencer Works	36	30	3	3	115	37	63
Blaina West Side	36	27	2	7	116	45	56
Port Talbot Athletic	36	22	6	8	75	33	50
Pontlottyn	36	19	8	9	82	46	46
Afan Lido FC	36	18	9	9	72	45	45
Cardiff College	36	19	7	10	85	57	45
Blaenavon Blues	36	16	7	13	72	75	39
BP Llandarcy	36	15	9	12	76	62	39
Pontyclun	36	12	7	17	53	58	31
Trelewis	36	14	3	19	72	95	31
Caerau Athletic	36	12	5	19	66	81	29
Abercynon Athletic	36	10	9	17	60	81	29
Garw	36	11	5	20	68	91	27
Tondu Robins	36	10	6	20	65	85	26
Seven Sisters	36	9	6	21	54	97	24
Morriston Town	36	5	8	23	54	117	18
Ystradgynlais	36	7	4	25	56	122	18
Semtex	36	1	3	32	21	153	5

WELSH LEAGUE SOUTH 1973-74

Premier Division

Team	P	W	D	L	F	A	Pts
Ton Pentre AFC	34	21	8	5	77	33	50
Pembroke Borough	34	17	12	5	79	35	46
Everwarm FC Bridgend	34	16	11	7	55	37	43
Newport County Reserves	34	17	8	9	61	28	42
Briton Ferry Athletic	34	16	8	10	59	44	40
Cardiff City Reserves	34	14	11	9	75	48	39
Cwmbran Town	34	14	11	9	61	42	39
Ammanford Town	34	14	11	9	54	47	39
Llanelli AFC	34	15	8	11	53	41	38
Ferndale Athletic	34	11	12	11	48	44	34
Cardiff Corinthians	34	11	8	15	60	63	30
Swansea City Reserves	34	12	6	16	61	72	30
Lewistown	34	12	6	16	43	65	30
Caerleon	34	8	13	13	48	58	29
Merthyr Tydfil AFC	34	10	7	17	51	71	27
Maesteg Park	34	7	11	16	32	48	25
Haverfordwest County	34	6	12	16	41	74	24
Cardiff University	34	2	3	29	22	130	7

Division 1

Team	P	W	D	L	F	A	Pts
Pontllanfraith	34	25	6	3	109	42	56
Sully	34	23	7	4	82	30	53
Spencer Works	34	21	7	6	109	59	49
Carmarthen Town	34	18	8	8	63	48	44
Barry Town	34	16	11	7	67	41	43
Swansea University	34	14	8	12	55	49	36
Aberaman Athletic	34	16	4	14	81	78	36
Tredomen Works	34	10	14	10	52	49	34
Tynte Rovers	34	14	5	15	68	70	33
Ynysybwl	34	10	11	13	53	59	31
Tonyrefail Welfare	34	12	6	16	59	72	30
Blaenrhondda	34	9	9	16	41	66	27
Treharris Athletic	34	9	9	16	46	76	27
Clydach United	34	8	8	18	40	70	24
Ebbw Vale AFC	34	10	3	21	53	73	23
Pontardawe Athletic	34	7	9	18	43	75	23
Abergavenny Thursdays	34	7	8	19	49	83	22
Panteg	34	6	9	19	40	70	21

Division 2

Team	P	W	D	L	F	A	Pts
Caerau Athletic	32	23	5	4	105	44	51
Afan Lido FC	32	23	3	6	74	29	49
Blaenavon Blues	32	22	4	6	83	31	48
BP Llandarcy	32	19	5	8	74	47	43
Pontlottyn	32	18	3	11	72	53	39
Blaina West Side	32	16	6	10	74	45	38
Abercynon Athletic	32	12	9	11	64	57	33
Pontyclun	32	12	9	11	50	54	33
Tondu Robins	32	11	9	12	51	53	31
Cardiff College	32	11	5	16	56	48	27
Seven Sisters	32	9	8	15	52	68	26
Port Talbot Athletic	32	8	10	14	26	47	26
Skewen Athletic	32	7	10	15	37	66	24
Garw	32	7	8	17	41	76	22
Morriston Town	32	9	4	19	51	95	22
Trelewis	32	5	6	21	39	85	16
Milford United	32	5	6	21	30	81	16

WELSH LEAGUE SOUTH 1974-75

Premier Division

Newport County Reserves	34	19	13	2	62	29	51
Ferndale Athletic	34	21	8	5	66	26	50
Everwarm FC Bridgend	34	16	11	7	55	35	43
Ton Pentre AFC	34	16	10	8	64	48	42
Llanelli AFC	34	16	8	10	62	35	40
Briton Ferry Athletic	34	17	6	11	70	46	40
Pontllanfraith	34	12	16	6	55	47	40
Sully	34	11	11	12	48	43	33
Pembroke Borough	34	12	9	13	51	53	33
Ammanford Town	34	11	10	13	63	71	32
Swansea City Reserves	34	11	10	13	46	56	32
Cardiff City Reserves	34	12	7	15	47	54	31
Merthyr Tydfil AFC	34	9	12	13	42	50	30
Lewistown	34	10	10	14	47	58	30
Caerleon	34	12	6	16	47	64	30
Cwmbran Town	34	8	9	17	38	62	25
Cardiff Corinthians	34	5	10	19	41	72	20
Maesteg Park	34	1	8	25	26	80	10

Division 1

Spencer Works	34	22	8	4	74	30	52
Haverfordwest County	34	21	8	5	63	35	50
Blaenrhondda	34	22	5	7	62	41	49
Barry Town	34	19	10	5	81	29	48
Afan Lido FC	34	18	9	7	58	34	45
Caerau Athletic	34	16	9	9	58	43	41
Tynte Rovers	34	15	9	10	76	52	39
Pontardawe Athletic	34	10	14	10	56	50	34
Swansea University	34	12	8	14	39	40	32
Ebbw Vale AFC	34	11	8	15	41	53	30
Tredomen Works	34	10	9	15	51	53	29
Tonyrefail Welfare	34	10	9	15	45	57	29
Treharris Athletic	34	10	8	16	51	64	28
Cardiff University	34	7	11	16	47	76	25
Carmarthen Town	34	6	13	15	41	72	25
Aberaman Athletic	34	6	9	19	57	90	21
Clydach United	34	5	10	19	36	71	20
Ynysybwl	34	4	7	23	40	86	15

Division 2

Blaenavon Blues	34	28	3	3	94	15	59
Cardiff College	34	27	5	2	112	22	59
Pontlottyn	34	25	5	4	124	41	55
Blaina West Side	34	18	9	7	72	40	45
Garw	34	16	7	11	53	57	39
Tondu Robins	34	14	10	10	65	50	38
Abercynon Athletic	34	15	7	12	60	51	37
Milford United	34	15	6	13	52	55	36
Pontyclun	34	9	14	11	52	51	32
Port Talbot Athletic	34	14	4	16	45	57	32
Skewen Athletic	34	9	11	14	33	50	29
BP Llandarcy	34	12	4	18	47	73	28
Abergavenny Thursdays	34	9	8	17	55	59	26
Brecon Corinthians	34	9	8	17	54	75	26
Trelewis	34	10	5	19	54	96	25
Panteg	34	8	7	19	42	72	23
Morriston Town	34	1	11	22	22	103	13
Seven Sisters	34	2	6	26	39	108	10

WELSH LEAGUE SOUTH 1975-76

Premier Division

Swansea City Reserves	34	22	7	5	91	32	51
Everwarm FC Bridgend	34	20	10	4	55	20	50
Sully	34	18	7	9	63	47	43
Ferndale Athletic	34	17	9	8	51	39	43
Ammanford Town	34	15	12	7	65	40	42
Cardiff City Reserves	34	15	10	9	57	48	40
Ton Pentre AFC	34	17	4	13	63	50	38
Pontllanfraith	34	14	8	12	53	47	36
Spencer Works	34	13	9	12	51	42	35
Briton Ferry Athletic	34	14	5	15	58	62	33
Newport County Reserves	34	11	10	13	33	33	32
Merthyr Tydfil AFC	34	12	7	15	42	51	31
Pembroke Borough	34	9	12	13	46	61	30
Llanelli AFC	34	10	8	16	36	62	28
Caerleon	34	7	10	17	44	69	24
Blaenrhondda	34	8	5	21	33	65	21
Lewistown	34	6	9	19	29	62	21
Haverfordwest County	34	4	6	24	25	65	14

Division 1

Cardiff College	34	25	4	5	108	22	54
Cwmbran Town	34	20	9	5	64	34	49
Afan Lido FC	34	19	9	6	79	31	47
Pontardawe Athletic	34	18	11	5	68	36	47
Pontlottyn	34	16	9	9	83	55	41
Blaenavon Blues	34	15	10	9	54	41	40
Cardiff Corinthians	34	15	8	11	71	45	38
Caerau Athletic	34	15	8	11	63	72	38
Tonyrefail Welfare	34	12	8	14	69	66	32
Tredomen Works	34	11	10	13	53	56	32
Barry Town	34	11	10	13	47	49	32
Maesteg Park	34	13	5	16	61	64	31
Treharris Athletic	34	14	1	19	68	90	29
Ebbw Vale AFC	34	11	3	20	58	78	25
Swansea University	34	9	7	18	51	79	25
Carmarthen Town	34	7	10	17	49	97	24
Tynte Rovers	34	5	6	23	38	95	16
Cardiff University	34	2	8	24	22	96	12

Division 2

Abergavenny Thursdays	34	25	6	3	104	32	56
Abercynon Athletic	34	23	6	5	84	27	52
Port Talbot Athletic	34	20	7	7	76	31	47
Pontyclun	34	17	11	6	65	39	45
Morriston Town	34	16	12	6	68	42	44
Tondu Robins	34	17	9	8	60	48	43
Milford United	34	17	7	10	73	35	41
Aberaman Athletic	34	13	13	8	82	63	39
Garw	34	13	7	14	65	63	33
Skewen Athletic	34	14	5	15	51	63	33
Clydach United	34	11	10	13	50	54	32
Seven Sisters	34	12	8	14	60	69	32
Blaina West Side	34	10	8	16	48	58	28
Ynysybwl	34	10	7	17	46	70	27
BP Llandarcy	34	8	4	22	41	78	20
Panteg	34	5	9	20	24	71	19
Brecon Corinthians	34	3	5	26	43	109	11
Trelewis	34	2	6	26	37	125	10

WELSH LEAGUE SOUTH 1976-77

Premier Division

Llanelli AFC	34	24	5	5	69	36	53
Bridgend Town	34	19	10	5	56	34	48
Afan Lido FC	34	17	11	6	51	35	45
Cardiff College	34	15	9	10	54	38	39
Ton Pentre AFC	34	15	7	12	51	46	37
Sully	34	12	12	10	55	47	36
Pontllanfraith	34	14	7	13	53	52	35
Swansea City Reserves	34	12	10	12	59	45	34
Merthyr Tydfil AFC	34	14	5	15	63	57	33
Newport County Reserves	34	14	5	15	45	45	33
Ferndale Athletic	34	13	7	14	43	51	33
Cardiff City Reserves	34	13	4	17	45	57	30
Ammanford Town	34	11	7	16	49	59	29
Cwmbran Town	34	8	12	14	24	37	28
Pembroke Borough	34	10	7	17	43	53	27
Briton Ferry Athletic	34	10	6	18	41	68	26
Spencer Works	34	7	12	15	21	39	26
Caerleon	34	6	8	20	37	61	20

Division 1

Caerau Athletic	34	24	5	5	69	25	53
Pontlottyn	34	20	8	6	75	39	48
Barry Town	34	18	10	6	66	27	46
Haverfordwest County	34	18	10	6	63	29	46
Port Talbot Athletic	34	12	13	9	42	35	37
Cardiff Corinthians	34	14	11	9	62	51	39
Treharris Athletic	34	13	11	10	56	55	37
Pontardawe Athletic	34	14	4	16	54	56	32
Blaenavon Blues	34	11	10	13	50	60	32
Tonyrefail Welfare	34	10	11	13	46	55	31
Swansea University	34	10	11	13	67	66	31
Maesteg Park	34	10	11	13	37	39	31
Tredomen Works	34	10	11	13	46	55	31
Blaenrhondda	34	8	11	15	44	63	27
Abercynon Athletic	34	11	5	18	50	77	27
Abergavenny Thursdays	34	8	9	17	50	69	25
Lewistown	34	6	8	20	33	68	20
Ebbw Vale AFC	34	6	7	21	32	86	19

Division 2

Milford United	34	26	4	4	112	37	56
Garw	34	20	9	5	109	49	49
Morriston Town	34	22	4	8	69	32	48
Tondu Robins	34	18	11	5	81	39	47
Aberaman Athletic	34	20	7	7	86	56	47
Ynysybwl	34	18	6	10	74	60	42
BP Llandarcy	34	15	9	10	53	40	39
Trelewis	34	13	8	13	54	58	34
Pontyclun	34	13	8	13	53	60	34
Seven Sisters	34	12	9	13	80	71	33
Carmarthen Town	34	13	6	15	61	74	32
Blaina West Side	34	12	5	17	57	71	29
Brecon Corinthians	34	9	6	19	56	96	24
Clydach United	34	8	7	19	43	65	23
Cardiff University	34	8	7	19	52	81	23
Skewen Athletic	34	8	6	20	48	91	22
Tynte Rovers	34	8	1	25	56	109	17
Panteg	34	2	9	23	39	94	13

WELSH LEAGUE SOUTH 1977-78

Premier Division

Llanelli AFC	34	23	8	3	63	20	54
Newport County Reserves	34	19	9	6	70	27	47
Pontllanfraith	34	19	6	9	66	38	44
Ton Pentre AFC	34	18	8	8	60	33	44
Ammanford Town	34	15	10	9	69	49	40
Pembroke Borough	34	13	10	11	51	48	36
Barry Town	34	11	12	11	42	39	34
Pontlottyn	34	11	12	11	55	55	34
Ferndale Athletic	34	13	8	13	41	43	34
Swansea City Reserves	34	14	5	15	57	66	33
Afan Lido FC	34	12	8	14	48	44	32
Sully	34	13	6	15	44	51	32
Cardiff College	34	11	7	16	48	57	29
Caerau Athletic	34	9	11	14	52	65	29
Merthyr Tydfil AFC	34	10	5	19	48	72	25
Bridgend Town	34	7	11	16	30	60	25
Cardiff City Reserves	34	6	10	18	38	72	22
Cwmbran Town	34	3	12	19	28	71	18

Division 1

Cardiff Corinthians	34	26	3	5	93	31	55
Milford United	34	24	6	4	85	34	54
Treharris Athletic	34	19	11	4	73	45	49
Haverfordwest County	34	21	6	7	72	37	48
Spencer Works	34	16	7	11	58	51	39
Maesteg Park	34	15	8	11	57	45	38
Blaenavon Blues	34	14	10	10	53	48	38
Briton Ferry Athletic	34	14	8	12	64	45	36
Abercynon Athletic	34	14	8	12	57	55	36
Caerleon	34	13	8	13	68	50	34
Port Talbot Athletic	34	12	9	13	50	60	33
Blaenrhondda	34	11	8	15	54	64	30
Garw	34	9	9	16	45	60	27
Pontardawe Athletic	34	10	4	20	44	78	24
Morriston Town	34	9	5	20	43	62	23
Tredomen Works	34	7	7	20	37	65	21
Swansea University	34	6	6	22	29	74	18
Tonyrefail Welfare	34	2	5	27	34	112	9

Division 2

Aberaman Athletic	38	29	6	3	112	44	64
Taffs Well AFC	38	30	4	4	102	41	64
BP Llandarcy	38	27	5	6	84	34	59
Lake United	38	23	11	4	80	27	57
Clydach United	38	20	8	10	69	47	48
Carmarthen Town	38	18	9	11	89	64	45
Tondu Robins	38	18	6	14	93	70	42
Pontyclun	38	14	10	14	64	62	38
Abergavenny Thursdays	38	13	12	13	51	56	38
Ebbw Vale AFC	38	14	8	16	68	71	36
Lewistown	38	13	8	17	51	58	34
Skewen Athletic	38	13	7	18	50	79	33
Brecon Corinthians	38	10	11	17	56	71	31
Trelewis	38	11	9	18	71	87	31
Tynte Rovers	38	12	6	20	69	91	30
Blaina West Side	38	13	2	23	39	70	28
Seven Sisters	38	9	6	23	60	87	24
Panteg	38	7	8	23	48	83	22
Ynysybwl	38	9	4	25	56	106	22
Cardiff University	38	4	6	28	55	119	14

WELSH LEAGUE SOUTH 1978-79

Premier Division

Team	P	W	D	L	F	A	Pts
Pontllanfraith	34	23	7	4	73	37	53
Cardiff Corinthians	34	20	4	10	77	45	44
Newport County Reserves	34	14	13	7	55	25	41
Afan Lido FC	34	17	7	10	43	37	41
Ton Pentre AFC	34	16	8	10	62	42	40
Swansea City Reserves	34	15	9	10	61	47	39
Ammanford Town	34	14	11	9	47	42	39
Pembroke Borough	34	16	6	12	63	50	38
Merthyr Tydfil AFC	34	15	7	12	61	58	37
Barry Town	34	12	11	11	54	45	35
Caerau Athletic	34	13	8	13	45	55	34
Sully	34	13	7	14	42	41	33
Milford United	34	12	8	14	55	45	32
Llanelli AFC	34	11	9	14	41	55	31
Pontlottyn	34	9	10	15	41	57	28
Treharris Athletic	34	9	8	17	43	65	26
Ferndale Athletic	34	3	6	25	36	90	12
Cardiff College	34	1	7	26	25	88	9

Division 1

Team	P	W	D	L	F	A	Pts
Maesteg Park Athletic	34	23	5	6	64	29	51
Cardiff City Reserves	34	17	14	3	75	33	48
Bridgend Town	34	20	6	8	66	42	46
Abercynon Athletic	34	20	6	8	73	53	46
BP Llandarcy	34	16	11	7	44	34	43
Blaenrhondda	34	15	11	8	59	40	41
Briton Ferry Athletic	34	15	8	11	62	47	38
Spencer Works	34	16	6	12	57	50	38
Blaenavon Blues	34	15	7	12	59	46	37
Haverfordwest County	34	12	8	14	64	48	32
Morriston Town	34	11	9	14	40	48	31
Taffs Well AFC	34	12	7	15	54	63	31
Aberaman Athletic	34	10	8	16	43	50	28
Caerleon	34	10	5	19	52	60	25
Cwmbran Town	34	8	8	18	34	53	24
Garw	34	8	4	22	41	64	20
Port Talbot Athletic	34	7	4	23	29	69	18
Pontardawe Athletic	34	5	5	24	26	113	15

Division 2

Team	P	W	D	L	F	A	Pts
Newport YMCA	38	30	5	3	113	33	65
Carmarthen Town	38	25	6	7	90	46	56
Tredomen Works	38	23	8	7	84	40	54
Clydach United	38	22	8	8	69	41	52
Lake United	38	23	4	11	85	37	50
Abergavenny Thursdays	38	21	8	9	75	46	50
Brecon Corinthians	38	20	9	9	102	57	49
Pontyclun	38	22	3	13	90	56	47
Trelewis	38	16	10	12	73	70	42
Swansea University	38	12	12	14	58	55	36
Tondu Robins	38	14	8	16	61	67	36
Blaina West Side	38	13	9	16	60	66	35
Skewen Athletic	38	11	9	18	44	72	31
Ebbw Vale AFC	38	10	10	18	62	76	30
Seven Sisters	38	8	10	20	60	88	26
Panteg	38	9	7	22	67	92	25
Lewistown	38	8	8	22	47	89	24
Tonyrefail Welfare	38	8	6	24	36	76	22
Tynte Rovers	38	7	3	28	57	155	17
Ynysybwl	38	4	5	29	48	119	13

WELSH LEAGUE SOUTH 1979-80

Premier Division

Team	P	W	D	L	F	A	Pts
Newport County Reserves	34	22	8	4	102	39	52
Maesteg Park Athletic	34	20	10	4	60	29	50
Cardiff City Reserves	34	15	13	6	53	32	43
Pontllanfraith	34	15	11	8	61	45	41
Swansea City Reserves	34	13	10	11	60	37	36
Ton Pentre AFC	34	14	8	12	58	47	36
Ammanford Town	34	11	13	10	50	54	35
Bridgend Town	34	12	10	12	51	48	34
Llanelli AFC	34	13	8	13	47	50	34
Milford United	34	12	9	13	46	42	33
Barry Town	34	9	15	10	46	44	33
Merthyr Tydfil AFC	34	11	10	13	60	56	32
Pontlottyn	34	11	8	15	46	72	30
Cardiff Corinthians	34	11	7	16	51	66	29
Pembroke Borough	34	9	7	18	37	74	25
Afan Lido FC	34	6	12	16	31	68	24
Sully	34	7	9	18	30	55	23
Caerau Athletic	34	7	8	19	38	69	22

Division 1

Team	P	W	D	L	F	A	Pts
Haverfordwest County	34	23	6	5	82	39	52
Caerleon	34	21	8	5	62	32	50
Briton Ferry Athletic	34	20	9	5	60	31	49
Tredomen Works	34	17	11	6	65	37	45
Newport YMCA	34	19	5	10	77	48	43
Spencer Works	34	14	12	8	66	46	40
BP Llandarcy	34	14	11	9	51	41	39
Aberaman Athletic	34	13	8	13	67	54	34
Blaenrhondda	34	14	6	14	58	50	34
Abercynon Athletic	34	12	8	14	51	47	32
Treharris Athletic	34	10	11	13	51	69	31
Carmarthen Town	34	11	8	15	59	73	30
Morriston Town	34	12	6	16	38	58	30
Taffs Well AFC	34	12	5	17	52	71	29
South Glamorgan Institute	34	7	13	14	37	62	27
Ferndale Athletic	34	7	12	15	48	65	26
Blaenavon Blues	34	4	5	25	44	79	13
Cwmbran Town	34	1	6	27	35	101	8

Division 2

Team	P	W	D	L	F	A	Pts
Lake United	38	33	2	3	131	33	68
Pontyclun	38	25	9	4	95	22	59
Brecon Corinthians	38	21	10	7	66	44	52
Pontardawe Athletic	38	19	12	7	85	34	50
Clydach United	38	21	7	10	78	53	49
Port Talbot Athletic	38	19	10	9	60	39	48
Tonyrefail Welfare	38	19	8	11	63	51	46
Tondu Robins	38	18	8	12	78	63	44
Garw	38	17	9	12	63	60	43
Abergavenny Thursdays	38	17	8	13	77	57	42
Trelewis	38	15	11	12	64	58	41
Swansea University	38	13	12	13	68	60	38
Ebbw Vale AFC	38	11	16	11	53	58	38
Tynte Rovers	38	12	7	19	68	83	31
Skewen Athletic	38	6	10	22	45	78	22
Panteg	38	7	7	24	44	112	21
Lewistown	38	4	12	22	39	92	20
Seven Sisters	38	4	11	23	41	96	19
Blaina West Side	38	4	9	25	44	98	17
Ynysybwl	38	1	10	27	36	107	12

WELSH LEAGUE SOUTH 1980-81

Premier Division

Haverfordwest County	34	19	10	5	61	39	48
Pontllanfraith	34	17	12	5	60	43	46
Ton Pentre AFC	34	17	6	11	45	48	40
Maesteg Park Athletic	34	14	11	9	60	41	39
Milford United	34	13	11	10	50	49	37
Briton Ferry Athletic	34	15	7	12	50	52	37
Swansea City Reserves	34	12	11	11	66	51	35
Caerleon FC	34	13	9	12	42	39	35
BarryTown	34	14	7	13	45	44	35
Newport County Reserves	34	12	11	11	41	40	35
Pontlottyn	34	10	12	12	41	41	32
Merthyr Tydfil	34	11	9	14	53	50	31
Ammanford Town	34	11	8	15	49	54	30
Cardiff Corinthians	34	12	6	16	47	55	30
Llanelli AFC	34	9	11	14	36	41	29
Bridgend Town	34	11	7	16	40	51	29
Pembroke Borough	34	8	11	15	44	52	27
Cardiff City Reserves	34	4	9	21	30	70	17

Division 1

Sully	34	22	6	6	75	26	50
Lake United	34	20	8	6	61	33	48
Newport YMCA	34	14	17	3	55	28	45
Spencer Works	34	16	13	5	57	36	45
South Glamorgan Institute	34	13	13	8	42	45	39
Blaenrhondda	34	14	9	11	40	43	37
TaffsWell	34	14	5	15	60	54	33
Brecon Corinthians	34	13	7	14	49	54	33
Tredomen Works	34	11	10	13	46	45	32
B.P. (Llandarcy)	34	12	7	15	42	43	31
Pontyclun	34	10	11	13	39	44	31
Carmarthen Town	34	8	14	12	47	57	30
Abercynon Athletic	34	10	9	15	38	41	29
Afan Lido FC	34	10	9	15	44	52	29
Caerau	34	7	12	15	47	54	26
Treharris Athletic	34	7	12	15	36	63	26
Aberaman Athletic	34	9	7	18	41	62	25
Morriston Town	34	8	7	19	32	71	23

Division 2

Trelewis	38	28	6	4	120	40	62
Pontardawe Athletic	38	28	6	4	93	28	62
Clydach United	38	26	7	5	99	37	59
Abergavenny Thursdays	38	26	4	8	115	54	56
Port Talbot Athletic	38	25	5	8	82	37	55
Tonyrefail Welfare	38	23	6	9	79	50	52
Ebbw Vale AFC	38	20	6	12	61	43	46
Garw	38	17	5	16	76	61	39
Ferndale Athletic	38	15	8	15	71	58	38
Tondu Robins	38	14	7	17	66	71	35
Swansea University	38	14	6	18	58	58	34
Panteg	38	11	11	16	55	74	33
Skewen Athletic	38	10	13	15	46	75	33
Seven Sisters	38	10	11	17	67	76	31
Tynte Rovers	38	13	5	20	71	92	31
Cwmbran Town	38	11	4	23	63	78	26
Ynysybwl	38	10	5	23	49	104	25
Blaina West Side	38	6	10	22	36	85	22
Blaenavon Blues	38	6	6	26	44	99	18
Lewistown	38	0	3	35	27	158	3

WELSH LEAGUE SOUTH 1981-82

Premier Division

TonPentre	34	21	7	6	84	46	70
Cardiff Corinthians	34	20	5	9	67	44	65
Caerleon	34	20	3	11	59	46	63
Haverfordwest County	34	19	3	12	60	42	60
Milford United	34	17	8	9	56	39	59
Sully	34	14	12	8	55	41	54
Ammanford Town	34	16	5	13	38	39	53
Maesteg Park	34	15	5	14	56	43	50
Merthyr Tydfil	34	14	6	14	43	42	48
Pembroke Borough	34	12	10	12	54	52	46
Pontllanfraith	34	13	7	14	49	56	46
Newport Y.M.C.A	34	12	9	13	43	52	45
BarryTown	34	13	5	16	67	60	44
Lake United	34	12	6	16	47	51	42
Llanelli	34	11	6	17	38	54	39
Bridgend Town	34	7	10	17	44	60	31
Briton Ferry Athletic	34	7	6	21	34	62	27
Pontlottyn	34	4	5	25	31	96	17

Division 1

Brecon Corinthians	34	26	4	4	74	30	82
Pontardawe Athletic	34	22	8	4	75	36	74
Blaenrhondda	34	21	10	3	74	27	73
Treharris Athletic	34	21	9	4	87	39	72
SpencerWorks	34	19	6	9	74	40	63
B.P. (Llandarcy)	34	15	8	11	58	41	53
Abercynon Athletic	34	13	10	11	61	48	49
Clydach United	34	13	7	14	48	53	46
South Glam. Institute	34	12	8	14	53	53	44
Caerau	34	11	10	13	59	50	43
Morriston Town	34	10	10	14	53	48	40
Trelewis	34	10	10	14	55	64	40
AfanLido	34	9	11	14	48	46	38
TaffsWell	34	10	5	19	43	63	35
Tredomen Works	34	9	4	21	40	92	31
Carmarthen Town	34	5	11	18	28	69	26
Aberaman	34	7	5	22	34	91	26
Pontyclun	34	3	4	27	28	102	13

Division 2

Ferndale Athletic	32	22	5	5	81	39	71
Cwmbran Town	32	20	8	4	77	27	68
EbbwVale	32	20	6	6	78	35	66
Tondu Robins	32	19	6	7	78	33	63
Abergavenny Thursdays	32	19	4	9	88	36	61
Tonyrefail Welfare	32	20	1	11	79	47	61
Port Talbot Athletic	32	16	7	9	56	37	55
Blaenavon Blues	32	15	8	9	64	46	53
Seven Sisters	32	14	7	11	75	59	49
Garw	32	12	8	12	68	57	44
Swansea University	32	9	6	17	42	75	33
Skewen Athletic	32	8	6	18	40	68	30
Panteg	32	8	5	19	44	68	29
Blaina West Side	32	7	3	22	37	98	24
Ynysybwl	32	7	2	23	35	96	23
TynteRovers	32	7	0	25	48	104	21
Lewistown	32	4	8	20	37	102	20

WELSH LEAGUE SOUTH 1982-83

Premier Division

Barry Town	34	26	3	5	103	35	81
Blaenrhondda	34	18	12	4	62	35	66
Newport Y.M.C.A	34	18	8	8	52	38	62
Maesteg Park Athletic	34	18	7	9	52	34	61
Lake United	34	17	8	9	61	43	59
Merthyr Tydfil	34	17	6	11	84	63	57
Sully	34	14	10	10	55	49	52
Caerleon	34	12	10	12	45	46	46
Ton Pentre	34	13	7	14	49	50	46
Pontllanfraith	34	12	9	13	61	49	45
Haverfordwest County	34	12	9	13	40	39	45
Brecon Corinthians	34	11	11	12	37	49	40
Pontardawe Athletic	34	10	5	19	33	57	35
Pembroke Boro	34	9	7	18	46	63	34
Milford United	34	9	6	19	41	76	33
Cardiff Corinthians	34	8	7	19	46	72	28
Llanelli	34	7	6	21	42	77	27
Ammanford Town	34	6	7	21	37	71	25

Cardiff Corinthians had 3 points deducted.
Brecon Corinthians had 4 points deducted.

Division 1

Abercynon Athletic	32	22	7	3	70	33	73
Caerau	32	19	11	2	63	28	68
TaffsWell	32	17	8	7	65	40	59
Morriston Town	32	17	7	8	61	36	58
Spencer Works	32	14	11	7	56	38	53
Treharris Athletic	32	15	8	9	62	45	53
B.P. (Llandarcy)	32	14	9	9	66	45	51
Cwmbran Town	32	13	8	11	60	48	47
Ferndale Athletic	32	10	10	12	47	48	40
Clydach United	32	10	10	12	50	52	40
EbbwVale	32	10	7	15	44	58	37
South Glamorgan Institute	32	16	5	11	71	54	33
Pontlottyn	32	8	5	19	53	77	29
Bridgend Town	32	7	4	21	40	92	25
Briton Ferry Athletic	32	5	8	19	43	78	23
Trelewis	32	6	5	21	40	82	23
AfanLido	32	5	5	22	41	78	20

South Glamorgan Institute had 20 points deducted.

Division 2

Tondu Robins	32	23	7	2	76	21	76
Port Talbot Athletic	32	22	7	3	70	23	73
Garw Athletic	32	20	7	5	73	29	67
Seven Sisters	32	19	6	7	64	38	63
Carmarthen Town	32	18	7	7	60	35	61
Blaenavon Blues	32	15	12	5	68	39	57
Tynte Rovers	32	14	7	11	73	56	49
Tonyrefail Welfare	32	14	6	12	51	45	48
Abergavenny Thursdays	32	10	11	11	44	50	41
Panteg	32	9	9	14	45	60	36
Swansea University	32	10	6	16	43	58	36
Ynysybwl	32	8	10	14	45	59	34
Pontyclun	32	8	10	14	49	66	34
Blaina West Side	32	7	8	17	41	60	29
Skewen Athletic	32	5	7	20	29	66	22
Lewistown	32	4	6	22	30	92	18
Aberaman	32	2	2	28	38	102	8

WELSH LEAGUE SOUTH 1983-84

National Division

BarryTown	30	21	5	4	85	24	68
Caerleon	30	19	5	6	58	28	62
Maesteg Park	30	15	8	7	62	37	53
Haverfordwest County	30	14	7	9	59	41	49
Blaenrhondda	30	14	7	9	55	44	49
Briton Ferry Athletic	30	14	6	10	46	36	48
Bridgend Town	30	14	6	10	39	30	48
Llanelli	30	13	8	9	35	26	47
Ton Pentre	30	13	6	11	43	40	45
Brecon Corinthians	30	13	4	13	49	42	43
Caerau	30	11	5	14	40	52	38
Cwmbran Town	30	10	4	16	40	50	34
Pontllanfraith	30	9	7	14	37	57	34
Pembroke Borough	30	7	8	15	31	47	29
EbbwVale	30	4	3	23	25	88	15
Milford United	30	3	3	24	19	81	12

Premier Division

Sully	36	26	6	4	89	32	77
Cardiff Corinthians	36	21	9	6	60	35	72
Port Talbot Athletic	36	20	11	5	69	33	71
Lake United	36	16	10	10	52	34	58
Newport Y.M.C.A	36	18	4	14	56	46	58
Merthyr Tydfil	36	17	6	13	75	56	57
B.P. (Llandarcy)	36	15	9	12	73	56	54
Morriston Town	36	15	9	12	58	47	54
South Glamorgan Institute	36	14	8	14	75	68	50
Spencer Works	36	12	10	14	54	64	46
Ferndale Athletic	36	12	9	15	52	60	45
Ammanford Town	36	13	6	17	48	63	45
Tondu Robins	36	12	8	16	51	60	44
Abercynon Athletic	36	12	7	17	54	55	43
Pontardawe Athletic	36	11	7	18	24	59	40
Clydach United	36	12	4	20	41	68	40
Treharris Athletic	36	10	7	19	45	72	37
TaffsWell AFC	36	10	6	20	54	70	36
Garw Athletic	36	6	4	26	38	100	22

Sully had 7 points deducted.

Division 1

Pontlottyn	36	28	3	5	99	36	87
Newport County	36	26	4	6	121	38	82
Blaenavon Blues	36	26	3	7	102	28	81
Afan Lido FC	36	20	8	8	76	41	68
Carmarthen Town	36	19	9	8	64	36	66
Tynte Rovers	36	19	6	11	77	54	63
Abergavenny Thursdays	36	18	4	14	73	49	58
Seven Sisters	36	15	7	14	65	56	52
Skewen Athletic	36	15	7	14	61	77	52
Tonyrefail Welfare	36	14	8	14	47	56	50
Ynysybwl	36	11	6	19	49	85	39
Aberaman	36	11	5	20	47	95	38
Panteg	36	9	9	18	40	64	36
Blaina West Side	36	9	9	18	39	66	36
Swansea University	36	10	6	20	42	71	36
Trelewis	36	9	7	20	53	75	34
Pontyclun	36	8	9	19	51	63	33
Lewistown	36	8	4	24	62	127	28
Tredomen Works	36	6	8	22	43	94	26

WELSH LEAGUE SOUTH 1984-85

National Division

Barry Town	32	21	8	3	91	29	71
Bridgend Town	32	19	9	4	69	35	66
Port Talbot Athletic	32	19	6	7	58	31	63
Haverfordwest County	32	18	8	6	60	46	62
Caerleon	32	18	7	7	57	31	61
Maesteg Park	32	16	8	8	55	29	56
Ton Pentre	32	16	4	12	60	37	52
Brecon Corinthians	32	14	9	9	46	37	51
Llanelli	32	11	14	7	55	46	47
Briton Ferry Athletic	32	10	6	16	47	54	36
Caerau	32	8	11	13	43	60	35
Blaenrhondda	32	8	8	16	51	60	32
Pontllanfraith	32	7	11	14	36	59	32
Pembroke Borough	32	6	7	19	29	61	25
Cwmbran Town	32	4	9	19	43	87	21
Ebbw Vale	32	4	8	20	45	86	20
Milford United	32	4	5	23	34	91	17

Premier Division

Cardiff Corinthians	34	27	1	6	97	35	82
Sully	34	20	6	8	76	41	66
AFC Cardiff	34	18	9	7	66	40	63
Clydach United	34	19	3	12	69	50	60
Newport County	34	16	6	12	73	52	54
Pontlottyn	34	14	9	11	61	57	51
Abercynon Athletic	34	13	7	14	69	65	46
Blaenavon Blues	34	13	7	14	63	62	46
Ammanford Town	34	11	9	14	46	46	42
South Glamorgan Institute	34	12	6	16	54	69	42
Merthyr Tydfil	34	11	8	15	51	62	41
Newport YMCA	34	10	11	13	45	62	41
Tondu Robins	34	12	5	17	43	66	41
Ferndale Athletic	34	11	7	16	59	67	40
Spencer Works	34	11	7	16	59	74	40
Pontardawe Athletic	34	10	9	15	33	57	39
BP (Llandarcy)	34	9	8	17	43	78	35
Morriston Town	34	8	4	22	44	68	27

Morriston Town had 1 point deducted.

Division 1

Taffs Well	32	23	4	5	89	20	73
Afan Lido FC	32	22	2	8	81	36	68
Aberaman Athletic	32	20	5	7	88	51	65
Garw Athletic	32	19	4	9	52	35	61
Tonyrefail Welfare	32	16	11	5	64	44	59
Skewen Athletic	32	15	4	13	55	41	49
Abergavenny Thursdays	32	14	6	12	62	48	48
Pontyclun	32	13	9	10	51	40	48
Seven Sisters	32	12	8	12	51	59	44
Ynysybwl	32	13	5	14	63	73	44
Treharris Athletic	32	12	4	16	48	61	40
Carmarthen Town	32	9	8	15	39	64	35
Trelewis	32	10	5	17	38	73	35
Blaina West Side	32	9	6	17	54	74	33
Tynte Rovers	32	8	8	16	55	77	32
Swansea University	32	4	5	23	48	93	17
Panteg	32	4	4	24	46	95	16

WELSH LEAGUE SOUTH 1985-86

National Division

Barry Town	32	23	9	0	84	26	78
Bridgend Town	32	19	6	7	69	42	63
Ebbw Vale	32	19	5	8	71	44	62
Brecon Corinthians	32	17	10	5	59	29	61
Cwmbran Town	32	16	7	9	68	43	55
Briton Ferry Athletic	32	15	9	8	66	50	54
Milford United	32	16	5	11	62	41	53
Ton Pentre	32	13	6	13	72	51	45
Haverfordwest County	32	10	15	7	49	40	45
Pembroke Borough	32	11	9	12	51	56	42
Maesteg Park	32	9	13	10	34	31	40
Blaenrhondda	32	7	10	15	48	82	31
Llanelli	32	7	9	16	51	65	30
Pontllanfraith	32	8	5	19	50	75	29
Caerleon	32	6	8	18	38	68	26
Caerau	32	3	7	22	32	94	16
Port Talbot Athletic	32	2	9	21	29	96	15

Premier Division

Sully	34	28	4	2	104	34	88
AFC Cardiff	34	27	6	1	87	16	87
Cardiff Corinthians	34	19	3	12	76	51	60
Taffs Well	34	18	5	11	75	51	59
Pontlottyn	34	16	7	11	46	44	55
Newport County	34	16	4	14	68	55	52
Blaenavon Blues	34	14	4	16	63	60	46
Clydach United	34	12	9	13	51	52	45
Ammanford Town	34	12	9	13	44	54	45
Newport YMCA	34	11	8	15	33	46	41
Ferndale Athletic	34	12	3	19	62	71	39
Abercynon Athletic	34	7	16	11	34	44	37
Spencer Works	34	10	7	17	46	56	37
Afan Lido FC	34	9	10	15	41	65	37
South Glamorgan Institute	34	9	9	16	46	80	36
Merthyr Tydfil	34	9	8	17	43	66	35
Aberaman Athletic	34	6	10	18	39	78	28
Tondu Robins	34	7	6	21	35	70	27

Division 1

South Wales Constabulary	30	23	5	2	88	24	74
Abergavenny Thursdays	30	23	5	2	95	37	74
Skewen Athletic	30	19	2	9	46	29	59
BP (Llandarcy)	30	17	2	11	50	40	53
Carmarthen Town	30	14	8	8	60	42	50
Treharris Athletic	30	13	8	9	55	47	47
Tonyrefail Welfare	30	14	4	12	56	48	46
Pontyclun	30	13	6	11	46	42	45
Morriston Town	30	13	4	13	52	52	43
Garw Athletic	30	12	4	14	35	47	40
Panteg	30	10	6	14	46	49	36
Ynysybwl	30	6	8	16	45	69	26
Seven Sisters	30	5	8	17	51	75	23
Pontardawe Athletic	30	6	5	19	35	65	23
Tynte Rovers	30	4	8	18	32	76	20
Trelewis	30	4	5	21	25	75	17

WELSH LEAGUE SOUTH 1986-87

National Division

Team	P	W	D	L	F	A	Pts
Barry Town	32	26	5	1	81	20	83
Ton Pentre	32	27	2	3	91	31	83
Cwmbran Town	32	18	8	6	60	31	62
Maesteg Park	32	19	5	8	48	32	62
Haverfordwest County	32	17	5	10	57	37	56
Ebbw Vale	32	16	7	9	72	42	55
Bridgend Town	32	15	7	10	58	46	52
Briton Ferry Athletic	32	14	8	10	46	41	50
Pontllanfraith	32	11	7	14	54	67	40
Brecon Corinthians	32	11	6	15	46	49	39
Milford United	32	11	5	16	38	52	38
Blaenrhondda	32	9	7	16	55	77	34
Llanelli	32	8	6	18	51	63	30
Caerleon	32	7	8	17	37	53	29
Port Talbot Athletic	32	5	7	20	40	85	22
Pembroke Borough	32	4	8	20	40	77	20
Caerau	32	2	3	27	26	97	9

Premier Division

Team	P	W	D	L	F	A	Pts
AFC Cardiff	34	27	4	3	101	23	87
Sully	34	22	4	8	97	45	70
South Wales Police	34	18	10	6	67	36	64
Taffs Well	34	19	6	9	70	47	63
Abergavenny Thursdays	34	18	6	10	76	54	60
Ammanford Town	34	16	9	9	54	35	57
Afan Lido FC	34	16	10	8	57	41	56
Newport County	34	16	5	13	65	56	53
Newport YMCA	34	14	6	14	47	49	48
Cardiff Corinthians	34	13	8	13	51	50	47
Abercynon Athletic	34	13	8	13	46	47	47
Ferndale Athletic	34	12	5	17	50	70	41
Spencer Works	34	8	10	16	41	58	34
Clydach United	34	10	4	20	45	80	34
Pontlottyn	34	9	4	21	45	80	31
Blaenavon Blues	34	7	8	19	39	64	29
Skewen Athletic	34	4	8	22	48	92	20
South Glamorgan Institute	34	4	5	25	26	98	17

Division 1

Team	P	W	D	L	F	A	Pts
BP (Llandarcy)	34	23	6	5	89	39	75
Panteg	34	23	2	9	77	44	71
Tonyrefail Welfare	34	19	5	10	75	39	62
Morriston Town	34	16	11	7	69	55	59
Ynysybwl	34	16	9	9	72	55	57
Aberaman Athletic	34	17	5	12	80	75	56
Pontyclun	34	16	7	11	66	48	55
Tondu Robins	34	16	7	11	63	52	55
Merthyr Tydfil	34	15	8	11	64	56	53
Caldicot Town	34	14	9	11	49	42	51
Garw Athletic	34	14	8	12	53	51	50
Trelewis	34	13	5	16	56	78	44
Treharris Athletic	34	10	8	16	53	64	38
Carmarthen Town	34	8	10	16	42	59	34
Pontardawe Athletic	34	7	11	16	44	60	32
Seven Sisters	34	6	4	24	45	80	22
Tynte Rovers	34	6	4	24	45	88	22
Blaina West Side	34	4	7	23	33	90	19

WELSH LEAGUE SOUTH 1987-88

National Division

Team	P	W	D	L	F	A	Pts
Ebbw Vale	34	26	4	4	82	30	82
Barry Town	34	25	5	4	85	31	80
Ton Pentre	34	24	4	6	75	25	76
Aberystwyth Town	34	19	7	8	80	43	64
Cwmbran Town	34	20	4	10	57	36	64
Haverfordwest County	34	19	6	9	82	45	63
AFC Cardiff	34	15	7	12	50	47	52
Pembroke Borough	34	14	8	12	53	45	50
Briton Ferry Athletic	34	13	10	11	49	47	49
Maesteg Park	34	9	11	14	51	62	38
Port Talbot Athletic	34	9	9	16	34	53	36
Brecon Corinthians	34	10	5	19	44	68	35
Pontllanfraith	34	9	7	18	43	79	34
Llanelli	34	9	6	19	51	81	33
Bridgend Town	34	8	8	18	50	62	32
Caerleon	34	6	8	20	35	63	26
Milford United	34	5	10	19	41	76	25
Blaenrhondda	34	2	9	23	33	104	15

Premier Division

Team	P	W	D	L	F	A	Pts
Afan Lido FC	34	28	3	3	80	25	87
Abergavenny Thursdays	34	23	4	7	77	40	73
Sully	34	21	5	8	77	37	68
Clydach United	34	16	5	13	88	57	53
Newport YMCA	34	13	12	9	46	52	51
Tonyrefail Welfare	34	14	8	12	53	48	50
Ferndale Athletic	34	13	9	12	69	56	48
BP (Llandarcy)	34	13	9	12	57	51	48
Cardiff Corinthians	34	11	13	10	49	54	46
Ammanford Town	34	12	8	14	33	49	44
Panteg	34	12	6	16	54	61	42
Newport County	34	11	8	15	59	59	41
South Wales Police	34	11	8	15	54	64	41
Abercynon Athletic	34	11	7	16	39	61	40
Spencer Works	34	11	4	19	59	67	37
Pontlottyn	34	9	10	15	35	56	36
Caerau	34	7	4	23	34	79	25
Taffs Well	34	5	7	22	40	87	22

Pontlottyn had 1 point deducted.

Division 1

Team	P	W	D	L	F	A	Pts
Merthyr Tydfil	34	23	7	4	83	27	76
Trelewis	34	21	6	7	71	49	69
Morriston Town	34	19	10	5	80	37	67
Caldicot Town	34	17	12	5	65	36	63
Aberaman Athletic	34	17	8	9	66	50	59
Skewen Athletic	34	16	6	12	58	44	54
Seven Sisters	34	15	7	12	56	51	52
Blaenavon Blues	34	14	8	12	61	45	50
Ynysybwl	34	14	7	13	71	68	49
Garw Athletic	34	13	8	13	45	51	47
Carmarthen Town	34	12	10	12	44	46	46
Tondu Robins	34	9	11	14	56	69	38
Pontyclun	34	10	6	18	53	62	36
Pontardawe Athletic	34	8	12	14	54	69	36
Treharris Athletic	34	8	9	17	46	62	33
Tynte Rovers	34	6	10	18	46	66	28
Blaina West Side	34	6	4	24	26	96	22
South Glamorgan Institute	34	2	11	21	24	77	17

WELSH LEAGUE SOUTH 1988-89

National Division

Barry Town	32	28	4	0	96	20	88
Aberystwyth Town	32	24	4	4	85	37	76
Haverfordwest	32	19	6	7	71	32	63
Ebbw Vale	32	18	2	12	60	47	56
Brecon Corinthians	32	16	7	9	54	44	55
Bridgend Town	32	14	7	11	49	46	49
Abergavenny Thursdays	32	13	8	11	52	53	47
Ton Pentre	32	13	4	15	51	48	43
Pembroke	32	11	7	14	38	41	40
Maesteg Park	32	10	6	16	39	48	36
Britol Ferry Athletic	32	10	6	16	45	58	36
Port Talbot	32	10	6	16	38	64	36
AFC Cardiff	32	8	10	14	37	60	34
Cwmbran Town	32	9	6	17	43	59	33
Pontllanfraith	32	7	5	20	39	71	26
Caerleon	32	6	7	19	40	68	25
Milford	32	7	3	22	37	76	24

Premier Division

Afan Lido FC	34	23	7	4	70	29	76
Sully	34	22	8	4	96	41	74
Ammanford	34	22	7	5	72	36	73
Cardiff Corinthians	34	17	8	9	64	36	59
Panteg	34	15	10	9	64	49	55
Ferndale	34	16	5	13	53	45	53
Llanelli	34	14	7	13	74	75	49
Clydach United	34	15	4	15	48	54	46
Newport YMCA	34	12	7	15	43	53	43
Llanwern	34	10	10	14	50	59	40
BP (Llandarcy)	34	10	9	15	37	49	39
Morriston	34	10	8	16	49	61	38
Tonyrefail	34	10	8	16	40	53	38
Blaenrhondda	34	8	13	13	47	68	37
Trelewis	34	9	8	17	47	62	35
Merthyr Tydfil	34	9	6	19	48	63	33
South Wales Police	34	7	10	17	51	83	31
Abercynon Athletic	34	6	7	21	39	76	25

Clydach United had 3 points deducted.

Division 1

Garw	34	23	6	5	78	32	75
Ynysybwl	34	21	6	7	82	43	69
Seven Sisters	34	19	10	5	89	48	67
Pontyclun	34	18	10	6	57	39	64
Carmarthen	34	19	6	9	62	38	63
Treharris	34	18	4	12	65	50	58
Aberaman Athletic	34	15	9	10	65	43	54
Caldicot	34	16	6	12	39	32	54
Skewen	34	14	9	11	58	50	51
Pontllotyn	34	16	3	15	49	53	51
Taffs Well	34	15	5	14	66	54	50
Tondu Robins	34	9	14	11	57	49	41
Blaenavon	34	8	11	15	45	86	35
Caerau	34	8	10	16	39	55	34
South Glamorgan Institute	34	9	6	19	40	74	33
Pontardawe	34	6	8	20	40	66	26
Tynte Rovers	34	4	4	26	40	82	16
Blaina	34	2	5	27	30	107	11

WELSH LEAGUE SOUTH 1989-90

National Division

Haverfordwest County	30	19	5	6	70	25	62
Aberystwyth Town	30	18	7	5	69	32	61
Abergavenny Thursdays	30	18	7	5	66	34	61
Cwmbran Town	30	19	3	8	55	33	60
Llanelli AFC	30	16	6	8	61	38	54
Briton Ferry Athletic	30	16	6	8	58	43	54
AFC Cardiff	30	14	6	10	44	40	48
Pembroke Borough	30	13	7	10	46	38	46
Ton Pentre AFC	30	11	6	13	44	54	39
Bridgend Town	30	9	8	13	38	49	35
Port Talbot Athletic	30	7	11	12	41	46	32
Brecon Corinthians	30	8	7	15	37	50	31
Maesteg Park AFC	30	6	9	15	31	38	27
Ammanford	30	7	6	17	32	54	27
Pontllanfraith	30	3	7	20	33	73	16
Ebbw Vale AFC	30	4	3	23	26	104	15

Premier Division

Sully AFC	34	24	6	4	120	38	78
Ferndale Athletic	34	22	7	5	73	34	73
Afan Lido FC	34	20	6	8	78	43	66
Milford United	34	19	6	9	73	38	63
Ynysybwl	34	18	5	11	67	56	59
Llanwern	34	17	5	12	62	51	56
Clydach United	34	15	8	11	63	60	53
Blaenrhondda	34	14	10	10	63	55	52
Seven Sisters	34	12	8	14	62	74	44
BP Llandarcy	34	12	7	15	48	59	43
Panteg	34	12	5	17	60	76	41
Garw	34	10	7	17	49	66	37
Morriston Town	34	10	7	17	56	81	37
Cardiff Corinthians	34	10	7	17	47	72	37
Newport YMCA	34	9	9	16	42	66	36
Caerleon	34	9	6	19	46	63	33
Tonyrefail Welfare	34	6	9	19	40	75	27
Trelewis	34	4	8	22	43	85	20

Division 1

Caldicot Town	32	20	5	7	66	32	65
Merthyr Tydfil	32	21	1	10	118	51	64
Aberaman Athletic	32	18	9	5	87	43	63
Blaenavon Blues	32	20	2	10	83	49	62
Taffs Well AFC	32	18	5	9	63	45	59
Carmarthen Town	32	16	3	13	68	56	51
South Wales Police	32	12	13	7	48	32	49
Treharris	32	15	4	13	65	51	49
Skewen Athletic	32	12	9	11	48	47	45
Pontlottyn Blast Furnace	32	12	6	14	54	62	42
Caerau	32	11	5	16	39	74	38
Pontardawe	32	9	9	14	47	67	36
Pontyclun FC	32	8	10	14	57	65	34
South Glamorgan Institute	32	9	6	17	40	63	33
Tondu Robins	32	9	5	18	57	68	32
Abercynon Athletic	32	7	8	17	48	90	29
Blaina	32	3	4	25	28	122	13

WELSH LEAGUE SOUTH 1990-91

National Division

	P	W	D	L	F	A	Pts
Abergavenny Thursdays	30	21	6	3	68	23	69
Aberystwyth Town	30	18	5	7	68	35	59
Haverfordwest County	30	16	6	8	56	34	54
Ton Pentre AFC	30	15	8	7	51	30	53
Maesteg Park AFC	30	15	5	10	50	41	50
Inter Cardiff	30	12	8	10	58	46	44
Briton Ferry Athletic	30	12	6	12	63	67	42
Brecon Corinthians	30	10	10	10	47	49	40
Cwmbran Town	30	11	6	13	63	58	39
Pembroke Borough	30	10	9	11	49	51	39
Bridgend Town	30	11	6	13	50	56	39
Afan Lido FC	30	9	8	13	44	62	35
Ferndale Athletic	30	9	7	14	39	54	34
Llanelli AFC	30	8	5	17	48	57	29
Port Talbot Athletic	30	8	5	17	31	56	29
Ammanford	30	2	6	22	20	86	12

Division 1

	P	W	D	L	F	A	Pts
Morriston Town	32	16	12	4	58	37	60
Caldicot Town	32	17	9	6	50	30	60
Ebbw Vale AFC	32	16	11	5	72	29	59
Llanwern	32	17	5	10	67	40	56
Aberaman Athletic	32	16	7	9	63	46	55
BP Llandarcy	32	13	5	14	55	61	44
Blaenrhondda	32	12	8	12	49	56	44
Seven Sisters	32	12	7	13	57	56	43
Newport YMCA	32	11	10	11	43	50	43
Garw	32	11	7	14	43	59	40
Pontypridd/Ynysybwl	32	11	4	17	55	60	37
Caerleon	32	9	9	14	39	51	36
Merthyr Tydfil	32	10	6	16	53	67	36
Pontllanfraith	32	11	3	18	39	60	36
Cardiff Corinthians	32	9	8	15	44	57	35
Panteg	32	9	8	15	47	64	35
Milford United	32	8	9	15	51	62	22

Milford United had 11 points deducted.

Division 2

	P	W	D	L	F	A	Pts
Cardiff Civil Service	32	25	3	4	100	36	78
Risca United	32	24	3	5	77	34	75
Taffs Well AFC	32	20	6	6	76	25	66
Caerau	32	17	6	9	41	30	57
Carmarthen Town	32	17	5	10	82	57	56
Treharris	32	16	3	13	65	68	51
Skewen Athletic	32	13	10	9	54	43	49
AFC Tondu	32	13	6	13	36	48	45
South Wales Police	32	12	5	15	48	55	41
Pontardawe	32	11	5	16	45	55	38
Blaenavon Blues	32	9	9	14	56	58	36
Cardiff Institute	32	11	3	18	40	70	36
Tonyrefail Welfare	32	8	11	13	38	44	35
Pontyclun FC	32	9	5	18	35	62	32
Abercynon Athletic	32	7	9	16	43	74	30
Trelewis	32	7	8	17	42	64	29
Pontllottyn Blast Furnace	32	2	5	25	32	87	11

WELSH LEAGUE SOUTH 1991-92

National Division

	P	W	D	L	F	A	Pts
Abergavenny Thursdays	30	23	5	2	64	24	74
Briton Ferry Athletic	30	23	1	6	72	43	70
Aberystwyth Town	30	18	6	6	65	35	60
Haverfordwest County	30	16	7	7	61	41	55
Ton Pentre AFC	30	16	6	8	51	43	54
Maesteg Park AFC	30	15	6	9	57	37	51
Cwmbran Town	30	11	12	7	51	42	45
Afan Lido FC	30	12	7	11	54	47	43
Pembroke Borough	30	10	7	13	50	48	37
Llanelli AFC	30	9	6	15	43	61	33
Ebbw Vale AFC	30	8	8	14	38	61	32
Inter Cardiff	30	7	8	15	32	45	29
Caldicot Town	30	6	6	18	36	60	24
Brecon Corinthians	30	6	5	19	36	61	23
Bridgend Town	30	4	8	18	25	58	20
Ferndale Athletic	30	4	6	20	31	63	18

Division 1

	P	W	D	L	F	A	Pts
Blaenrhondda	32	18	8	6	76	47	62
Morriston Town	32	18	3	11	58	37	57
Ammanford	32	16	9	7	55	35	57
Port Talbot Athletic	32	15	9	8	57	41	54
Caerleon	32	15	8	9	58	34	53
Pontypridd/Ynysybwl	32	15	4	13	57	53	49
Aberaman Athletic	32	14	6	12	52	48	48
Cardiff Civil Service	32	13	9	10	51	48	48
Taffs Well AFC	32	13	7	12	42	41	46
Risca United	32	12	6	14	51	52	42
Llanwern	32	10	9	13	40	44	39
BP Llandarcy	32	11	5	16	47	54	38
Newport YMCA	32	11	5	16	41	54	38
Cardiff Corinthians	32	9	9	14	50	60	36
Pontllanfraith	32	8	10	14	38	60	34
Seven Sisters	32	8	7	17	37	62	31
Garw	32	5	8	19	30	73	23

Division 2

	P	W	D	L	F	A	Pts
AFC Porth	32	28	3	1	79	20	87
Carmarthen Town	32	22	6	4	71	19	72
Skewen Athletic	32	18	7	7	51	33	61
Tonyrefail Welfare	32	16	8	8	54	36	56
Caerau	32	16	8	8	52	39	56
South Wales Police	32	15	8	9	50	39	53
Pontyclun FC	32	13	9	10	51	39	48
Treharris	32	12	7	13	51	54	43
Pontardawe	32	12	5	15	43	52	41
Pontllottyn Blast Furnace	32	10	9	13	42	42	39
Goytre United	32	10	8	14	40	47	38
Milford United	32	11	5	16	48	68	38
Panteg	32	8	5	19	37	63	29
Cardiff Institute	32	7	7	18	41	67	28
AFC Tondu	32	5	9	18	39	61	24
Abercynon Athletic	32	6	6	20	38	69	24
Trelewis	32	4	8	20	26	65	20

WELSH LEAGUE SOUTH 1992-93

Division 1

Ton Pentre AFC	26	22	1	3	71	20	67
Brecon Corinthians	26	17	4	5	74	40	55
Pontypridd Town	26	14	9	3	53	24	51
Caldicot Town	26	14	4	8	50	31	46
Aberaman Athletic	26	13	3	10	54	47	42
Ammanford	26	11	7	8	38	44	40
Pembroke Borough	26	11	3	12	46	51	36
Cardiff Civil Service	26	11	2	13	40	36	35
Port Talbot Athletic	26	10	4	12	48	49	34
Morriston Town	26	9	5	12	46	66	32
Caerleon	26	8	2	16	37	54	26
Blaenrhondda	26	6	5	15	32	50	23
Bridgend Town	26	6	5	15	38	58	23
Ferndale Athletic	26	2	2	22	119	76	8

Division 2

AFC Porth	26	20	4	2	81	25	64
Caerau	26	16	5	5	61	30	53
Llanwern	26	15	6	5	43	22	51
Risca United	26	15	4	7	44	29	49
Carmarthen Town	26	10	8	8	51	43	38
Taffs Well AFC	26	11	5	10	48	42	38
Skewen Athletic	26	11	2	13	46	48	35
BP Llandarcy	26	9	8	9	35	41	35
Tonyrefail Welfare	26	7	9	10	38	42	30
Garw	26	6	8	12	40	55	26
Fields Park Pontllanfraith	26	7	4	15	33	43	25
Cardiff Corinthians	26	7	7	12	33	69	25
Newport YMCA	26	6	3	17	37	64	21
Seven Sisters	26	4	3	19	24	61	15

Division 3

Treowen Stars	26	21	4	1	61	14	67
Pontyclun FC	26	16	5	5	58	32	53
Milford United	26	15	2	9	74	36	47
Penrhiwceiber	26	13	8	5	57	44	47
Cardiff Institute	26	11	6	9	63	49	39
Panteg	26	10	8	8	44	39	38
Pontardawe	26	9	9	8	46	44	36
Goytre United	26	11	3	12	48	49	36
Pontlottyn Blast Furnace	26	7	9	10	35	44	30
Abercynon Athletic	26	7	8	11	35	47	29
AFC Tondu	26	6	8	12	43	60	26
Treharris	26	6	5	15	40	51	23
South Wales Constabulary	26	4	8	14	34	63	20
Trelewis	26	3	3	20	27	93	12

WELSH LEAGUE SOUTH 1993-94

Division 1

Barry Town	34	27	4	3	94	28	85
Aberaman Athletic	34	20	4	10	71	49	64
AFC Porth	34	19	6	9	68	38	63
Caldicot Town	34	16	11	7	83	59	59
Pontypridd Town	34	15	8	11	53	43	53
Pembroke Borough	34	15	6	13	59	49	51
Cardiff Civil Service	34	15	6	13	59	50	51
Llanwern	34	13	7	14	50	53	46
Ammanford	34	13	6	15	52	55	45
Caerleon	34	12	9	13	50	59	45
Morriston Town	34	11	10	13	45	49	43
Brecon Corinthians	34	11	8	15	57	68	41
Caerau	34	10	10	14	46	50	40
Abergavenny Thursdays	34	10	9	15	40	68	39
Ferndale Athletic	34	7	13	14	36	62	34
Port Talbot Athletic	34	9	7	18	43	71	34
Blaenrhondda	34	8	8	18	47	64	32
Bridgend Town	34	6	6	22	43	81	24

Division 2

Taffs Well AFC	26	17	5	4	66	25	56
Treowen Stars	26	17	5	4	52	25	56
Carmarthen Town	26	15	3	8	58	47	48
Risca United	26	14	3	9	50	34	45
BP Llandarcy	26	12	6	8	50	37	42
Fields Park Pontllanfraith	26	10	9	7	42	36	39
Garw	26	11	6	9	41	35	39
Skewen Athletic	26	10	8	8	44	43	38
Cardiff Corinthians	26	10	4	12	34	51	34
Pontyclun FC	26	7	7	12	33	37	28
Newport YMCA	26	7	6	13	36	50	27
Seven Sisters	26	7	1	18	30	54	22
Tonyrefail Welfare	26	6	3	17	36	54	21
Milford United	26	3	6	17	28	72	15

Division 3

Penrhiwceiber	26	19	4	3	75	23	61
Grange Harlequins	26	19	3	4	92	29	60
Goytre United	26	18	3	5	81	31	57
Porth Tywyn	26	15	3	8	60	34	48
Tondu Robins	26	14	4	8	57	38	46
Pontlottyn Blast Furnace	26	12	8	6	49	36	44
Pontardawe	26	11	5	10	45	50	38
Treharris	26	11	3	12	60	62	36
Albion Rovers	26	8	4	14	46	57	28
Abercynon Athletic	26	4	10	12	33	61	22
South Wales Constabulary	26	5	5	16	43	71	20
Cardiff Institute	26	4	6	16	28	72	18
Panteg	26	3	8	15	34	67	17
Trelewis	26	5	2	19	25	87	17

WELSH LEAGUE SOUTH 1994-95

Division 1

	P	W	D	L	F	A	Pts
Briton Ferry Athletic	36	29	4	3	118	40	91
Haverfordwest County	36	22	7	7	108	51	73
Carmarthen Town	36	20	9	7	89	45	69
Abergavenny Thursdays	36	20	5	11	68	45	65
Caldicot Town	36	20	4	12	69	46	64
Treowen Stars	36	17	9	10	69	51	60
AFC Porth	36	18	5	13	85	69	59
Taffs Well AFC	36	15	10	11	68	53	55
Llanwern	36	14	12	10	70	48	54
Aberaman Athletic	36	15	8	13	82	67	53
Pontypridd Town	36	16	2	18	67	58	50
Brecon Corinthians	36	14	6	16	66	75	48
Cardiff Civil Service	36	12	11	13	67	65	47
Caerleon	36	12	9	15	54	69	45
Ammanford	36	12	8	16	43	52	44
Morriston Town	36	12	4	20	56	82	40
Caerau	36	6	11	19	39	102	29
Ferndale Athletic	36	2	2	32	23	123	5
Pembroke Borough	36	2	2	32	33	133	2

Ferndale Athletic had 3 points deducted.
Pembroke Borough had 6 points deducted.

Division 2

	P	W	D	L	F	A	Pts
Penrhiwceiber	26	17	6	3	67	22	57
Risca United	26	16	6	4	50	29	54
Cardiff Corinthians	26	16	2	8	50	48	50
Goytre United	26	14	4	8	48	31	46
BP Llandarcy	26	13	6	7	46	38	45
Grange Harlequins	26	13	5	8	55	34	44
Garw	26	12	6	8	49	40	42
Port Talbot Athletic	26	10	4	12	60	42	34
Bridgend Town	26	7	7	12	44	47	28
Blaenrhondda	26	7	7	12	32	38	28
Pontyclun FC	26	7	5	14	27	48	26
Fields Park Pontllanfraith	26	6	6	14	34	56	24
Skewen Athletic	26	5	6	15	20	48	21
Milford United	26	3	2	21	26	87	11

Division 3

	P	W	D	L	F	A	Pts
Pontardawe	30	20	4	6	77	44	64
Porth Tywyn	30	18	6	6	66	39	60
Porthcawl Town	30	18	5	7	82	46	59
Cardiff Institute	30	17	8	5	82	35	55
Monkton Swifts	30	17	3	10	66	40	54
Pontlottyn Blast Furnace	30	12	12	6	53	34	48
Albion Rovers	30	14	4	12	66	71	46
Tondu Robins	30	11	9	10	43	45	42
Tonyrefail Welfare	30	12	6	12	63	73	42
Seven Sisters	30	9	8	13	55	62	35
Newport YMCA	30	8	7	15	41	56	31
Panteg	30	7	10	13	43	62	31
Treharris	30	7	8	15	56	72	29
Abercynon Athletic	30	7	5	18	39	71	26
Trelewis	30	6	4	20	47	80	22
South Wales Police	30	5	5	20	35	84	20

Cardiff Institute had 4 points deducted.

WELSH LEAGUE SOUTH 1995-96

Division 1

	P	W	D	L	F	A	Pts
Carmarthen Town	34	25	7	2	101	37	82
Haverfordwest County	34	23	7	4	116	34	76
Maesteg Park AFC	34	20	8	6	73	47	68
Cardiff Civil Service	34	19	6	9	82	47	63
Treowen Stars	34	18	6	10	67	46	60
Llanwern	34	15	7	12	57	55	52
Penrhiwceiber	34	14	9	11	69	58	51
Taffs Well AFC	34	14	9	11	66	63	51
Caldicot Town	34	14	4	16	60	68	46
AFC Porth	34	11	10	13	57	67	43
Risca United	34	12	6	16	50	67	42
Aberaman Athletic	34	11	7	16	64	79	40
Cardiff Corinthians	34	11	7	16	46	56	40
Abergavenny Thursdays	34	10	8	16	50	62	38
Pontypridd Town	34	12	7	15	58	73	36
Brecon Corinthians	34	8	3	23	47	90	27
Ammanford	34	6	5	23	43	105	23
Caerleon	34	2	6	26	30	82	12

Pontypridd Town had 7 points deducted

Division 2

	P	W	D	L	F	A	Pts
Grange Harlequins	30	21	2	7	97	39	65
Goytre United	30	19	6	5	84	36	63
Port Talbot	30	19	5	6	69	32	62
Pontardawe	30	21	3	6	77	37	59
BP Llandarcy	30	18	4	8	69	38	58
Porthcawl Town	30	15	7	8	61	32	52
Porth Tywyn	30	13	8	9	51	35	47
Pontyclun	30	12	9	9	48	48	45
Bridgend Town	30	12	5	13	52	44	41
Caerau	30	12	5	13	46	45	41
Skewen	30	8	8	14	59	65	32
Fields Park Pontllanfraith	30	9	3	18	46	71	30
Morriston	30	9	2	19	40	55	29
Blaenrhondda	30	6	7	17	50	79	25
Garw	30	7	1	22	30	84	22
Ferndale Athletic	30	1	1	28	27	166	4

Pontardawe had 7 points deducted.

Division 3

	P	W	D	L	F	A	Pts
Cardiff Institute	28	26	2	0	104	16	80
Treharris	28	23	3	2	118	30	72
Hoover Sports	28	22	3	3	102	27	65
Abercynon Athletic	28	16	2	10	66	55	50
Tonyrefail	28	16	1	11	73	71	49
Newport YMCA	28	11	6	11	68	56	39
Monkton Swifts	28	11	5	12	71	56	38
Albion Rovers	28	11	5	12	48	52	38
Pontlottyn Blast Furnace	28	10	3	15	63	77	33
Seven Sisters	28	10	2	16	48	57	32
Panteg	28	8	6	14	48	58	30
Milford United	28	9	2	17	63	66	29
South Wales Police	28	9	1	18	38	67	28
Trelewis	28	5	2	21	42	108	17
Tondu Robins	28	1	1	26	19	175	4

Hoover Sports had 4 points deducted

WELSH LEAGUE SOUTH 1996-97
Division 1

Haverfordwest County	34	25	4	5	111	24	79
Llanelli	34	21	6	7	76	43	69
AFC Rhondda	34	20	8	6	65	30	68
Treowen Stars	34	19	8	7	74	39	65
Goytre	34	20	5	9	67	43	65
Afan Lido FC	34	18	9	7	60	31	63
Cardiff Corinthians	34	16	6	12	44	56	54
Grange Harlequins	34	15	5	14	75	58	47
Maesteg Park	34	11	11	12	53	52	44
Port Talbot	34	12	7	15	38	49	43
Cardiff Civil Service	34	12	6	16	50	61	42
Llanwern	34	10	9	15	49	53	39
Aberaman Athletic	34	10	8	16	48	63	38
Taffs Well	34	9	8	17	39	60	35
Abergavenny Thursdays	34	10	3	21	39	68	33
Risca	34	8	5	21	32	69	29
Penrhiwceiber	34	6	5	23	31	103	23
Caldicot Town	34	4	7	23	37	86	19

Grange Harlequins had 3 points deducted.

Division 2

Bridgend Town	30	22	5	3	74	18	71
Univ. Wales Insitute Cardiff	30	20	5	5	80	25	65
Porthcawl Town	30	17	7	6	79	38	58
Pontardawe	30	17	4	9	88	49	55
Porth Tywyn	30	16	7	7	61	39	55
Treharris	30	17	4	9	65	48	55
BP Llandarcy	30	16	4	10	94	46	52
Hoover Sports	30	15	4	11	73	55	49
Caerau	30	13	4	13	62	56	43
Pontyclun	30	9	10	11	44	54	36
Pontypridd	30	9	4	17	46	71	31
Ammanford	30	7	6	17	45	82	27
Brecon Corinthians	30	8	3	19	48	126	27
Skewen	30	7	5	18	42	65	26
Caerleon	30	3	6	21	25	76	15
Fields Park Pontllanfraith	30	2	6	22	34	112	12

Pontyclun had 1 point deducted.

Division 3

Gwynfi United	30	25	3	2	99	23	78
Blaenrhondda	30	21	5	4	88	32	68
Albion Rovers	30	18	4	8	76	35	58
Milford United	30	14	7	9	55	52	49
Monkton Swifts	30	12	7	11	50	59	43
Newport YMCA	30	11	7	12	54	52	40
Garw	30	10	8	12	51	64	38
Panteg	30	10	7	13	44	53	37
Pontlottyn Blast Furnace	30	11	4	15	49	59	37
Tonyrefail	30	11	4	15	44	60	37
Morriston	30	9	9	12	45	51	36
Ferndale Athletic	30	10	4	16	57	57	34
Abercynon Athletic	30	10	4	16	44	62	34
South Wales Police	30	10	4	16	45	76	34
Seven Sisters	30	8	7	15	43	73	31
Trelewis	30	5	6	19	41	77	21

WELSH LEAGUE SOUTH 1997-98
Division 1

Ton Pentre	36	28	4	4	122	39	88
Afan Lido FC	36	27	4	5	86	26	85
Llanelli	36	26	4	6	88	30	82
Treowen Stars	36	24	2	10	76	43	74
Port Talbot	36	22	5	9	70	51	71
Goytre	36	20	3	13	89	42	63
Univ. Wales Insitute Cardiff	36	18	7	11	59	35	61
AFC Rhondda	36	15	13	8	73	51	58
Bridgend Town	36	14	7	15	80	65	48
Maesteg Park	36	13	8	15	82	73	47
Grange Harlequins	36	13	6	17	54	66	45
Porthcawl	36	13	3	20	63	78	42
Cardiff Corinthians	36	9	12	15	63	66	39
Briton Ferry Athletic	36	12	3	21	63	94	39
Cardiff Civil Service	36	11	5	20	50	83	38
Aberaman Athletic	36	9	4	23	43	77	31
Taffs Well	36	6	9	21	46	83	27
Llanwern	36	6	10	20	53	79	25
Abergavenny Thursdays	36	0	3	33	31	210	3

Bridgend Town had 1 point deducted.
Llanwern had 3 points deducted.

Division 2

Pontardawe	30	20	6	4	81	37	66
Port Tywyn	30	19	5	6	86	41	62
BP Llandarcy	30	19	5	6	84	48	62
Gwynfi United	30	18	4	8	78	48	58
Risca United	30	16	7	7	67	35	55
Hoover Sports	30	16	7	7	83	59	55
Treharris Athletic	30	13	9	8	67	45	48
Ammanford	30	13	5	12	45	58	44
Blaenrhondda	30	12	5	13	58	52	41
Caldicot Town	30	8	11	11	50	50	35
Penrhiwceiber	30	9	7	14	62	85	34
Pontypridd	30	10	2	18	41	85	32
Albion Rovers	30	8	7	15	53	71	31
Pontyclun	30	6	4	20	37	72	22
Caerau	30	5	3	22	39	82	18
Brecon Corinthians	30	2	5	23	35	98	11

Division 3

Milford United	30	23	3	4	88	37	72
Chepstow Town	30	21	5	4	84	43	68
Morriston Town	30	20	6	4	85	36	66
Fields Park Pontllanfraith	30	20	5	5	66	29	65
Ely Rangers	30	14	7	9	71	47	49
Caerleon	30	11	9	10	49	45	39
Monkton Swifts	30	11	5	14	54	59	38
Newport YMCA	30	10	7	13	49	55	37
Skewen Athletic	30	11	4	15	59	65	37
Garw	30	10	7	13	53	57	36
Pontlottyn Blast Furnace	30	9	7	14	52	61	34
South Wales Police	30	9	3	18	47	72	30
Abercynon Athletic	30	9	3	18	39	70	30
Panteg	30	9	2	19	38	71	29
Tonyrefail	30	8	2	20	48	84	26
Ferndale Athletic	30	6	3	21	36	85	21

Caerleon had 3 points deducted.
Garw had 1 point deducted.

WELSH LEAGUE SOUTH 1998-99

Division 1

Team							
Ton Pentre	34	25	5	4	79	32	80
Llanelli	34	21	5	9	79	45	68
AFC Rhondda	34	19	7	8	78	46	64
BP Llandarcy	34	19	4	11	69	47	61
Univ. Wales Insitute Cardiff	34	15	8	11	49	44	53
Pontardawe	34	15	8	11	55	54	53
Bridgend Town	34	14	10	10	76	48	52
Maesteg Park	34	13	12	9	51	43	51
Port Talbot	34	15	4	15	54	56	49
Treowen Stars	34	12	10	12	57	52	46
Goytre	34	13	5	16	50	50	44
Cardiff Civil Service	34	12	4	18	41	64	40
Aberaman Athletic	34	10	7	17	53	74	37
Briton Ferry Athletic	34	9	9	16	46	66	36
Cardiff Corinthians	34	9	8	17	51	70	35
Porth Tywyn	34	7	11	16	57	66	32
Grange Harlequins	34	6	10	17	46	83	28
Porthcawl	34	6	5	23	35	86	23

Division 2

Team							
Penrhlwceiber	30	21	5	4	83	30	68
Gwynfi United	30	19	6	5	79	36	63
Ammanford	30	18	5	7	71	30	59
Taffs Well	30	17	6	7	67	35	57
Risca United	30	15	6	9	51	41	51
Milford United	30	14	8	8	68	38	50
Chepstow Town	30	14	8	8	75	46	50
Hoover Sports	30	15	4	11	89	57	49
Llanwern	30	14	3	13	68	64	45
Blaenrhondda	30	11	6	13	41	50	39
Caldicot Town	30	10	7	13	59	73	37
Abergavenny Thursdays	30	11	3	16	51	75	36
Morriston Town	30	7	6	17	34	73	27
Albion Rovers	30	5	3	22	34	85	18
Treharris Athletic	30	5	3	22	44	113	18
Pontypridd	30	4	1	25	43	111	13

Division 3

Team							
Caerleon	32	27	1	4	114	39	82
Tredegar Town	32	24	4	4	101	40	76
Fields Park Pontllanfraith	32	24	3	5	77	30	75
Garw	32	22	1	9	98	41	67
Ely Rangers	32	20	5	7	88	39	65
Caerau Ely	32	16	7	9	96	50	55
Skewen Athletic	32	17	1	14	73	63	52
Pontyclun	32	14	4	14	53	52	46
Pontlottyn Blast Furnace	32	13	5	14	67	71	44
Newport YMCA	32	12	5	15	57	61	41
Caerau	32	9	8	15	55	73	35
Seven Sisters	32	9	4	19	64	83	31
Abercynon Athletic	32	9	3	20	43	88	30
Monkton Swifts	32	7	5	20	39	79	26
S W Police	32	7	4	21	40	110	25
Panteg	32	5	6	21	38	96	21
Brecon Corinthians	32	1	6	25	25	113	9

WELSH LEAGUE SOUTH 1999-00

Division 1

Team							
Ton Pentre	34	25	5	4	111	34	80
Port Talbot	34	22	9	3	85	33	75
Maesteg Park	34	18	11	5	67	41	65
BP Llandarcy	34	17	5	12	96	57	56
Cardiff Civil Service	34	15	9	10	70	49	54
AFC Rhondda	34	17	3	14	67	61	54
Bridgend Town	34	15	5	14	67	72	50
Britol Ferry Athletic	34	14	6	14	47	55	48
Gwynfi United	34	14	5	15	73	79	47
Penrhiwceiber	34	13	6	15	61	65	45
Goytre	34	13	6	15	64	70	45
Porth Tywyn	34	12	7	15	60	70	43
Treowen Stars	34	12	6	16	61	74	42
Pontardawe	34	11	8	15	56	63	41
Univ. Wales Insitute Cardiff	34	10	8	16	50	82	38
Ammanford	34	10	6	18	41	54	36
Cardiff Corinthians	34	9	7	18	45	71	34
Aberaman	34	2	2	30	47	138	8

Division 2

Team							
Fields Park Pontllanfraith	30	20	5	5	103	30	65
Milford United	30	19	5	6	77	43	62
Caerleon	30	17	9	4	75	40	60
Porthcawl	30	16	7	7	66	40	55
Chepstow Town	30	15	8	7	78	55	53
Hoover Sports	30	15	6	9	87	61	51
Taffs Well	30	15	5	10	63	50	50
Tredegar Town	30	17	3	10	94	56	48
Risca United	30	12	4	14	53	61	40
Llanwern	30	9	8	13	63	55	35
Caldicot	30	9	6	15	50	51	33
Portos Grange Harlequins	30	9	5	16	60	73	32
Albion Rovers	30	8	7	15	48	72	31
Blaenrhondda	30	5	8	17	46	72	23
Morriston Town	30	5	4	21	36	117	19
Abergavenny Thursdays	30	2	4	24	25	148	10

Tredegar Town had 6 points deducted.

Division 3

Team							
Garw	28	24	2	2	101	25	74
Ely Rangers	28	23	4	1	94	27	73
Garden Village	28	17	4	7	56	31	55
AFC Llwydcoed	28	17	3	8	72	56	54
Seven Sisters	28	14	5	9	64	58	47
Treharris Athletic	28	14	3	11	70	54	45
Skewen Athletic	28	13	2	13	74	68	41
Caerau	28	11	7	10	50	43	40
Caerau Ely	28	10	4	14	63	71	34
Newport YMCA	28	11	0	17	46	76	33
Pontyclun	28	9	3	16	45	61	30
Pontypridd	28	6	10	12	54	62	28
Abercynon	28	6	3	19	45	84	21
Monkton Swifts	28	4	3	21	35	99	15
Pontlottyn	28	3	3	22	39	93	12

WELSH LEAGUE SOUTH 2000-01

Division 1

Ton Pentre	34	20	11	3	81	28	71
Maesteg Park	34	21	8	5	61	28	71
Fields Park Pontllanfraith	34	21	5	8	77	39	68
Goytre United	34	21	5	8	72	52	68
Caerleon	34	17	12	5	55	37	63
Pontardawe	34	13	9	12	64	50	48
Cardiff Corinthians	34	12	8	14	50	49	44
AFC Rhondda	34	11	10	13	47	54	43
Ammanford	34	11	8	15	45	56	41
Neath	34	10	10	14	49	53	40
Penrhiwceiber	34	11	7	16	62	73	40
Gwynfl United	34	12	3	19	47	73	39
Milford United	34	10	8	16	44	58	38
Bridgend Town	34	10	8	16	47	65	38
Cardiff Civil Service	34	8	13	13	47	51	37
Porth Tywyn	34	10	7	17	35	63	37
Britol Ferry Athletic	34	9	8	17	49	66	35
Treowen Stars	34	6	6	22	35	72	24

Division 2

Garw	30	24	1	5	93	33	73
Llanwern	30	18	5	7	65	37	59
Ely Rangers	30	18	4	8	61	30	58
Porthcawl	30	16	4	10	58	46	52
Chepstow Town	30	18	3	9	57	48	51
Blaenrhondda	30	14	6	10	49	52	48
Tredegar Town	30	13	4	13	66	54	43
Garden Village	30	11	8	11	50	54	41
Taffs Well	30	10	10	10	49	52	40
Merthyr Saints	30	12	3	15	41	58	39
Aberaman	30	11	3	16	55	64	36
Portos Grange Harlequins	30	9	6	15	50	55	33
Morriston Town	30	9	6	15	49	68	33
Risca United	30	8	5	17	46	55	29
Caldicot	30	8	4	18	60	66	28
Albion Rovers	30	3	4	23	22	99	13

Chepstow Town had 6 points deducted.

Division 3

Bettws	30	19	4	7	73	35	61
AFC Llwydcoed	30	18	5	7	66	37	59
Treharris Athletic	30	17	5	8	77	50	56
Dinas Powys	30	17	4	9	72	35	55
Caerau Ely	30	16	6	8	72	48	54
Newport YMCA	30	15	5	10	60	45	50
Pontlottyn	30	14	6	10	54	42	48
Newcastle Emlyn	30	15	3	12	54	55	48
Pontyclun	30	12	11	7	66	40	47
Pontypridd	30	10	10	10	40	47	40
Cwmtillery	30	11	3	16	56	63	36
Abercynon	30	10	5	15	62	80	35
Skewen Athletic	30	8	5	17	49	72	29
Seven Sisters	30	7	6	17	48	69	27
Caerau	30	6	8	16	47	61	26
Abergavenny Thursdays	30	1	2	27	21	138	5

WELSH LEAGUE SOUTH 2001-02

Division 1

Ton Pentre	36	26	6	4	81	22	84
Pontardawe	36	27	2	7	94	36	83
Univ. Wales Insitute Cardiff	36	23	7	6	81	45	76
Garw	36	18	10	8	74	49	64
Neath	36	19	7	10	64	47	64
Maesteg Park	36	18	6	12	61	53	60
Goytre United	36	14	13	9	61	49	55
Ely Rangers	36	15	9	12	69	52	54
Llanwern	36	13	8	15	76	62	47
Gwynfl United	36	14	6	16	66	69	45
Caerleon	36	12	6	18	48	55	42
Penrhiwceiber	36	12	6	18	69	100	42
Cardiff Corinthians	36	12	5	19	54	66	41
Milford United	36	10	9	17	43	64	39
Cardiff Civil Service	36	10	7	19	54	62	37
Fields Park Pontllanfraith	36	10	7	19	50	76	37
AFC Rhondda	36	9	4	23	30	80	31
Ammanford	36	8	5	23	40	85	29
Bridgend Town	36	7	7	22	50	93	28

Gwynfl United had 3 points deducted.

Division 2

Garden Village	30	21	2	7	69	38	65
Bettws	30	21	1	8	85	41	64
Britol Ferry Athletic	30	18	6	6	62	30	60
Porth Tywyn	30	18	4	8	58	48	58
Aberaman	30	15	5	10	71	52	50
Taffs Well	30	13	7	10	74	54	46
AFC Llwydcoed	30	12	6	12	65	55	42
Blaenrhondda	30	13	6	11	66	54	41
Tredegar Town	30	17	2	11	68	60	41
Porthcawl	30	12	5	13	63	60	41
Portos Grange Harlequins	30	11	5	14	52	61	38
Morriston Town	30	8	7	15	52	67	31
Merthyr Saints	30	8	7	15	63	82	31
Treharris Athletic	30	7	5	18	49	72	26
Treowen Stars	30	7	3	20	31	83	24
Chepstow Town	30	1	5	24	41	112	8

Blaenrhondda had 4 points deducted.
Tredegar Town had 12 points deducted.

Division 3

Newport YMCA	34	27	3	4	90	33	84
Dinas Powys	34	26	5	3	96	25	83
Pontypridd	34	20	9	5	77	32	69
Caldicot	34	21	4	9	77	34	67
Newcastle Emlyn	34	18	4	12	64	59	58
Seven Sisters	34	15	10	9	86	62	55
Pontyclun	34	16	6	12	59	48	54
Tillery	34	15	7	12	70	52	52
Risca United	34	14	7	13	50	52	49
Pentwyn Dynamo	34	13	6	15	79	71	45
Troedyrhiw	34	10	12	12	56	53	42
Caerau Ely	34	11	8	15	58	64	41
Skewen Athletic	34	10	8	16	47	66	38
Pontlottyn	34	8	12	14	49	62	36
Albion Rovers	34	9	5	20	51	63	32
RTB Ebbw Vale	34	8	8	18	52	75	32
Caerau	34	6	3	25	50	106	21
Abercynon	34	0	1	33	21	175	1

WELSH LEAGUE SOUTH 2002-03

Division 1

Bettws	34	24	5	5	89	30	77
Neath	34	24	5	5	71	29	77
Univ. Wales Insitute Cardiff	34	23	7	4	67	33	76
Ton Pentre	34	22	3	9	86	35	69
Goytre United	34	19	3	12	56	39	60
Garw	34	16	5	13	61	57	53
Britol Ferry Athletic	34	14	4	16	50	53	46
Cardiff Civil Service	34	12	9	13	45	52	45
Maesteg Park	34	13	6	15	44	57	45
Pontardawe	34	12	7	15	51	49	43
Cardiff Corinthians	34	12	6	16	40	59	42
Caerleon	34	10	10	14	49	48	40
Llanwern	34	11	5	18	44	64	38
Gwynfi United	34	10	7	17	56	57	37
Ely Rangers	34	10	6	18	46	52	36
Garden Village	34	9	7	18	39	65	34
Penrhiwceiber	34	9	7	18	48	81	34
Milford United	34	1	8	25	26	108	11

Division 2

Dinas Powys	34	24	7	3	97	31	79
Grange Harlequins	34	22	6	6	95	46	72
Bridgend Town	34	21	9	4	73	33	72
AFC Llwydcoed	34	18	11	5	67	33	65
Taffs Well	34	15	7	12	65	54	52
Newport YMCA	34	15	7	12	50	46	52
Pontypridd	34	12	15	7	62	41	51
Aberaman	34	14	8	12	69	65	50
Tredegar Town	34	14	6	14	70	63	48
Ammanford	34	14	5	15	65	63	47
Blaenrhondda	34	13	4	17	45	70	43
Treharris Athletic	34	10	10	14	55	55	40
Morriston Town	34	11	6	17	55	76	39
Merthyr Saints	34	11	5	18	50	69	38
Porthcawl	34	10	4	20	55	98	34
Porth Tywyn	34	9	5	20	52	79	32
AFC Rhondda	34	8	7	19	48	73	31
Fields Park Pontllanfraith	34	3	2	29	36	114	11

Division 3

Pontyclun	34	21	7	6	73	39	70
Skewen Athletic	34	22	4	8	77	43	70
Caldicot	34	19	8	7	67	42	65
Caerau Ely	34	19	7	8	77	46	64
Bryntirion	34	19	4	11	70	41	61
Seven Sisters	34	15	7	12	59	53	52
Troedyrhiw	34	15	5	14	53	52	50
Pontlottyn	34	14	8	12	70	72	50
Treowen Stars	34	13	7	14	50	48	46
Tillery	34	11	10	13	64	72	43
Albion Rovers	34	11	7	16	54	64	40
Risca United	34	10	9	15	53	65	39
Cwmmaman	34	11	5	18	57	70	38
Chepstow Town	34	10	8	16	67	84	38
Pentwyn Dynamo	34	9	8	17	59	70	35
Newcastle Emlyn	34	10	5	19	51	75	35
RTB Ebbw Vale	34	10	3	21	52	82	33
Caerau	34	8	6	20	58	93	30

WELSH LEAGUE SOUTH 2003-04

Division 1

Llanelli	34	26	4	4	74	28	82
Goytre United	34	22	9	3	73	24	75
Grange Harlequins	34	22	8	4	74	26	74
Univ. Wales Insitute Cardiff	34	21	6	7	72	33	69
Ton Pentre	34	20	6	8	96	38	66
Dinas Powys	34	14	11	9	58	41	53
Maesteg Park	34	14	11	9	39	36	53
Neath	34	15	5	14	65	56	50
Britol Ferry Athletic	34	11	11	12	53	45	44
Bridgend Town	34	12	7	15	50	60	43
Garw	34	11	5	18	46	66	38
Caerleon	34	10	7	17	56	62	37
Bettws	34	9	5	20	39	66	32
Ely Rangers	34	8	7	19	42	64	31
Gwynfi United	34	8	7	19	37	77	31
Cardiff Corinthians	34	7	6	21	39	65	27
Pontardawe	34	7	6	21	37	103	27
Llanwern	34	6	5	23	36	96	23

Division 2

Skewen Athletic	32	23	7	2	72	26	76
Taffs Well	32	22	7	3	97	43	73
AFC Llwydcoed	32	23	3	6	83	36	72
Newport YMCA	32	22	4	6	88	46	70
Merthyr Saints	32	15	4	13	65	63	49
Pontyclun	32	15	3	14	48	50	48
Morriston Town	32	13	8	11	51	51	47
Garden Village	32	13	4	15	55	56	43
Aberaman	32	11	9	12	58	68	42
Ammanford	32	10	7	15	52	66	37
Caldicot	32	8	10	14	46	51	34
Porthcawl	32	9	5	18	58	76	32
Tredegar Town	32	8	7	17	50	69	31
Penrhiwceiber	32	7	9	16	38	70	30
Pontypridd Town	32	8	5	19	39	58	29
Blaenrhondda	32	8	5	19	48	68	29
Treharris Athletic	32	5	7	20	41	92	22

Division 3

Bryntirion Athletic	30	24	3	3	105	28	75
Seven Sisters	30	21	3	6	69	34	66
Tillery	30	18	4	8	62	42	58
Treowen Stars	30	17	4	9	54	32	55
Troedyrhiw	30	17	2	11	67	47	53
Pentwyn Dynamo	30	13	5	12	59	63	44
Goytre	30	12	7	11	44	44	43
Caerau Ely	30	11	8	11	48	46	41
Chepstow Town	30	11	4	15	56	63	37
Cwmamman United	30	11	4	15	54	63	37
Newcastle Emlyn	30	9	10	11	50	60	37
Risca & Gelli	30	10	5	15	35	38	35
AFC Rhondda	30	8	10	12	35	51	34
Fields Park Pontllanfraith	30	8	7	15	40	63	31
Llantwit Fardre	30	6	3	21	38	60	21
Albion Rovers	30	4	1	25	26	108	13

WELSH LEAGUE SOUTH 2004-05

Division 1

Ton Pentre AFC	34	24	7	3	91	33	79
Grange Harlequins	34	23	4	7	76	23	73
AFC Llwydcoed	34	20	6	8	65	35	66
Skewen Athletic	34	17	8	9	56	32	59
Goytre United	34	17	7	10	63	48	58
Maesteg Park AFC	34	18	3	13	58	47	57
Bridgend Town	34	16	8	10	60	43	56
Taffs Well	34	15	6	13	71	48	51
Univ. Wales Insitute Cardiff	34	15	6	13	65	49	51
Briton Ferry Athletic	34	15	4	15	61	55	49
Barry Town	34	14	5	15	45	44	47
Bettws	34	14	5	15	47	51	47
Caerleon	34	11	11	12	44	47	44
Ely Rangers	34	11	5	18	54	62	38
Dinas Powys	34	10	8	16	43	51	38
Neath	34	10	4	20	38	71	31
Gwynfi United	34	2	4	28	25	124	7
Garw Athletic	34	3	1	30	12	111	7

Gwynfi United and Garw Athletic both had 3 points deducted. Skewen Athletic and Neath AFC merged to become Neath Athletic before the 2005-06 season.

Division 2

Pontardawe Town	34	24	7	3	88	32	79
Newport YMCA	34	23	6	5	89	36	75
Bryntirion Athletic	34	23	2	9	79	40	71
Tredegar Town	34	21	5	8	64	37	68
Pontypridd Town	34	20	6	8	79	44	66
Garden Village	34	17	8	9	60	55	59
Penrhiwceiber Rangers	34	13	12	9	66	54	48
Caldicot Town	34	14	4	16	47	48	46
Porthcawl	34	12	8	14	43	52	44
Merthyr Saints	34	12	4	18	51	59	40
Pontyclun	34	11	5	18	47	56	38
Ento Aberaman Athletic	34	11	4	19	45	75	37
Morriston Town	34	10	6	18	43	58	36
Tillery FC	34	11	1	22	49	98	34
Cardiff Corinthians	34	9	6	19	40	72	33
Ammanford AFC	34	8	8	18	46	65	32
Seven Sisters	34	8	7	19	41	71	31
Llanwern	34	6	7	21	44	69	25

Penrhiwceiber Rangers had 3 points deducted.

Division 3

Troedyrhiw	34	24	7	3	79	27	79
Croesyceiliog	34	23	6	5	81	35	75
Caerau Ely	34	20	7	7	80	50	67
Treharris Athletic	34	19	7	8	85	49	64
Chepstow Town	34	15	7	12	72	66	52
AFC Porth	34	15	7	12	58	59	52
Penrhiwfer	34	14	5	15	74	74	47
Treowen Stars	34	14	5	15	53	59	47
Pentwyn Dynamo	34	13	6	15	73	76	45
Goytre AFC	34	12	7	15	53	59	43
Blaenrhondda	34	12	7	15	50	60	43
Llantwit Fardre	34	12	6	16	62	61	42
Ystradgynlais	34	11	9	14	63	67	42
Cwmamman	34	11	6	17	49	59	39
Newcastle Emlyn	34	10	6	18	72	102	36
Risca United	34	7	11	16	32	52	32
Albion Rovers	34	8	5	21	52	89	29
Fields Park Pontllanfraith	34	6	6	22	43	87	24

WELSH LEAGUE SOUTH 2005-06

Division 1

Goytre United	34	22	9	3	82	42	75
Neath Athletic	34	22	7	5	76	32	73
Pontardawe Town	34	18	9	7	57	35	63
Maesteg Park	34	18	9	7	61	40	63
Univ. Wales Insitute Cardiff	34	16	6	12	61	52	54
Bridgend Town	34	16	6	12	55	47	54
Afan Lido	34	13	8	13	46	41	47
Dinas Powys	34	13	8	13	42	44	47
Bryntirion Athletic	34	13	6	15	62	56	45
Newport YMCA	34	11	11	12	48	54	44
Barry Town	34	11	10	13	39	50	43
Ely Rangers	34	12	5	17	47	59	41
Ton Pentre	34	11	5	18	51	60	38
Caerleon	34	11	4	19	33	58	37
Taffs Well	34	9	9	16	46	62	36
Bettws	34	10	5	19	46	63	35
Briton Ferry Athletic	34	9	6	19	43	64	33
AFC Llwydcoed	34	8	3	23	35	69	27

Division 2

Pontypridd Town	34	26	6	2	91	20	84
Croesyceiliog	34	24	3	7	92	65	75
Garw	34	24	2	8	69	39	74
ENTO Aberaman	34	19	10	5	57	25	67
Troedyrhiw	34	20	3	11	77	40	63
Garden Village	34	18	6	10	58	40	60
Morriston Town	34	17	5	12	68	51	56
Penrhiwceiber Rangers	34	16	7	11	84	57	55
Caldicot Town	34	15	10	9	71	54	55
Tredegar Town	34	12	6	16	50	66	42
Merthyr Saints	34	11	5	18	49	69	38
Ammanford	34	10	7	17	44	61	37
Cardiff Corinthians	34	9	4	21	47	70	31
Caerau Ely	34	11	7	16	65	80	30
Pontyclun	34	8	4	22	43	65	28
Abertillery Excels	34	5	9	20	45	77	24
Porthcawl Town	34	6	5	23	34	72	23
Gwynfi United	34	3	5	26	30	123	8

Caerau Ely had 10 points deducted.
Gwynfi United had 6 points deducted.

Division 3

West End	34	25	2	7	98	50	77
Cambrian & Clydach Vale BGC	34	23	6	5	83	36	75
Treharris Athletic	34	22	5	7	87	47	71
Newcstle Emlyn	34	21	3	10	79	62	66
Pentwyn Dynamoes	34	16	10	8	70	52	58
Llanwern	34	18	3	13	67	60	57
Ystradgynlais	34	16	5	13	62	62	53
Cwmamman United	34	12	9	13	67	66	45
Risca United	34	13	5	16	54	68	44
AFC Porth	34	12	7	15	50	59	43
Goytre FC	34	10	8	16	52	56	38
Chepstow Town	34	11	5	18	59	72	38
Seven Sisters	34	11	4	19	47	67	37
Llantwit Fardre	34	9	9	16	38	53	36
Cwmbran Celtic	34	11	3	20	43	60	36
Blaenrhondda	34	10	6	18	42	64	36
Treowen Stars	34	10	5	19	34	54	35
Penrhiwfer	34	5	7	22	52	96	22

WELSH LEAGUE SOUTH 2006-07

Division 1

Neath Athletic	36	29	5	2	100	32	92
Goytre United	36	24	8	4	86	32	80
Pontypridd Town	36	24	8	4	88	37	80
Ton Pentre	36	21	9	6	68	32	72
Afan Lido	36	19	9	8	66	45	66
ENTO Aberaman Athletic	36	18	6	12	53	45	60
Maesteg Park	36	17	4	15	47	49	55
Bryntirion Athletic	36	14	5	17	56	62	47
Croesyceiliog	36	13	7	16	53	57	46
Caerleon	36	14	4	18	52	58	46
Bridgend Town	36	13	6	17	67	61	45
Taffs Well	36	12	7	17	60	68	43
Dinas Powys	36	11	7	18	45	67	40
Newport YMCA	36	10	9	17	55	69	39
Pontardawe Town	36	11	6	19	33	54	39
Univ. Wales Insitute Cardiff	36	9	6	21	46	74	33
Ely Rangers	36	7	8	21	52	77	29
Grange Harlequins	36	7	9	20	34	72	29
Barry Town	36	5	5	26	33	103	20

Grange Harlequins had 1 point deducted.

Division 2

Garw Athletic	34	24	7	3	73	21	79
Cambrian & Clydach Vale BGC	34	23	4	7	78	39	73
Caldicot Town	34	19	10	5	75	40	67
Bettws	34	20	5	9	52	32	65
West End	34	18	7	9	81	53	61
Ammanford	34	15	9	10	63	63	54
Troedyrhiw	34	14	12	8	53	53	54
Britol Ferry Athletic	34	14	5	15	54	56	47
Garden Village	34	12	9	13	64	64	45
Cardiff Corinthians	34	13	8	13	54	46	40
Tredegar Town	34	12	6	16	46	54	39
Pontyclun	34	11	6	17	47	63	39
Caerau Ely	34	10	8	16	56	75	38
Treharris Athletic	34	9	8	17	46	52	35
Merthyr Saints	34	9	6	19	50	72	33
Penrhiwcelber Rangers	34	11	5	18	54	70	31
Morriston Town	34	7	5	22	41	78	26
AFC Llwydcoed	34	4	2	28	28	84	14

Tredegar Town had 3 points deducted.
Cardiff Corinthians and Penrhiwceiber Rangers each had 7 points deducted.

Division 3

Cwmbran Celtic	32	20	10	2	68	35	70
Llanwern	32	20	8	4	75	35	68
Llangeinor	32	19	7	6	73	52	64
Pentwyn Dynamo	32	17	9	6	75	46	59
Llantwit Fardre	32	14	9	9	51	40	51
Aberbargoed Buds	32	13	8	11	60	51	47
Ystradgynlais	32	14	5	13	77	71	47
Newcastle Emlyn	32	12	8	12	76	66	44
Seven Sisters	32	11	6	15	51	61	39
Cwmamman United	32	11	5	16	55	62	38
Goytre	32	11	5	16	49	60	38
Risca United	32	11	4	17	46	62	37
Porthcawl Town	32	10	4	18	46	62	34
Abertillery Excelsiors	32	9	6	17	61	83	33
Llansawel	32	8	9	15	51	73	33
Chepstow Town	32	8	5	19	46	84	29
AFC Porth	32	7	6	19	57	74	27

Pentwyn Dynamo had 1 point deducted.
Gwynfi United withdrew from the League during the season and their record was expunged.

WELSH LEAGUE SOUTH 2007-08

Division 1

Goytre United	34	25	3	6	101	30	78
Dinas Powys FC	34	25	1	8	92	34	76
Ton Pentre AFC	34	22	7	5	102	33	73
ENTO Aberaman	34	21	6	7	75	40	69
Bryntirion Athletic	34	20	5	9	82	35	65
Afan Lido FC	34	17	11	6	58	31	62
Newport YMCA	34	19	4	11	88	70	61
Caerleon FC	34	16	7	11	60	42	55
Cambrian & Clydach Vale BGC	34	13	10	11	59	47	49
Bridgend Town	34	13	6	15	84	68	45
Caldicot Town	34	13	3	18	54	65	42
Taffs Well FC	34	11	7	16	53	70	40
Pontardawe Town	34	11	6	17	47	55	39
Cwmbran Town	34	10	8	16	56	50	38
Croesyceiliog FC	34	9	5	20	60	80	32
Maesteg Park AFC	34	7	6	21	43	83	27
Pontypridd Town	34	3	4	27	38	116	13
Garw Athletic	34	1	1	32	14	217	4

Division 2

Bettws AFC	34	22	9	3	79	35	75
Barry Town	34	21	6	7	74	35	69
Cardiff Corinthians	34	19	6	9	77	59	63
West End FC	34	17	6	11	78	57	57
Univ. Wales Insitute Cardiff	34	15	11	8	59	42	56
Garden Village	34	16	8	10	70	59	56
Ely Rangers	34	16	6	12	63	57	54
Llanwern	34	11	14	9	58	55	47
Cwmbran Celtic	34	12	8	14	52	60	44
Caerau Ely FC	34	11	10	13	63	64	43
Ammanford	34	11	7	16	67	74	40
Grange Harlequins	34	10	9	15	56	65	39
Llangeinor	34	10	7	17	60	68	37
Treharris Athletic	34	10	7	17	61	94	36
Tredegar Town	34	9	7	18	55	71	34
Briton Ferry Athletic	34	8	8	18	43	63	32
Pontyclun FC	34	9	5	20	41	67	32
Troedyrhiw	34	8	8	18	44	75	32

Treharris Athletic had 1 point deducted

Division 3

Pentwyn Dynamos	34	24	4	6	94	49	76
Newcastle Emlyn	34	21	5	8	96	54	68
Penrhiwceiber	34	21	3	10	99	60	66
AFC Llwydcoed	34	19	6	9	84	52	63
Cwmaman Institute	34	18	7	9	84	60	61
Aberbargoed Buds	34	18	5	11	82	61	59
Llantwit Fardre	34	16	7	11	63	43	55
Porthcawl Town	34	15	7	2	66	73	52
Risca United	34	15	6	13	54	47	51
Monmouth Town	34	13	7	14	73	64	46
Cwmamman United	34	14	3	17	79	85	45
Goytre FC	34	11	6	17	69	75	39
Merthyr Saints	34	15	2	17	74	85	37
Llansawel	34	10	6	18	58	76	36
Seven Sisters	34	7	10	17	35	68	28
Ystradgynlais	34	6	10	18	54	105	28
Abertillery Excelsiors	34	6	6	22	42	101	24
Morriston Town	34	6	2	26	37	85	20

Seven Sisters had 3 points deducted.
Merthyr Saints had 10 points deducted.

WELSH LEAGUE SOUTH 2008-09
Division 1

	P	W	D	L	F	A	Pts
ENTO Aberaman	34	24	5	5	73	33	77
Goytre United	34	24	4	6	90	39	76
Barry Town	34	22	7	5	63	26	70
Bettws FC	34	18	8	8	64	32	62
Bridgend Town	34	18	6	10	65	49	60
Cambrian & Clydach Vale BGC	34	16	9	9	62	48	57
Afan Lido FC	34	15	9	10	70	49	54
Pontardawe Town	34	14	10	10	48	32	52
Ton Pentre	34	14	7	13	59	51	49
Cardiff Corinthians	34	13	7	14	51	53	46
Bryntirion Athletic	34	12	8	14	54	58	44
Dinas Powys FC	34	10	5	19	43	73	35
Caldicot Town	34	9	7	18	41	67	34
Carleon	34	9	7	18	36	64	34
Taffs Well	34	8	9	17	43	58	33
Newport YMCA	34	8	4	22	41	76	28
Croesyceiliog FC	34	7	5	22	45	82	26
Cwmbran Town	34	3	7	24	32	90	16

Barry Town had 3 points deducted.

Division 2

	P	W	D	L	F	A	Pts
West End FC	34	22	5	7	102	49	71
Ely Rangers	34	21	6	7	79	38	69
Garden Village	34	21	6	7	90	55	69
Penrhiwceiber Rangers	34	21	3	10	67	39	66
Llanwern AFC	34	17	9	8	75	46	60
Cwmbran Celtic	34	17	7	10	69	51	58
Newcastle Emlyn FC	34	17	7	10	72	61	58
Ammanford AFC	34	15	10	9	73	52	55
Tredegar Town	34	13	8	13	51	55	47
Univ. Wales Insitute Cardiff	34	14	4	16	76	67	46
Grange Harlequins	34	12	8	14	53	70	41
Treharris Athletic	34	11	3	20	60	95	36
Maesteg Park AFC	34	9	7	18	40	64	34
Llangeinor FC	34	9	5	20	42	71	32
Caerau (Ely)	34	9	3	22	46	83	30
Pentwyn Dynamos	34	8	8	18	65	78	28
Garw BCG	34	6	13	15	44	69	28
Pontypridd Town	34	5	6	23	39	100	21

Grange Harlequins and Garw BCG each had 3 points deducted.
Pentwyn Dynamos had 4 points deducted.

Division 3

	P	W	D	L	F	A	Pts
AFC Llwydcoed	34	26	6	2	126	31	84
AFC Porth	34	25	5	4	91	33	80
Porthcawl Town	34	21	7	6	65	36	70
Cwmmaman United	34	19	5	10	76	65	62
Newport Civil Service	34	19	4	11	72	52	61
Llantwit Fardre	34	17	7	10	81	42	58
Aberbargoed Buds	34	17	5	12	71	71	56
Pontyclun FC	34	16	5	13	80	58	53
Monmouth Town	34	14	4	16	79	64	46
Troedyrhiw	34	14	3	17	69	69	45
Briton Ferry Athletic	34	13	5	16	61	52	44
Goytre FC	34	11	9	14	49	50	42
Cwmaman Institute	34	9	9	16	50	59	36
Seven Sisters FC	34	10	5	19	39	71	35
Risca United	34	9	8	17	46	83	35
Llansawel FC	34	7	8	19	42	63	29
Ystradgynlais	34	4	5	25	36	119	17
Merthyr Saints	34	4	2	28	39	154	11

Merthyr Saints had 3 points deducted.

WELSH LEAGUE SOUTH 2009-10
Division 1

	P	W	D	L	F	A	Pts
Goytre United	34	19	12	3	86	47	69
Cambrian & Clydach Vale BGC	34	19	11	4	73	42	68
Afan Lido	34	19	6	9	74	37	63
Caldicot Town	34	16	7	11	78	54	55
Bryntirion Athletic	34	15	9	10	67	60	54
Taffs Well	34	15	5	14	72	60	50
Barry Town	34	12	13	9	46	41	49
Pontardawe Town	34	13	8	13	59	56	47
Bridgend Town	34	12	9	13	57	55	45
Aberaman Athletic	34	12	8	14	56	68	44
West End	34	12	8	14	62	84	44
Cardiff Corinthians	34	12	7	15	63	69	43
Garden Village	34	12	6	16	46	52	42
Ton Pentre	34	11	8	15	56	65	41
Ely Rangers	34	10	6	18	46	67	36
Bettws	34	9	9	16	38	59	36
Dinas Powys	34	9	4	21	50	83	31
Caerleon	34	8	6	20	37	67	30

Division 2

	P	W	D	L	F	A	Pts
Penrhiwceiber Rangers	34	21	8	5	79	53	71
Cwmbran Celtic	34	21	6	7	75	33	69
Caerau (Ely)	34	18	7	9	82	53	61
AFC Llwydcoed	34	17	4	13	74	62	55
Ammanford	34	16	6	12	67	47	54
Croesyceiliog	34	13	13	8	58	42	52
Treharris Athletic Western	34	15	6	13	69	67	51
AFC Porth	34	14	7	13	47	49	49
Llangeinor	34	15	2	17	47	59	47
Newport YMCA	34	11	13	10	54	52	46
Newcastle Emlyn	34	13	6	15	54	57	45
Univ. Wales Insitute Cardiff	34	11	11	12	57	59	44
Cardiff Bay Harlequins	34	11	9	14	52	66	42
Cwmbran Town	34	10	7	17	47	62	37
Llanwern	34	10	7	17	52	77	37
Tredegar Town	34	6	14	14	35	46	32
Maesteg Park	34	7	11	16	51	72	32
Porthcawl Town	34	6	5	23	34	78	23

Division 3

	P	W	D	L	F	A	Pts
Aberbargoed Buds	34	21	7	6	74	41	70
Abertillery Bluebirds	34	22	3	9	81	38	69
Cwmaman Institute	34	19	11	4	70	34	68
Briton Ferry Llansawel	34	19	7	8	65	48	64
Pontypridd Town	34	18	9	7	67	41	63
Corus Steel	34	16	8	10	53	42	56
Cwmamman United	34	16	8	10	61	55	56
Monmouth Town	34	15	6	13	82	71	51
Goytre	34	14	6	14	66	69	48
South Gower	34	13	8	13	61	63	47
Newport Civil Service	34	14	4	16	50	55	46
Seven Sisters	34	13	6	15	62	58	45
Pontyclun	34	12	5	17	58	62	41
Troedyrhiw	34	10	7	17	56	75	37
Llantwit Fardre	34	9	9	16	46	60	36
Risca United	34	8	7	19	47	65	31
Pentwyn Dynamos	34	5	3	26	56	109	18
Garw	34	3	4	27	50	119	13

WELSH LEAGUE SOUTH 2010-2011
Division 1

	P	W	D	L	F	A	Pts
Bryntirion Athletic	30	23	1	6	76	27	70
Afan Lido	30	20	5	5	63	28	65
Cambrian & Clydach Vale BGC	30	17	6	7	68	37	57
Pontardawe Town	30	15	6	9	54	44	51
Caerau (Ely)	30	15	4	11	66	52	49
Bridgend Town	30	14	5	11	60	47	47
West End	30	13	6	11	57	47	45
Cardiff Corinthians	30	12	4	14	58	52	40
Taffs Well	30	12	3	15	47	57	39
Aberaman Athletic	30	12	3	15	58	74	39
Goytre United	30	10	8	12	47	53	38
Cwmbran Celtic	30	10	7	13	45	50	37
Barry Town	30	9	8	13	39	55	35
Caldicot Town	30	8	3	19	37	48	27
Garden Village	30	6	7	17	41	75	25
Penrhiwceiber Rangers	30	4	4	22	27	97	16

Division 2

	P	W	D	L	F	A	Pts
Ton Pentre	30	22	8	0	98	34	74
Cwmaman Institute	30	19	4	7	70	37	61
AFC Porth	30	16	7	7	49	35	55
Croesyceiliog	30	15	9	6	73	46	54
Aberbargoed Buds	30	13	7	10	64	52	46
Ely Rangers	30	12	9	9	56	50	45
Dinas Powys	30	12	8	10	47	42	44
Caerleon	30	12	7	11	44	37	43
Newport YMCA	30	12	6	12	55	49	42
Bettws	30	12	5	13	38	49	41
Newcastle Emlyn	30	10	8	12	54	58	38
Ammanford	30	10	6	14	40	50	36
Treharris Athletic Western	30	9	6	15	49	55	33
Abertillery Bluebirds	30	9	5	16	58	74	32
AFC Llwydcoed	30	3	8	19	30	65	17
Llangeinor	30	1	3	26	20	112	6

Division 3

	P	W	D	L	F	A	Pts
Monmouth Town	34	19	9	6	96	64	66
Corus Steel	34	18	10	6	64	40	64
Caerau	34	18	9	7	83	51	63
Goytre	34	19	6	9	82	53	63
Pontypridd Town	34	19	6	9	73	50	63
Newport Civil Service	34	17	6	11	78	54	57
Briton Ferry Llansawel	34	17	5	12	68	54	56
Risca United	34	16	4	14	74	61	52
Univ. Wales Insitute Cardiff	34	14	7	13	59	48	49
Treowen Stars	34	13	6	15	48	68	45
Cardiff Grange Harlequins	34	10	11	13	57	58	41
Pontyclun	34	12	3	19	62	72	39
Llanwern	34	9	10	15	56	65	37
Tredegar Town	34	9	9	16	46	65	36
Cwmamman United	34	10	6	18	51	88	36
South Gower	34	8	10	16	52	77	34
Cwmbran Town	34	7	11	16	38	59	32
Porthcawl Town Athletic	34	4	6	24	31	91	18

WELSH LEAGUE SOUTH 2011-2012
Division 1

	P	W	D	L	F	A	Pts
Cambrian & Clydach Vale BGC	30	16	10	4	78	26	58
Taffs Well	30	16	4	10	60	42	52
Haverfordwest County	30	15	7	8	58	43	51
Bryntirion Athletic	30	16	3	11	52	43	51
AFC Porth	30	13	9	8	54	36	48
Barry Town	30	12	10	8	48	37	46
Goytre United	30	12	8	10	71	55	44
Bridgend Town	30	13	5	12	50	41	44
Ton Pentre	30	9	16	5	48	40	43
Pontardawe Town	30	11	9	10	48	53	42
West End	30	11	5	14	53	62	38
Cwmbran Celtic	30	12	2	16	32	54	38
Aberaman Athletic	30	8	9	13	46	56	33
Cwmaman Institute	30	7	8	15	36	59	29
Cardiff Corinthians	30	8	10	14	50	67	28
Caerau (Ely)	30	4	3	23	37	109	15

Division 2

	P	W	D	L	F	A	Pts
Monmouth Town	30	22	4	4	102	33	70
Tata Steel	30	23	1	6	80	36	70
Caerleon	30	18	8	4	68	25	62
Newport YMCA	30	18	3	9	60	38	57
Dinas Powys	30	17	5	8	54	35	56
Penrhiwceiber Rangers	30	13	5	12	50	47	44
Croesyceiliog	30	12	6	12	55	54	42
Garden Village	30	11	8	11	57	50	41
Caldicot Town	30	12	3	15	42	63	39
Caerau	30	11	5	14	44	58	35
Ely Rangers	30	9	7	14	51	62	34
Ammanford	30	9	6	15	44	67	33
Aberbargoed Buds	30	9	5	16	47	59	32
Bettws	30	7	4	19	31	65	25
Newcastle Emlyn	30	6	3	21	35	66	21
Treharris Athletic Western	30	4	5	21	30	92	17

Caerau had 3 points deducted.

Division 3

	P	W	D	L	F	A	Pts
Undy Athletic	28	20	3	5	70	32	63
Goytre	28	19	3	6	65	39	60
Briton Ferry Llansawel	28	17	7	4	72	39	58
Bridgend Street	28	16	7	5	73	42	55
Pontypridd Town	28	16	4	8	69	38	52
Univ. Wales Insitute Cardiff	28	13	5	10	49	51	44
Abertillery Bluebirds	28	13	4	11	45	44	43
Risca United	28	12	5	11	58	49	41
Cardiff Grange Harlequins	28	11	3	14	53	58	36
Llanwern	28	7	9	12	44	57	30
Newport Civil Service	28	7	7	14	46	68	28
Tredegar Town	28	5	8	15	31	53	23
Treowen Stars	28	6	5	17	29	70	23
AFC Llwydcoed	28	6	3	19	40	67	21
Pontyclun	28	2	7	19	32	69	13

Llangeinor withdrew during season and their record was expunged.

WELSH LEAGUE SOUTH 2012-2013

Division 1

West End	28	18	4	6	64	29	58
Cambrian & Clydach Vale BGC	28	17	5	6	56	26	56
Taffs Well	28	14	7	7	57	39	49
Haverfordwest County	28	13	8	7	63	35	47
Aberdare Town	28	13	8	7	45	35	47
AFC Porth	28	13	7	8	39	34	46
Monmouth Town	28	13	6	9	54	43	42
Bryntirion Athletic	28	10	9	9	38	40	39
Ton Pentre	28	9	9	10	39	39	36
Pontardawe Town	28	10	5	13	34	39	35
Goytre United	28	10	4	14	33	51	34
Cwmbran Celtic	28	9	5	14	41	52	32
Bridgend Town	28	8	7	13	28	51	31
Tata Steel	28	5	6	17	28	61	21
Caerleon	28	1	4	23	18	63	7

Monmouth Town had 3 points deducted.
Barry Town withdrawn before the end of the season and their record was expunged.

Division 2

Goytre	30	23	3	4	78	32	72
Aberbargoed Buds	30	15	10	5	49	33	55
Caerau (Ely)	30	14	10	6	66	37	52
Undy Athletic	30	15	6	9	60	35	51
Caerau	30	14	8	8	70	52	50
Ammanford	30	13	7	10	54	49	46
Garden Village	30	13	6	11	42	44	45
Briton Ferry Llansawel	30	13	5	12	71	57	44
Penrhiwceiber Rangers	30	12	7	11	61	58	43
Caldicot Town	30	11	10	9	51	54	43
Croesyceiliog	30	10	10	10	65	64	40
Newport YMCA	30	12	4	14	42	45	40
Dinas Powys	30	9	12	9	63	43	39
Ely Rangers	30	6	7	17	55	77	25
Cardiff Corinthians	30	3	7	20	33	81	16
Cwmaman Institute	30	0	2	28	21	120	2

Division 3

Cardiff Metropolitan University	30	23	3	4	98	41	72
AFC Llwydcoed	30	19	3	8	74	51	60
Chepstow Town	30	19	2	9	81	49	59
Pontypridd Town	30	17	8	5	54	30	59
Risca United	30	14	11	5	56	29	53
Llantwit Major	30	15	5	10	62	43	50
Llanwern	30	13	5	12	54	58	44
Newport Civil Service	30	10	9	11	60	64	39
Bridgend Street	30	11	5	14	53	56	38
Abertillery Bluebirds	30	9	8	13	44	56	35
Treowen Stars	30	9	6	15	32	56	33
Cardiff Grange Harlequins	30	9	5	16	43	57	32
Tredegar Town	30	9	3	18	44	61	30
Newcastle Emlyn	30	8	2	20	37	86	26
Treharris Athletic Western	30	6	7	17	50	68	25
Bettws	30	6	4	20	42	79	22

WELSH LEAGUE SOUTH 2013-2014

Division 1

Monmouth Town	30	21	2	7	78	33	65
Taffs Well	30	19	6	5	63	30	63
Penybont	30	17	4	9	77	44	55
Haverfordwest County	30	16	7	7	59	37	55
Goytre	30	15	9	6	49	43	54
Cambrian & Clydach Vale BGC	30	15	5	10	60	44	50
Caerau (Ely)	30	12	10	8	52	51	46
Aberdare Town	30	13	5	12	49	48	44
Goytre United	30	11	6	13	56	43	39
AFC Porth	30	10	9	11	48	49	39
Ton Pentre	30	9	11	10	36	47	38
Pontardawe Town	30	9	6	15	34	60	33
Cwmbran Celtic	30	7	5	18	40	58	26
Tata Steel	30	6	7	17	29	65	25
Aberbargoed Buds	30	4	8	18	35	65	20
West End	30	5	2	23	36	84	17

Division 2

Cardiff Metropolitan University	30	20	6	4	86	24	66
Garden Village	30	20	4	6	93	34	64
Briton Ferry Llansawl	30	21	3	6	84	42	66
Chepstow Town	30	19	7	4	84	36	64
Undy Athletic	30	19	6	5	70	32	63
Caldicot Town	30	15	8	7	78	34	53
Ely Rangers	30	12	7	11	62	56	43
Croesyceiliog	30	13	4	13	72	75	43
Penrhiwceiber Rangers	30	12	4	14	50	52	40
Caerleon	30	11	6	13	63	63	39
AFC Llwydcoed	30	11	4	15	63	57	37
Dinas Powys	30	8	9	13	39	46	33
Ammanford	30	7	7	16	49	55	28
Cardiff Corinthians	30	5	6	19	42	83	21
Newport YMCA	30	4	3	23	37	99	15
Caerau	30	1	0	29	31	215	3

Division 3

Barry Town United	36	29	3	4	116	29	90
Llanwern	36	27	7	2	112	41	88
Risca United	36	23	6	7	96	51	75
Cwmamman United	36	23	4	9	106	63	73
Lliswerry	36	15	11	10	76	56	56
Llanelli Town	36	16	6	14	75	59	54
Rhoose	36	14	8	14	82	66	50
Tredegar Town	36	14	8	14	66	76	50
Cardiff Grange Harlequins	36	13	9	14	71	67	48
Newport Civil Service	36	12	5	19	65	79	41
Treowen Stars	36	12	5	19	49	84	41
Bridgend Street	36	11	7	18	58	73	40
Bettws	36	11	6	19	61	85	39
Llantwit Major	36	12	5	19	50	72	38
Pontypridd Town	36	10	8	18	46	81	38
Treharris Athletic Western	36	9	10	17	61	91	37
Abertillery Bluebirds	36	9	10	17	52	88	37
Cwmaman Institute	36	10	4	22	50	102	34
Newcastle Emlyn	36	8	6	22	50	79	30

Llantwit Major had 3 points deducted.

WELSH LEAGUE SOUTH 2014-2015

Division 1

Caerau (Ely)	30	21	5	4	75	39	68
Haverfordwest County	30	19	6	5	69	32	63
Cardiff Metropolitan University	30	19	6	5	57	20	63
Goytre United	30	16	8	6	74	41	56
Penybont	30	17	5	8	73	52	56
Monmouth Town	30	16	3	11	57	35	51
Briton Ferry Llansawel	30	13	9	8	52	37	48
Taffs Well	30	15	2	13	61	45	47
Ton Pentre	30	12	4	14	44	54	40
Goytre	30	11	3	16	46	47	36
Aberdare Town	30	10	5	15	48	68	35
Garden Village	30	8	10	12	49	61	34
Afan Lido	30	9	6	15	40	60	33
Cambrian & Clydach Vale BGC	30	7	7	16	45	46	28
Pontardawe Town	30	4	6	20	28	66	18
AFC Porth	30	0	1	29	16	131	1

Division 2

Barry Town United	30	22	6	2	77	32	72
Aberbargoed Buds	30	20	4	6	76	31	64
Risca United	30	18	5	7	70	38	59
Caldicot Town	30	17	7	6	51	24	58
Llanwern	30	14	6	10	72	50	48
Undy Athletic	30	15	6	9	61	42	48
Cwmbran Celtic	30	11	14	5	53	31	47
Croesyceiliog	30	12	6	12	51	56	42
AFC Llwydcoed	30	12	4	14	63	77	40
Chepstow Town	30	9	8	13	49	70	35
West End	30	10	5	15	43	67	35
Tata Steel	30	8	6	16	34	57	30
Penrhiwceiber Rangers	30	7	7	16	40	67	28
Dinas Powys	30	7	3	20	36	67	24
Caerleon	30	5	5	20	36	66	20
Ely Rangers	30	5	4	21	45	82	19

Undy Athletic had 3 points deducted.

Division 3

Llanelli Town	34	27	3	4	105	31	84
Cwmamman United	34	24	6	4	101	40	78
Ammanford	34	22	4	8	89	55	70
Tredegar Town	34	20	4	10	73	45	64
Rhoose	34	18	7	9	75	49	61
Lliswerry	34	17	4	13	74	56	55
Pontypridd Town	34	16	6	12	71	50	54
Bridgend Street	34	14	12	8	62	46	54
Cardiff Corinthians	34	16	2	16	68	63	50
Cwm Welfare	34	11	7	16	64	84	40
Panteg	34	11	6	17	52	71	39
Caerau	34	10	8	16	49	78	38
Newport YMCA	34	12	2	20	49	95	38
Llantwit Major	34	10	7	17	48	59	37
Treowen Stars	34	10	6	18	48	73	36
Bettws	34	9	4	21	49	72	31
Treharris Athletic Western	34	6	6	22	42	89	24
Newport Civil Service	34	5	2	27	31	94	17

Cardiff Grange Harlequins withdrew from the league during the season.

WELSH LEAGUE SOUTH 2015-2016

Division 1

Cardiff Metropolitan University	30	19	5	6	63	26	62
Barry Town United	30	16	10	4	62	33	58
Goytre	30	17	5	8	72	36	56
Caerau (Ely)	30	15	5	10	59	43	50
Cambrian & Clydach Vale BGC	30	15	5	10	48	39	50
Taffs Well	30	14	5	11	57	51	47
Goytre United	30	13	4	13	45	47	43
Afan Lido	30	11	9	10	53	53	42
Ton Pentre	30	12	4	14	45	52	40
Risca United	30	12	3	15	48	48	39
Penybont	30	11	6	13	53	56	39
Monmouth Town	30	10	9	11	56	60	39
Briton Ferry Llansawel	30	10	9	11	41	49	39
Aberdare Town	30	11	4	15	34	56	37
Aberbargoed Buds	30	8	3	19	42	63	27
Garden Village	30	1	4	25	27	93	7

Division 2

Caldicot Town	30	24	1	5	68	28	73
Cwmbran Celtic	30	24	0	6	89	33	72
Undy Athletic	30	22	5	3	76	24	71
Pontardawe Town	30	16	9	5	55	37	57
Ammanford	30	16	3	11	59	44	51
Cwmamman United	30	15	5	10	71	48	50
Llanelli Town	30	15	3	12	59	44	48
AFC Llwydcoed	30	13	4	13	52	52	43
AFC Porth	30	11	4	15	49	51	37
Tata Steel	30	9	8	13	42	60	35
West End	30	9	5	16	46	76	32
Croesyceiliog	30	8	6	16	38	60	30
Llanwern	30	8	5	17	43	55	29
Dinas Powys	30	8	2	20	36	70	26
Penrhiwceiber Rangers	30	4	6	20	46	91	18
Chepstow Town	30	3	4	23	37	93	13

Division 3

Pontypridd Town	34	25	6	3	99	31	81
Abergavenny Town	34	24	5	5	98	48	77
Bridgend Street	34	22	6	6	81	50	72
STM Sports	34	21	4	9	103	65	67
Caerau	34	20	5	9	108	69	65
Llantwit Major	34	18	11	5	71	39	65
Panteg	34	17	6	11	88	67	57
Cwm Welfare	34	15	5	14	79	71	50
Treharris Athletic Western	34	13	6	15	72	60	45
Tredegar Town	34	12	7	15	51	51	43
Treowen Stars	34	12	7	15	53	77	43
Caerleon	34	11	8	15	62	72	41
Ely Rangers	34	11	8	15	64	77	41
Bettws	34	10	5	19	65	87	35
Lliswerry	34	9	3	22	47	71	30
Newport YMCA	34	7	6	21	44	91	27
Cardiff Corinthians	34	3	8	23	45	104	17
Newport Civil Service	34	2	2	30	39	139	8

WELSH LEAGUE SOUTH 2016-17

Division 1

Barry Town United	30	20	6	4	69	18	66
Penybont	30	19	4	7	73	41	61
Goytre	30	18	4	8	80	49	58
Haverfordwest County	30	16	6	8	55	47	54
Caerau (Ely)	30	13	9	8	57	50	48
Cwmbran Celtic	30	14	3	13	60	50	45
Undy Athletic	30	13	2	15	53	53	41
Afan Lido	30	13	5	12	46	49	41
Taffs Well	30	12	4	14	40	48	40
Goytre United	30	10	9	11	44	37	39
Cambrian & Clydach Vale BGC	30	10	7	13	41	49	37
Ton Pentre	30	10	6	14	51	61	36
Port Talbot Town	30	10	5	15	41	57	35
Monmouth Town	30	9	6	15	49	74	33
Caldicot Town	30	7	2	21	36	65	23
Risca United	30	6	2	22	38	85	20

Afan Lido had 3 points deducted.

Division 2

Llanelli Town	30	23	7	0	108	29	76
Briton Ferry Llanswel	30	18	8	4	57	33	62
Cwmamman United	30	18	4	8	74	49	58
Pontypridd Town	30	16	9	5	66	38	57
AFC Porth	30	15	7	8	70	42	52
Ammanford	30	15	5	10	66	47	50
Aberdare Town	30	11	8	11	46	42	41
AFC Llwydcoed	30	12	1	17	49	75	37
Croesyceiliog	30	10	6	14	39	50	36
Pontardawe Town	30	9	7	14	47	58	34
Abergavenny Town	30	9	5	16	45	57	32
Dinas Powys	30	10	1	19	42	67	31
Garden Village	30	8	4	18	45	58	28
West End	30	8	7	15	40	72	28
Aberbargoed Buds	30	7	6	17	39	64	27
Newport City	30	6	5	19	28	80	20

West End and Newport City each had 3 points deducted.

Division 3

Llantwit Major	30	22	6	2	68	24	72
STM Sports	30	21	4	5	91	38	64
Caerau	30	16	2	12	71	65	50
Chepstow Town	29	14	5	10	66	57	47
Treharris Athletic Western	29	14	5	10	53	50	47
Panteg	30	15	1	14	67	63	46
Penrhiwceiber Rangers	30	13	5	12	50	60	44
Bridgend Street	30	12	7	11	64	41	43
Ely Rangers	30	11	7	12	67	70	40
Treowen Stars	30	11	6	13	45	59	39
Trethomas Bluebirds	30	11	5	14	49	61	38
Trefelin Boys & Girls Club	30	8	12	10	48	49	36
Ynysygerwn	30	9	5	16	46	61	32
Tredegar Town	30	9	2	19	42	66	29
Caerleon	30	7	3	20	39	81	24
Cwm Welfare	30	6	5	19	50	71	23

STM Sports had 3 points deducted.

WELSH LEAGUE SOUTH 2017-2018

Division 1

Llanelli Town	30	24	3	3	87	33	75
Haverfordwest County	30	19	3	8	65	37	60
Pen-y-Bont	30	18	6	6	64	37	57
Cambrian & Clydach Vale BGC	30	17	3	10	58	39	54
Afan Lido	30	15	4	11	61	48	49
Goytre	30	15	3	12	51	62	48
Goytre United	30	13	8	9	53	52	47
Cwmbran Celtic	30	14	4	12	67	51	46
Undy Athletic	30	13	5	12	62	60	44
Taffs Well	30	11	5	14	52	48	38
Briton Ferry Llansawel	30	10	7	13	58	64	37
Cwmamman United	30	8	6	16	38	59	30
Port Talbot Town	30	9	11	10	58	53	29
Monmouth Town	30	7	4	19	44	73	25
Caerau (Ely)	30	5	3	22	32	78	18
Ton Pentre	30	1	7	22	26	82	10

Pen-y-Bont had 3 points deducted
Port Talbot Town had 9 points deducted

Division 2

Llantwit Major	30	21	6	3	70	27	69
Pontypridd Town	30	22	1	7	93	31	67
Ammanford	30	20	3	7	74	37	63
STM Sports	30	18	6	6	94	36	60
Aberbargoed Buds	30	18	3	9	54	33	57
Garden Village	30	17	3	10	59	46	54
Caldicot Town	30	17	2	11	50	35	53
Risca United	30	13	7	10	53	48	46
Pontardawe Town	30	13	3	14	51	51	42
Abergavenny Town	30	11	6	13	43	48	39
Aberdare Town	30	9	6	15	42	56	33
Croesyceiliog	30	9	2	19	36	56	29
AFC Llwydcoed	30	8	4	18	41	60	28
West End	30	8	5	17	40	80	26
Dinas Powys	30	4	3	23	25	80	15
AFC Porth	30	1	2	27	24	125	5

West End had 3 points deducted.

Division 3

Swansea University	30	24	3	3	100	27	75
Bridgend Street	30	23	5	2	105	41	74
Trefelin Boys & Girls Club	30	23	5	2	81	33	74
Treharris Athletic Western	30	17	3	10	76	64	54
Penrhiwceiber Rangers	30	12	6	12	59	60	42
Pontyclun	30	11	8	11	53	61	41
Ynysygerwn	30	10	10	10	53	53	40
Trethomas Bluebirds	30	11	5	14	50	48	38
Panteg	30	11	5	14	59	70	38
Tredegar Town	30	10	7	13	48	58	37
Caerau	30	11	2	17	48	72	35
Newport City	30	9	5	16	52	69	32
Treowen Stars	30	9	3	18	42	68	30
Chepstow Town	30	7	6	17	57	84	27
Ely Rangers	30	6	3	21	44	92	21
Neuadd Wen	30	4	8	18	44	71	20

NORTH WALES COAST FOOTBALL LEAGUE

Formation and History

By Mr. H.R. WILLIAMS, League Secretary, Bangor.
(This article has been taken verbatim from the North Wales Football Annual 1934).

This league was formed in 1893, and as the first Minute Book is not available, we have to rely on the Rhyl Journal of March 25th, 1893, for the year of its birth. The Rhyl Journal states that A Meeting was held at the Lorne Hotel, Rhyl, for the purpose of forming a North Wales Football League for next season. At this memorable meeting there were present Messrs. Barber (Flint), Dolan (Holywell), J. Ll. Williams (Holywell). Hampshire (Bangor), Williams (St. Asaph). Prenton, A.J. Jones and Robinson (Rhyl). A resolution that such a League be formed, subject to the approval of the Welsh F.A., was proposed by Mr. Hampshire, and seconded by Mr. Robinson. The original promoters of the League were Mr. Barber (Flint), and Messrs. Williams and Dolan (Holywell) and it was at their initiative the meeting was called. Mr. Barber was the first Secretary, and is now [1934] an Alderman and the present Mayor of Flint. He and Mr. Robinson still take an interest in the game.

The Mr Williams of Holywell is now known to everybody connected with or interested in football as Lt. Col. T. Llewelyn Williams, Honorary Secretary of the North Wales Coast Football Association since its inception in 1894 and it can safely be said that this Association is the offspring of the League. In his younger days Colonel Williams was a well-known player within the area for many years, and as a half-back he held his own with the best of his day. Afterwards be did not shirk the responsibility of officiating as referee. It is further interesting to note that Colonel Williams is the Treasurer of the Football Association of Wales, and has been a prominent and hard working member of that body for the last 30 years. He, with the late Mr. H Miller of Shotton, initiated the original Flintshire League.

Throughout all these years Colonel Williams name can be found in the Minute Books, which are available from 1896, and on more than our occasion he has come to the assistance of the League by carrying on, pro-tem the duties of Secretary. Today, He is the honoured President of the League. The Minute Book for 1896 shows that the Annual Meeting of the League was held on September 1st of that year, and Mr. C. W. Berrie of Rhyl, was appointed Secretary in place of Mr. Barber, who resigned at the meeting, Mr. Hampshire was appointed Treasurer, and Mr. T. B. Farrington, C.E., of Conway, was elected President, and he held this office until the season 1900-01.

I find in the minutes of 1896 an amazing decision. Bangor drew with Flint 1-1, and Bangor claimed that they should have had a penalty which might have won the match for them. The Committee made the amazing decision that Bangor should be awarded a penalty, which should be taken at the start of the next game and this should decide the match. This decision was not carried out as it was rescinded before the game was played. One kick to decide a match would have been a unique record. Mr. R. John Hughes, the present excellent Chairman, attended League Meetings as far back as 1898, and he was chairman of a meeting held on July 19th of that year. At that time he lived at Rhyl but later he moved to Penmaenmawr, and he now lives at Deganwy.

Mr. Hughes name appears continually in the minute books, and in 1903-04 he was the President. Holywell resigned from the League in 1898, and it was during this year that Holyhead and Llanrwst were admitted into membership. It was also during this season that Llandudno F.C. presented the Russell Cup to the League, and it was won by Caernarvon, who beat Bangor for the championship on goal average. Caernarvons record was 20 points for 14 matches played, and a goal average of 54 for and 28 against. Bangors goal average was 36 for and 29 against. The other clubs in the League finished in the following order: Llanrwst, Colwyn Bay, Holyhead, Rhyl, Llandudno, and Menai Bridge.

In season 1899-1900 Captain Jones of Caernarvon was appointed treasurer, with Mr. J.C. Jones, of Bangor, as secretary. During this season Denbigh became members of the League, and Holywell were re-admitted. 1900-01 shows Mr. Hampshire back as Treasurer, and Mr. C.E. Peart Jones, Holywell, became Secretary. It was during this season that Colwyn Bay failed to get a ground, and were compelled to resign. Flint also resigned, and a club from Connah's Quay was expelled. A team from the R.W.F. (Volunteers) at Penmaenmawr were admitted into membership, but they did not win a match throughout the season, and they finished the season with only two points.

In the 1901-02 season Mr C.W. Berrie, of Rhyl, was the President, with the same Treasurer and Secretary, but during the season, the Secretary resigned, and from January 1902 to the end of the season this office was held by Colonel Williams. It was at the end of this season that Rhyl resigned, and their place was taken by Rhyl Athletic.

1902-03 saw Mr. Henry Lloyd, of Llanrwst as President, with Mr. Henry Jones, of the same town, as Secretary, and Mr H.T. Angel, Caernarvon as Treasurer. This was the first season for an East v West match to be played, and this game took place at Bangor, on April 1st, 1903. The selected teams were: East: – B. Hayes (Llanrwst); Chas Roberts (Llandudno), Edgar Allen (Colwyn Bay): T.W. Ellis (Rhyl), A.D. Thomas (Llanrwst) Jim Parry (Llandudno); W. Owen (Llanrwst), J.E. Williams (Llandudno), Wellings (Colwyn Bay), Wilson (Conway), and Evan Jones (Llanrwst).

West: – Evan Davies (Portmadoc); W. Evans (Bangor), W. Edwards (Penmaenmawr) Foulkes (Penmaenmawr), J.R. Jones (Portmadoc), Oldfield (Caernarvon), A.T. Evans (Bangor) Moseley Jones (Portmadoc), Owen Jones (Portmadoc), H. Moran (Bangor) and W. Jones (Caernarvon).

The referee was Mr. E. Lloyd Williams.

There was a loss of £2 10s 3d shown on this game, but on the match Champions v Rest of the League, played at the end of the season, there was a profit of £4.

As already stated Mr R. John Hughes became President in 1903-04, Mr. Henry Lloyd was the Treasurer, and Mr D. Ll. Hughes, Portmadoc, Secretary. New rules were adopted for this season, and the League was governed by a Council consisting of Messrs. R.W. Parry, Bangor, F. Beech, Rhyl, D.M. Roberts, Colwyn Bay, Henry Jones, Llanrwst, and K. Lloyd Williams, Bangor.

In 1904-5 the officials were Mr. T.O. Morgan, Conway, as President; Mr. W. Ll. Jones, Llanrwst, Treasurer; Mr. K. Lloyd Williams, Bangor, Secretary. The Executive Committee were Messrs. H. Lloyd, Conway; H. Jones, Llanrwst; G.T. Phillips, Penmaenmawr; D. Ll. Hughes, Portmadoc and Mr. F.J.H. Beech, Rhyl. During this season Holyhead Swifts were re-admitted to the League and Blaenau Ffestiniog became members.

1905-6 saw Mr. D. Ll. Hughes, Portmadoc, elected President, with Mr. W. Ll. Jones, Llanrwst, as Treasurer; and Mr. F.J.H. Beach, Rhyl, as Secretary. The Executive Committee were Messrs. R. Ll. Williams, Bangor; T.O. Morgan, Conway; H. Heap, Colwyn Bay; N.J. Campbell, Holyhead; and J.R. Vincent, Llandudno.

Efforts were made at this time to form a Second Division divided into East and West sections, but it was not a success in the West. An Eastern section was operated with four clubs in membership [Editors note; this is mistaken; there were seven clubs in membership]. The North Wales Chronicle Co. presented a Silver Challenge Cup in this season to the League with certain conditions attached to it. The Cup was returned to the donors in 1911-12 with the best thanks of the League for its use for six years.

The records between October 1905 and May 1906, have been torn from the Minute Book, but it can be traced that seven clubs in Division 1 completed their programme. The same officials were in office during 1906-7, but it was during this season that a proposal by the Llandudno club that a representative from each club form the Executive Committee came into operation.

Season 1907-8 saw Sir Richard Williams-Buckley, Bart., of Beaumaris elected President, and he remained in this office until the end of season 1909-10. Mr W Llewelyn Jones, of Llanrwst, still retained the office of Treasurer, and Mr. Reach of Rhyl was the efficient Secretary. It was decided to appoint a Chairman for the season, and Mr R.D. Richards, Bangor, was appointed. Mr Richards proved such a capable official that he was asked to remain in office for another season, but he declined this honour. He however accepted office again in 1909-10, 1910-11, 1911-12, 1912-13, 1913-14 and 1914-15. The office was held open for him in 1919-20, but his military duties prevented his attendance at the meeting. Mr P. Weekes, of Holyhead, proved a very efficient deputy during the first post-war season. Mr. Weekes was also the Chairman

In season 1908-9, Mr R.D. Richards was the Treasurer, and Mr E. Lloyd Williams, Bangor, was the Secretary. Mr Lloyd Williams held this office until May 1st, 1914, when he resigned on accepting an appointment in South Wales. During Mr. Williams secretaryship the League prospered considerably. There were 11 clubs In membership during 1909-10, and Beaumaris – in their first season – carried off the championship. Mr T.E. Purdy, of Colwyn Bay, was the Treasurer during seasons 1909-10 and 1910-11, and 1909-10 was the only season a team from the University College of North Wales took part in the competition. It proved to be such a good team that it carried off the championship. A western section of Division II was formed in this season, but it was In 1910-11 that this section with nine clubs, came into its own. Glasinfryn Swifts carried off the championship, with Llandndno Amateurs the champions of ten clubs in Divison I. It was in season 1910-11 that Mr Thos. F. Dargie, of Bangor became President, and the records show that he was in constant attendance at the several meetings. The famous L.R. Roose signed a League Form for Blaenau Festiniog in this season, and an application by the Blaenau Festiniog club to have this form returned to them was refused by the management committee.

With the object of getting players in this area recognised as likely candidates for international honours, the League invited the F.A.W. Council to attend the annual East v West match. The fame of the League must have spread to England during this time, as applications from Birmingham and Leeds Amateur FAs were received for inter-league matches during Easter, but congestion of figures – even in those days – prevented serious consideration being given to them.

Thanks to the efficient work of the officials and splendid donations from the President (Mr. Dargie), the Vice-Presidents and the clubs, a new solid silver cup was purchased from Messrs. Fattorini of Bolton.

Mr H.J. Williams, Llandudno, was appointed Hon. Treasurer in 1911-12 and he held this office for several seasons. It was in May 1914 that I took over the reins of office, and after I had made all the necessary preparations for season 1914-15 war broke out. On September 2nd 1914, the clubs agreed, on the motion of Mr P. Weekes, on behalf of the Holyhead club, "That Football and Football Management, as controlled by the North Wales Coast Football League, be suspended during the currency of the War". It was not until August 16th, 1920, that the clubs met in Committee again and at this meeting the officials for the forthcoming season were appointed. The President was Mr. Thos. F. Davies, Bangor; Chairman, Mr. R.D. Richards, Bangor; Hon. Treasurer, Mr. Walter J. Parry, Conway; Secretary myself. There were 11 clubs in Division I, and 10 clubs in Division II (West). The President at the close of the season subscribed £5, the Coast Association £6, the Hon. Secretary of the Coast Association and all the clubs in both Divisions of the League subscribed handsomely towards the funds of the League and for the purchase of medals to the champions of both Divisions.

Season 1920-21 was probably the best season the League ever experienced. There were 12 clubs in Division I, and 14 in Division II.

Division I: Holyhead. Holywell, Denbigh, Bangor, Blaenau Festiniog, Llandudno, Colwyn Bay, Conway, Caernarvon, Llanrwst, Portmadoc, Ogwen Valley.

Division II: Llechid Celts, Glasinfryn Swifts, Abergele, Pemnaenmnwr, Holyhead R.I. Reserves, Bangor Athletic Reserves, Llanfairfechan, Caernarvon Athletic Reserves, Nantlle Vale, Menai Bridge, Llanberis Comrades, Dolgarrog. Llangefni, Rhiwlas Athletic.

Mr. E. Bithell, of Colwyn Bay, was appointed Chairman, and the other officials remained as in the previous season. During this season the FAW played several international trial matches, and Messrs. Ted Parry, of Colwyn Bay, Jackie Jones, Abergele, C. Edwards, Holywell, and Idwal Davies, Conway, received their Amateur international caps. J. Neal of Llandudno and Bangor UCNW was selected as first reserve. Everton F.C. sent a strong team to Colwyn Bay on December 8th, 1920, to play a representative side of the League, and were successful by one goal to nil. The nett financial result of this match was a profit of £51 13s 1d. to the League. The League from time to time applied to the Coast Association for financial assistance, and always the response was most favourable, this season the response was £15. The financial position of the League was sound with a credit balance of £71 10s 5d in the General Account and £65 11s in the Deposit Account. After allowing for all liabilities, there was a balance of £85 4s 10d, assets in excess of liabilities. This was the healthy state of football on the North Wales Coast when the Football Association of Wales decided to form the Welsh National League with a North and South section. The Northern Section was further divided Into Division I and Division II and III, and the lower Divisions were further divided into East and West sections. A meeting at Bangor, addressed by Mr. Robblns, the FAW Secretary, on June 23rd, 1921, decided to join the new league.

The Coast League clubs faithfully carried out their obligations to the new body, and it was no fault of theirs that the League was not the success anticipated. It can be truthfully said that Divisions II and III Western area were the main support of the new League with 23 clubs in membership; they also assisted in forming Divisions in Anglesey and in South Caernarvonshire.

The Welsh [National] League was disbanded in 1930, and after a trial had been given to the resuscitated Football Combination and the Welsh Combination, the clubs decided to resuscitate the old North Wales Coast League. During the time the clubs were members of the Welsh League (Divisions II and III West) Mr. Richard Owen, Bangor was the Chairman, and I was the Secretary. The last few seasons have been carried on under some difficulty, but it is hoped that the road is now clear for this old League to carry on and to improve on its old grand traditions.

Note added in 2006:

A meeting was held on 27th March 1930, at a time when the dissolution of the Welsh National League was imminent, with a view to investigate the possibility of reviving the North Wales Coast League. It was resolved to call a meeting before the commencement of the 1930-31 season with the intention of re-establishing the League.

This meeting was held at Bangor on Saturday 30th August "in accordance with the resolution of 27th March last, to call a meeting of North Wales football club representatives to consider the question of the resuscitation of the old North Wales Coast Football League". Only five clubs were represented, though apologies were received from two or three others for their absence.

The North Wales Observer reported that Mr Richard Owen, chairman of Bangor City FC was voted in as Chairman and the March resolution formally confirmed. The meeting then proceeded to consider alterations and amendments to the rules of the now dissolved Welsh National League which had been prepared by a sub-committee and submitted for discussion.

The main object of debate was the amendment submitted to the effect that the League shall be governed by an independent management committee. On the motion of Mr Stythe of Caernarvon, seconded by Mr Glanfab Jones of Bangor, it was decided that "the league shall be governed by a committee of management consisting of a president, five vice-presidents, treasurer and secretary together with six representatives to be appointed by clubs in membership."

The rule amendments submitted by the sub-committee and from the floor were adopted as the constitution of the new League, subject to FAW approval.

The area of the league, as proposed by Glanfab Jones, would be west of a line drawn between Colwyn Bay to Portmadoc. Clubs from within the area were invited to join namely: Portmadoc, Pwllheli, Penygroes, Caernarvon, Bangor City, Bethesda, Menai Bridge, Holyhead, Penmaenmawr, Conway, Llandudno, Colwyn Bay, Llanrwst, Festiniog and either Llangefni or Beaumaris. Applications were to be in to the Secretary Mr H.R. Williams by the following Saturday. The election of the officials and members of the management committee was deferred to the next meeting, which took place on 25th September at Bangor. Mr H.R. Williams reported as Secretary that Llandudno, Penmaenmawr, Conway and Colwyn Bay had applied for permission to enter an organisation in another area and he had written to Mr Ted Robbins FAW Secretary asking him to deal with the actions of these clubs by compelling them to join the Coast League in whose area they were located. The meeting backed his actions.

The chairman made it known that only six clubs had thus far formally applied for membership and that one of the six, Festiniog, had a ground to which players with the other five objected. It was obvious to Mr Owen, who was formally elected as League Chairman at this meeting, that they could not form a league with only five clubs. A suggestion from the floor that Festiniog be admitted on condition they rectify the complaints against the ground. The Festiniog representatives agreed to this by guaranteeing to the satisfaction of the committee that they would carry out the work and they became the sixth member. The League thus had six members committed to the revived League and it was proposed that the other four mentioned earlier might now "see their way to throw in their lot with the other six clubs" bringing the membership up to a more viable ten clubs. The four plus other clubs in the area were to be contacted and it was agreed that the League would carry on with six clubs in the meantime. As players were eager to start playing the first six fixtures were set for the 27th and comprised:

Bangor City Reserves v Festiniog

Bethesda v Caernarvon

Holyhead v Menai Bridge

All three were played but mysteriously no other mention is made of this incarnation of the Coast League in any newspaper checked thus far.

The cups used by this league are believed to have been as follows:

1893 – 1898 no trophy

1898 – 1906 The Russell Cup, donated by Llandudno, which may have been used as the Division II championship trophy from 1906.

1906 – 1911 The North Wales Chronicle Cup

1911 – 1921 A cup commissioned from Fattorinis of Bradford which is now the current North Wales Coast F.A. Challenge Cup

Sources: Main section as stated; additional information gleaned from North Wales Weekly News at Llandudno Library and North Wales Observer at Library of the University of Wales Bangor

Additional research by Mel Thomas and Ian Garland.

NORTH WALES COAST LEAGUE
1893-94

Fflint FC	12	10	2	0	45	6	22
Llandudno Swifts	12	9	2	1	41	7	20
Bangor FC	11	4	3	4	26	32	11
Holywell FC	12	5	0	7	27	27	10
Caledfryn Rangers	12	3	1	8	10	36	7
Rhyl FC	11	3	0	8	21	31	6
Bagillt FC	10	2	0	5	14	41	4

Connahs Quay FC withdrew before the start of the season and their place was taken by Caledfryn Rangers.
Not all fixtures were completed.

NORTH WALES COAST LEAGUE
1894-95

Rhyl FC	9	6	1	2	27	16	13
Fflint FC	10	5	1	4	39	13	11
Llandudno Swifts	8	5	1	2	21	15	11
Bangor FC	10	2	4	4	17	18	8
Holywell FC	8	2	1	5	8	33	5
Ruthin FC	7	2	0	5	11	28	4

Llandudno Swifts v Ruthin FC was not played after Ruthin failed to appear.
Table shown is one found from 30th March 1895 with the Swifts vs Fflint (4-0) game from 20th April 1895 also added.

NORTH WALES COAST LEAGUE
1895-96

Bangor FC	10	7	2	1	26	11	16
Fflint FC	10	6	2	2	29	20	14
Caernarfon Ironopolis	10	4	2	4	20	16	10
Llandudno Swifts	10	3	1	6	14	18	7
Holywell FC	10	3	1	6	15	31	7
Rhyl FC	10	3	1	7	13	31	6

NORTH WALES COAST LEAGUE
1896-97

Llandudno Swifts	10	8	1	1	37	15	17
Bangor FC	10	7	2	1	34	12	16
Fflint FC	9	6	0	3	30	20	12
Caernarfon Ironopolis	9	2	2	5	16	24	6
Holywell FC	10	2	1	7	17	28	5
Rhyl FC	9	1	0	8	13	41	2

Table shown as at 27th March 1897.

NORTH WALES COAST LEAGUE
1897-98

Llandudno Swifts	9	7	1	2	31	8	13
Rhyl Town	10	5	2	3	19	16	12
Bangor FC	10	5	1	4	30	17	11
Rhyl Amateurs	10	3	1	6	15	37	7
Caernarfon Ironopolis	8	2	2	4	11	16	6
Holywell FC	7	2	1	4	9	21	5

Table shown as at 2nd April 1898.

NORTH WALES COAST LEAGUE
1898-99

Llanrwst Town	14	9	0	5	48	33	18
Bangor FC	11	8	0	3	23	24	16
Colwyn Bay FC	14	7	0	7	33	22	14
Caernarfon Ironopolis	9	6	0	3	33	24	12
Rhyl FC	13	6	0	7	38	44	12
Holyhead Railway Institute	9	4	0	5	22	20	8
Llandudno Swifts	10	3	1	6	21	23	7
Menai Bridge FC	13	3	1	9	16	42	7

Table shown as at 29th April 1899.

NORTH WALES COAST LEAGUE
1899-00

Bangor FC	14	12	0	2	55	11	24
Llanrwst Town	14	9	0	5	37	32	18
Holywell FC	14	8	0	6	29	22	16
Rhyl United	14	6	2	6	28	25	14
Llandudno Swifts	14	5	2	7	25	25	12
Caernarfon Ironopolis	14	6	2	6	11	24	12
Colwyn Bay FC	14	3	1	10	21	28	7
Holyhead Railway Institute	14	3	1	10	15	54	7

Caernarfon Ironopolis had 2 points deducted.

NORTH WALES COAST LEAGUE
1900-01

Bangor FC	13	8	2	3	43	18	18
Rhyl FC	13	7	2	4	32	20	16
Holyhead FC	14	7	2	5	47	34	16
Caernarfon Ironopolis	13	7	0	6	34	24	14
Holywell FC	13	6	2	5	38	32	14
Llandudno Swifts	13	5	3	5	26	35	13
Llanrwst Town	12	4	1	7	32	27	9
Penmaenmawr R.W.F.	11	0	2	9	15	76	2

Penmaenmawr Royal Welch Fusiliers FC took over from Colwyn Bay FC who resigned from the League.
Llanrwst Town vs Llandudno, Penmaenmawr vs Bangor, Penmaenmawr vs Rhyl and Penmaenmawr vs Caernarfon were not played. Holywell FC vs Llanrwst Town was abandoned after two attempts.

NORTH WALES COAST LEAGUE
1901-02

Caernarfon Ironopolis	12	9	1	2	38	15	19
Bangor FC	12	8	2	2	37	23	18
Colwyn Bay FC	13	7	3	3	44	28	17
Rhyl FC	12	6	2	4	51	34	14
Llandudno FC	13	6	1	6	28	35	13
Holyhead FC	10	3	0	7	19	53	6
Llanrwst Town	12	2	2	8	28	33	6
Llanberis	12	0	1	11	16	42	1

The table shown is calculated to known results up to 24th April 1902.

NORTH WALES COAST LEAGUE
1902-03

Portmadoc	18	13	2	7	62	22	28
Bangor FC	18	11	2	4	58	27	24
Colwyn Bay FC	18	9	3	6	60	42	21
Llanrwst Town	18	9	3	6	44	38	21
Llandudno FC	17	7	2	8	43	39	16
Penmaenmawr FC	18	7	1	10	41	51	15
Llanberis FC	17	5	3	9	36	53	13
Caernarfon Ironopolis	14	5	2	7	30	31	14
Rhyl Athletic	14	4	2	8	30	56	10
Conwy FC	17	4	0	13	28	78	8

Not all fixtures were completed.

NORTH WALES COAST LEAGUE
1903-04

Bangor FC	16	14	0	2	54	17	28
Portmadoc	15	11	0	4	64	24	22
Conwy FC	16	10	0	6	46	36	20
Colwyn Bay FC	16	8	2	6	43	34	18
Llandudno FC	16	8	1	7	43	41	17
Llanberis FC	15	6	1	8	45	53	15
Llanfairpwll FC	16	4	2	10	22	37	10
Llanrwst Town	16	2	4	10	17	52	8
Penmaenmawr FC	16	2	2	12	20	57	6

Llanberis vs Portmadoc was not played.

NORTH WALES COAST LEAGUE
1904-05

Bangor FC Reserves	14	12	0	2	66	18	24
Portmadoc	13	9	2	2	45	15	20
Colwyn Bay FC	14	7	2	5	46	32	16
Llandudno FC	14	6	2	6	35	38	14
Holyhead Swifts	11	5	0	6	23	47	10
Conwy FC	14	4	0	10	28	52	8
Llanfairfechan FC	14	4	0	10	22	56	8
Llanrwst Town	12	3	0	9	18	43	6

Portmadoc vs Holyhead Swifts, Holyhead Swifts vs Llanrwst Town and Llanrwst Town vs Holyhead Swifts were not played.

NORTH WALES COAST LEAGUE
1905-06

Division 1

Bangor FC	12	9	1	2	38	14	19
Holyhead Swifts	12	8	3	1	36	18	19
Colwyn Bay FC	12	7	1	4	35	19	15
Portmadoc	12	5	3	4	20	16	13
Llandudno Amateurs	12	4	2	6	22	26	10
Llanrwst Town	12	1	2	9	14	40	4
Blaenau Ffestiniog	12	1	2	9	13	45	4

Division 2

Rhyl Victoria	12	9	2	1	30	12	20
Prestatyn Town	12	7	3	2	28	16	15
Denbigh FC	12	5	4	3	22	17	14
Rhyl Church Guild FC	12	3	4	5	18	18	10
Llandudno Amateurs Reserves	12	3	2	7	22	31	8
Ruthin FC	12	3	2	7	14	24	8
Abergele FC	12	2	3	7	15	31	7

Prestatyn Town had 2 points deducted for fielding an ineligible player.
Colwyn Bay FC Reserves resigned from Division 2 during the season and their record was deleted.

NORTH WALES COAST LEAGUE
1906-07

Division 1

Holyhead Swifts	12	8	3	1	49	20	19
Llandudno Amateurs	12	6	2	4	21	22	14
Caernarfon United	12	5	3	4	26	26	13
Conwy FC	12	5	2	5	32	34	12
Colwyn Bay FC	12	4	3	5	24	33	11
Blaenau Ffestiniog	12	3	2	7	22	32	8
Bangor FC Reserves	12	2	3	7	25	38	7

Portmadoc resigned from Division 1 during the season.

Division 2

Rhyl Victoria	10	8	1	1	38	10	17
Ruthin FC	10	5	2	3	26	11	12
Denbigh FC	10	6	0	4	14	18	12
Rhyl Church Guild FC	10	3	2	5	17	22	8
Llandudno Amateurs Reserves	10	2	4	4	14	22	8
Rhuddlan Conservatives	10	1	1	8	8	33	3

NORTH WALES COAST LEAGUE
1907-08

Division 1

Bangor FC Reserves	20	14	4	2	68	27	32
Holyhead Swifts	20	13	0	7	71	48	26
Beaumaris FC	20	11	2	7	53	36	24
Colwyn Bay United	20	9	3	8	58	45	21
Llandudno Amateurs	20	9	3	8	29	39	21
Rhyl Athletic Reserves	20	8	3	9	55	36	19
Conwy FC	20	7	2	11	41	58	16
Caernarfon United	19	8	2	9	41	63	16
Denbigh United	20	7	1	12	33	47	15
Blaenau Ffestiniog	20	7	1	12	39	74	15
Llanrwst Town	19	4	4	11	19	54	8

Caernarfon United had 2 points deducted for fielding an ineligible player.
Match Llanrwst Town vs Caernarfon United was not played.

Division 2

Ruthin Town	6	4	1	1	17	8	9
Denbigh Church Guild	6	3	1	2	12	12	7
Denbigh United Reserves	6	2	1	3	15	17	5
Corwen FC Reserves	6	1	1	4	8	14	3

Rhuddlan Conservatives resigned from Division 2 during the season.

NORTH WALES COAST LEAGUE
1908-09

Division 1

Beaumaris FC	20	15	2	3	74	29	32
Caernarfon United	20	12	4	4	57	29	28
Llandudno Amateurs	20	10	4	6	30	33	24
Bangor FC Reserves	20	11	1	9	45	33	23
Pwllheli Town	20	10	3	7	40	46	23
Holyhead Swifts	20	8	2	10	71	39	18
Conwy FC	20	8	2	10	41	52	18
Denbigh United	20	6	6	8	34	47	18
Colwyn Bay United	20	3	7	10	33	49	13
Llanrwst Town	20	4	4	12	22	65	12
Blaenau Ffestiniog	20	5	1	14	37	62	11

Division 2

Ruthin Town	6	6	0	0	15	6	12
Denbigh Church Guild	6	2	2	2	17	13	6
Colwyn Bay United Reserves	6	1	2	3	6	11	4
Denbigh United Reserves	6	0	2	4	7	15	0

Denbigh United Reserves had 2 points deducted for fielding an ineligible player.

NORTH WALES COAST LEAGUE
1909-10
Division 1

U.C.N.W. Bangor	18	13	3	2	86	31	29
Caernarfon United	18	12	1	5	57	30	25
Holyhead Swifts	18	8	5	5	49	27	21
Llanrwst Town	17	9	3	5	33	26	21
Bangor FC Reserves	17	7	3	7	43	34	17
Llandudno Amateurs	18	7	4	7	37	38	16
Colwyn Bay United	18	6	2	10	43	59	14
Pwllheli Town	18	6	1	11	27	37	13
Blaenau Ffestiniog	18	6	0	12	36	49	12
Llanberis United	18	2	4	12	31	91	8

Llandudno Amateurs had 2 points deducted for fielding an
ineligible player.
Bangor FC Reserves vs Llanrwst Town was not played.
Conway FC withdrew from Division 1 during the season.

Division 2

Holyhead Swifts Reserves	12	7	3	2	52	22	17
Glasinfryn Swifts	12	5	4	3	37	23	14
Llechid Swifts	12	5	3	4	30	38	13
Menai Bridge Tigers	12	4	3	5	27	32	11
Llangefni United	12	4	2	6	24	30	10
Caernarfon United Reserves	12	5	2	5	25	35	10
Llandudno Amateurs Reserves	12	3	1	8	20	35	7

Caenarfon United Reserves had 2 points deducted for fielding an
ineligible player.

NORTH WALES COAST LEAGUE
1910-11
Division 1

Llandudno Amateurs	18	12	5	1	47	16	29
Caernarfon United	18	12	2	4	56	27	26
Colwyn Bay United	18	9	4	5	39	27	22
Llandudno Junction FC	18	10	2	6	41	33	22
Holyhead Swifts	18	10	0	8	43	24	20
Llanrwst Town	18	8	1	10	32	31	15
Bangor FC Reserves	18	7	2	9	33	34	14
Blaenau Ffestiniog	18	4	6	8	31	49	14
Pwllheli Town	18	4	1	13	19	65	9
Llanberis United	18	2	3	13	35	70	7

Bangor FC Reserves had 2 points deducted for fielding an
ineligible player.

Division 2

Glasinfryn Swifts	16	13	1	2	85	25	27
Llechid Swifts	16	10	4	2	38	24	24
Holyhead Swifts Reserves	16	10	0	6	64	36	29
Menai Bridge Tigers	16	9	1	6	50	40	19
Penmaenmawr FC	16	7	2	7	37	39	16
Llanfairfechan FC	16	5	1	10	26	51	11
Llandudno Amateurs Reserves	16	5	1	10	19	50	11
Llandudno Junction FC Res.	16	3	3	10	18	44	9
Colwyn Bay FC Celts	16	2	3	11	18	46	7

Bangor FC Juniors resigned from Division 2 during the season.

NORTH WALES COAST LEAGUE
1911-12
Division 1

Caernarfon United	20	15	1	4	65	36	31
Bangor Town Reserves	20	15	0	5	122	23	30
Holyhead Swifts	20	13	2	5	63	21	28
Denbigh United	20	9	3	8	39	36	21
Ffestiniog Town	20	10	1	9	42	41	21
Rhyl United	20	8	4	8	35	51	21
Llandudno Amateurs	20	7	5	8	36	53	19
Colwyn Bay United	20	7	3	10	26	40	17
Llandudno Junction FC	20	5	3	12	29	56	13
Llanrwst Town	20	4	4	12	34	78	12
Llanberis United	20	3	2	15	34	90	8

Division 2

Glasinfryn Swifts	14	10	2	2	53	17	22
Bangor FC Reserves	14	10	1	3	34	21	21
Llechid Swifts	14	5	3	6	26	22	13
Tregarth Celts	14	5	2	7	21	30	12
Penmaenmawr FC	14	5	2	7	20	27	12
Llanfairfechan FC	14	4	3	7	36	41	11
Holyhead Swifts Reserves	14	5	1	8	25	45	11
Menai Bridge Tigers	14	5	0	9	23	34	8

Llandudno Amateurs Reserves, Llandudno Junction Reserves
and Colwyn Bay United Reserves all withdrew from Division 2
during the season.

NORTH WALES COAST LEAGUE
1912-13
Division 1

Ffestiniog Town	20	13	4	3	63	39	30
Caernarfon United	20	14	0	6	59	33	28
Rhyl United	20	12	0	8	67	36	24
Denbigh United	20	9	3	8	47	31	21
Colwyn Bay United	20	9	2	9	34	35	20
Llandudno Junction FC	19	8	3	8	33	28	19
Holyhead Swifts	18	7	3	8	41	39	17
Holywell United	19	7	3	9	42	42	17
Bangor Town Reserves	18	7	2	9	31	44	16
Llanrwst Town	18	4	2	12	23	62	8
Llanberis United	18	4	1	13	31	76	7

LLanrwst Town and Llanberis United each had 2 points deducted
for fielding an ineligible player.

Division 2

Tregarth FC	13	10	3	0	42	10	23
Holyhead Swifts Reserves	10	4	5	1	24	18	13
Glasinfryn Swifts	12	6	1	5	27	29	13
Llechid Swifts	13	5	2	6	31	34	12
Penmaenmawr FC	11	5	1	5	23	16	11
Llanfairfechan FC	12	3	4	5	24	26	10
Menai Bridge Tigers	14	3	4	7	25	37	10
Glascoed FC	11	2	0	9	12	43	4

A number of fixtures were not played..
Llandudno FC Reserves resigned from Division 2 during the
season.
The table shown is the probable Final Table as no further results
have been found.

NORTH WALES COAST LEAGUE
1913-14
Division 1

Holywell United	17	15	1	1	57	16	31
Denbigh United	18	11	2	5	46	24	24
Colwyn Bay United	18	8	6	4	27	18	23
Rhyl United	18	10	1	7	42	36	21
Holyhead Swifts	18	8	3	7	31	40	19
Bangor Town	18	7	1	10	37	40	15
Ffestiniog Town	17	6	2	9	44	25	14
Llandudno Junction FC	18	4	4	10	20	51	12
Llanrwst Town	17	3	4	11	28	54	10
Caernarfon United	17	5	0	13	24	52	10

Llanrwst Town vs Caernarfon United and Holywell United vs Ffestiniog Town were not played.

Division 2

Bangor Railway Institute	22	19	1	2	90	17	39
Bangor Town Reserves	22	17	3	2	88	19	37
Penmaenmawr FC	22	12	4	6	51	32	28
Bethesda United	22	11	5	6	50	28	27
Llanfairfechan FC	22	12	1	9	62	49	25
Menai Bridge Tigers	22	8	4	10	54	54	20
Holyhead Swifts Reserves	21	7	5	9	40	47	19
Llechid Celts	22	6	4	12	37	64	16
Caernarfon United Reserves	22	6	4	12	32	60	14
Glasinfryn Swifts	21	5	2	14	38	69	12
Llangefni United	20	4	3	13	26	71	11
Dolgarrog United	20	4	0	16	23	81	8

Caernarfon United Reserves had 2 points deducted.
The Final Table is shown as not all fixtures were completed.
Llanberis United resigned from Division 2 during the season and their record was expunged.

NORTH WALES COAST LEAGUE
1919-20
Division 1

Bangor Comrades	18	13	2	3	69	26	28
Bangor Railway Institute	18	12	4	2	68	28	28
Holyhead Railway Institute	18	9	5	4	38	22	23
Colwyn Bay FC	18	10	2	6	69	51	22
Denbigh United	18	8	4	6	31	35	20
Conwy FC	18	7	1	10	42	45	15
Blaenau Ffestiniog Comrades	18	7	1	10	47	56	15
Llanrwst Town	18	5	2	11	39	56	12
Caernarfon Athletic	18	4	2	12	36	55	10
Portmadoc	18	3	1	14	28	93	7

Division 2

Holyhead Railway Institute Res.	18	15	1	2	56	23	31
Abergele FC	18	14	2	2	75	22	30
Bethesda Comrades	18	9	3	6	37	43	21
Glasinfryn Swifts	18	9	2	7	44	31	20
Penmaenmawr FC	18	7	5	6	39	30	19
Llechid Celts	18	7	3	8	30	31	17
Bangor Comrades Reserves	18	6	3	9	43	45	15
Dolgarrog FC	18	4	3	11	33	46	11
Llanfairfechan FC	18	5	1	12	30	50	11
Nantlle Vale FC	18	1	2	15	24	90	4

Bangor Railway Institute Reserves resigned from Division 2 during the season.
Bethesda Comrades vs Holyhead Railway Institute Reserves was abandoned when Bethesda and the home crowd disputed Holyhead's third goal. They would not let the match continue and the referee abandoned the game. A subsequent NWCFA meeting censured Bethesda and the match and championship was awarded to Holyhead. Abergele lodged a protest about this decision.

NORTH WALES COAST LEAGUE
1920-21
Division 1

Holyhead Railway Institute	22	17	2	3	70	22	36
Holywell United	22	15	3	4	92	37	33
Denbigh United	22	12	4	6	57	35	28
Bangor Athletic	22	11	4	7	64	60	26
Blaenau Festiniog Comrades	22	11	3	8	58	40	25
Llandudno FC	22	10	4	8	50	57	24
Colwyn Bay FC	22	10	3	9	60	48	23
Conwy FC	22	10	2	10	44	57	22
Caernarfon Athletic	22	7	2	13	44	65	16
Llanrwst Town	22	4	5	13	38	66	13
Portmadoc	22	4	3	15	40	76	11
Ogwen Valley FC	22	1	4	17	23	77	6

Division 2

Llechid Celts	26	19	4	3	74	30	42
Glasinfryn Swifts	25	19	3	3	90	29	41
Abergele FC	25	19	2	5	105	29	38
Penmaenmawr FC	26	18	2	5	80	37	38
Holyhead Railway Institute Res.	26	14	3	9	64	53	31
Bangor Athletic Reserves	26	11	4	11	54	46	26
Llanfairfechan FC	26	10	5	11	55	53	25
Caernarfon Athletic Reserves	26	8	8	10	48	53	24
Nantlle Vale FC	26	7	6	13	44	64	20
Menai Bridge Tigers	26	6	8	12	43	69	20
Llanberis Comrades FC	26	9	2	15	43	74	20
Dolgarrog FC	26	7	5	14	54	74	19
Llangefni FC	26	7	2	17	40	77	16
Rhiwlas Athletic	26	0	2	24	26	132	2

Abergele FC and Glasinfryn Swifts failed to agree on a date for their match after a replay was ordered by the League.

In 1921 the League was absorbed into the newly established Welsh National League but an effort was made in 1930 to resurrect it.

NORTH WALES COAST LEAGUE
1930-31

Bethesda Victoria	1	1	0	0	9	0	2
Bangor City Reserves	1	1	0	0	4	1	2
Menai Bridge	1	1	0	0	2	1	2
Holyhead	1	0	0	1	1	2	0
Blaenau Festiniog	1	0	0	1	1	4	0
Caernarfon Town	1	0	0	1	0	9	0

Only one round of matches was played. No evidence of further games has been found and the League may have folded.

NORTH WALES COAST LEAGUE
1933-34

Rhyl Athletic Reserves	18	15	1	2	82	27	31
Llanfairfechan FC	18	11	3	4	57	34	25
Portmadoc	18	10	3	5	68	39	23
Llandudno FC	18	10	3	5	59	40	23
Blaenau Ffestiniog	18	9	2	7	57	41	20
Bangor City Reserves	18	8	1	9	39	55	17
Bethesda Victoria	18	5	3	10	37	65	13
Llanrwst Town	18	5	3	10	35	63	13
Holyhead Town	18	3	4	11	31	56	10
Colwyn Bay FC Reserves	18	1	3	14	20	65	5

Pwllheli FC resigned during season and their record was expunged.

NORTH WALES COAST LEAGUE
1934-35

Llanfairfechan FC	10	8	1	1	31	15	17
Bangor City Reserves	12	6	2	4	34	33	14
Llandudno FC	10	4	3	3	47	27	11
Portmadoc	10	4	3	3	32	32	11
Blaenau Ffestiniog	10	3	2	5	25	32	8
Rhyl Athletic Reserves	12	2	1	9	24	49	5
Colwyn Bay FC Reserves	4	1	0	3	5	10	2

Colwyn Bay FC Reserves did not fulfil their fixtures against Llanfairfechan, Llandudno, CPD Porthmadog and Blaenau Ffestiniog.

The League disbanded in 1935 with the formation of the Welsh League (North) which runs to this day under the name Welsh Alliance League.

NORTH WALES FOOTBALL COMBINATION

Formation

Following the demise of the Welsh National League structure in 1930, senior clubs in the area demanded to a strong and competitive league. Football in North Wales had begun to decline and the intention was that this league would replicate the old Combination and provide a strong competition for clubs in north Wales and the borders.

The early discussions between officials of the Welsh League and Cheshire League to develop a cross-border competition were secretive. The proposals that emerged were put to a meeting of clubs at the Albion Hotel, Chester on the 5th of July 1930 and duly accepted. Nineteen clubs were given permission to apply, but with no guarantee of acceptance as other clubs were waiting to apply for membership of what was envisaged as initially an 18 club League. As it turned out the following clubs were accepted into membership: Buckley, Ellesmere Port Town, Bangor, Caernarvon Athletic, Flint Town, Blaenau Festiniog, Holywell Town, Llandudno, Mold Town, New Brighton Reserves, Rhyl Athletic, Wrexham Reserves and Colwyn Bay. Three clubs, namely Stockport County, Shell-Mex and Northern Nomads, who had originally intended to participate resigned for various reasons and Blaenau Festiniog resigned on financial grounds before the season started. Buckley, Holywell, Flint and Mold also resigned with only Llanfairfechan and Holyhead Town stepping in to make a less impressive ten-club league. Lt Col. J Llewelyn Williams of Holywell became president and H.R. Williams of Bangor took on the role of secretary. In November 1930, Caernarvon Athletic went into liquidation and their fixtures were taken over by Bethesda Victoria. During the 1930-31 season, clubs played each other twice home and away but this was not a financial success.

As the Combination had not drawn in clubs from Cheshire, FAW secretary Ted Robbins, suggested at a meeting in Bangor on 13th July 1931, that an east and west league should be formed in North Wales with Llandudno or Colwyn Bay as the dividing line. It was decided to call the new league the Welsh Combination. Five clubs in the North Wales Football Combination then decided to resign and join the new league. The new structure covered an area from Llandudno to Holyhead, Portmadoc, Pwllheli and Blaenau Ffestiniog. By the following week no clubs were left in the original league and it was wound up.

For the 1931-32 season, champions Colwyn Bay, Rhyl Athletic, New Brighton, and Ellesmere Port all resigned. New members were elected: Blaenau Festiniog, Penmaenmawr FC, Pwllheli and Conway FC. At the end of the season only Penmaenmawr dropped out but the league increased in size with the addition of Llanrwst Town and Caernarvon Athletic.

At the AGM at the end of the third season, a change of name to the North Wales Coast League was proposed and accepted, thus closing another chapter in the history of league football in North Wales.

NORTH WALES FOOTBALL COMBINATION LEAGUE 1930-31

Colwyn Bay FC	18	12	3	3	71	20	27
Bangor City	18	11	2	5	55	34	24
Rhyl Athletic	18	11	1	6	56	34	23
New Brighton FC	18	10	1	7	50	52	21
Wrexham AFC Reserves	18	8	4	6	42	39	20
Ellesmere Port Town	18	7	2	9	54	67	16
Llanfairfechan FC	18	6	3	9	44	63	15
Holyhead Town	18	5	3	10	51	67	13
Llandudno FC	18	5	1	12	27	58	11
Bethesda Victoria	18	3	4	11	33	49	10

Bethesda Victoria took over the fixtures of Caernarvon Athletic who went bankrupt

NORTH WALES FOOTBALL COMBINATION LEAGUE 1931-32

Bethesda Victoria	16	12	1	3	64	30	25
Holyhead Town	16	9	4	3	53	25	22
Blaenau Ffestiniog	16	10	2	4	57	41	22
Llandudno FC	16	9	1	6	51	39	19
Llanfairfechan FC	16	8	1	7	46	40	17
Penmaenmawr FC	16	6	2	8	56	47	14
Bangor City	16	5	2	9	42	55	12
Pwllheli FC	16	4	2	10	28	58	10
Conwy FC	16	1	1	14	19	81	3

NORTH WALES FOOTBALL COMBINATION LEAGUE 1932-33

Caernarfon Athletic	18	12	3	3	64	26	27
Llanfairfechan FC	18	10	4	4	60	34	24
Holyhead Town	18	11	2	5	48	36	24
Llanrwst Town	18	10	1	7	37	35	21
Llandudno FC	18	6	6	6	48	53	18
Bangor City Reserves	18	7	3	8	35	36	17
Pwllheli FC	18	7	1	10	44	52	15
Conwy FC	18	6	1	11	41	51	13
Bethesda Victoria	18	6	1	11	20	43	13
Blaenau Ffestiniog	18	2	4	12	37	67	8

WELSH FOOTBALL LEAGUE

Formation

As the Welsh National League collapsed at the end of the 1929-30 season, new Leagues sprang up all over North Wales as clubs consolidated.

Division II East of the Northern Section of the Welsh National League had actually enjoyed an excellent season and, due to hard working administrators, had completed their fixtures in full and in good time. The Division had eleven members – Prestatyn Town, Denbigh Mental Hospital, Llanddulas FC, Bettisfield FC, Holywell Arcadians, Abergele FC, Ruthin FC, Denbigh Juniors, Llysfaen FC, Kinmel Bay FC, and Rhuddlan FC – and on 23rd of July 1930 the membership and administrators held a meeting at the Imperial Hotel, Rhyl.

As reported in the North Wales Weekly News of July 31st the meeting was chaired by Mr W.H. Jones of Abergele, President of the League.

A detailed financial statement was read out and explained by W. Morris, Treasurer and Acting Hon Secretary. The League was in a strong financial position, a cash credit of £110 being disclosed and Mr Morris's services to the League were recognised by several present. It was unanimously decided to make him a presentation as a token of the Leagues regard for the painstaking manner in which he had carried out his duties.

Several accounts were passed for payment and the representatives of the Prestatyn and Bettisfield clubs were handed the respective trophies and medals which they had won.

By seven votes to six it was decided to apply for permission to the FA of Wales to re-name the League "The Welsh League" as the Welsh National League was in the hands of trustees. The opinion was expressed that as Division II East was the only league in North Wales to complete its fixtures last season it was entitled to claim itself as being the best organised and controlled league in the area, and, as such, to claim a title that was more in keeping with its high position.

It was decided to advertise in several newspapers for three more clubs in order to bring up the total to fourteen.

The retiring vice-presidents were re-elected en bloc. On the position of the Llysfaen representative it was decided to ask Messrs S. Millington and E. Bithell to act as vice-presidents.

The name change was sanctioned by the FAW and four new clubs were admitted – Conwy Casuals, Colwyn Bay FC Reserves, Penmaenmawr FC and Rhyl Amateurs – one of whom replaced Rhuddlan FC who resigned before the start of the season.

The League ran for five years before running down to eight clubs at the end of 1934-35 season when yet another reconstruction of the League system condemned the league to history.

See the Welsh League North history overleaf for further details.

WELSH FOOTBALL LEAGUE 1930-31

Holywell Arcadians	26	20	4	2	125	46	44
Bettisfield FC	26	17	5	4	86	34	39
Conwy Casuals	26	16	5	5	74	42	37
Prestatyn Town	26	14	5	7	82	45	33
Colwyn Bay FC Reserves	26	16	1	9	70	52	33
Denbigh Juniors	26	14	4	8	60	42	32
Llanddulas FC	26	14	1	11	74	65	29
Kinmel Bay FC	26	9	4	13	72	84	22
Denbigh Mental Hospital	26	8	5	13	58	69	21
Abergele FC	26	11	1	14	79	77	21
Ruthin FC	26	8	3	15	71	92	19
Penmaenmawr FC	26	7	2	20	39	83	14
Llysfaen FC	26	4	2	20	46	122	10
Rhyl Amateurs	26	3	2	21	37	115	8

Abergele FC had 2 points deducted.

WELSH FOOTBALL LEAGUE 1931-32

Rhyl FC A	24	18	3	3	83	31	39
Holywell Arcadians	24	18	1	5	124	43	37
Abergele FC	24	14	2	8	84	62	28
Llanddulas FC	24	9	9	6	95	63	27
Denbigh Juniors	24	11	5	8	64	72	27
Bettisfield FC	24	11	3	10	68	52	25
Denbigh Mental Hospital	24	9	7	8	68	65	25
Colwyn Bay FC Reserves	24	9	3	12	63	74	21
Kinmel Bay FC	24	8	4	12	80	79	20
Conwy FC	24	8	4	12	43	66	20
Llysfaen FC	24	7	2	15	66	92	16
Llandudno FC	24	5	3	16	45	118	13
Ruthin FC	24	5	2	17	50	106	12

Llandudno FC and Conwy FC played in both the Welsh League and Combination

WELSH FOOTBALL LEAGUE 1932-33

Holywell Arcadians	20	15	4	1	84	34	34
Abergele FC	20	11	3	6	50	31	25
Llanddulas FC	20	11	2	7	56	47	24
Rhyl Corinthians	20	9	6	5	35	19	24
Rhyl FC Reserves	20	11	1	8	59	48	23
Bethesda Victoria	20	11	1	8	59	48	23
Colwyn Bay FC Reserves	20	9	2	9	38	51	20
Denbigh Mental Hospital	20	8	1	11	49	59	17
Denbigh Town	20	6	2	12	36	48	14
Bettisfield FC	20	5	1	14	34	60	11
Llysfaen FC	20	3	2	15	37	99	8

WELSH FOOTBALL LEAGUE 1933-34

Fflint Town	18	16	1	1	99	11	33
Rhyl Athletic Reserves	18	13	2	3	50	29	27
Abergele FC	18	10	3	5	50	31	23
Llanddulas FC	18	7	6	5	44	45	20
Denbigh Mental Hospital	18	8	3	7	32	37	19
Bettisfield FC	18	8	2	8	46	51	18
Prestatyn Town	18	7	2	9	48	49	16
Denbigh Town	18	3	5	10	28	51	11
Rhuddlan Town	18	3	2	13	33	75	8
Llysfaen FC	18	1	3	14	30	69	5

WELSH FOOTBALL LEAGUE 1934-35

Abergele FC	14	12	0	2	67	16	24
Fflint Town	13	11	1	1	57	11	23
Ruthin FC	14	7	1	6	43	45	15
Prestatyn Town	14	6	2	6	30	33	14
Denbigh Mental Hospital	13	5	0	8	38	38	10
Llanfairfechan FC	14	4	2	8	34	55	10
Llanddulas FC	14	4	1	9	35	50	9
Llysfaen FC	14	2	0	12	22	69	4

Not all fixtures were completed.

WELSH LEAGUE (NORTH)

Formation and History

At the beginning of the 1934-35 season, senior football in the North Wales coast area was covered by two senior Leagues – the North Wales Coast League and the Welsh League, largely split along geographic lines. Both competitions had been formed following the collapse of the Welsh National League set-up in 1930, the former under the title of North Wales Football Combination.

By 1934 stagnation had once more crept in to the game in the north and, at a meeting held at the Royal Hotel, Colwyn Bay in October of that year, a proposal formulated by Col. J Llewelyn Williams of Holywell (then FAW Treasurer) was put to a meeting of both the aforementioned leagues, convened by the FAW.

Originally put together in July 1933, the plan had been discussed on September the 5th by a special sub-committee made up of four prominent members of the North Wales Coast League, namely D.A. Rodger (Rhyl), Percy Weekes (Holyhead), E.W. Hughes (Bangor) and Hugh R. Williams (Bangor).

Following the meeting they submitted a report which the North Wales Weekly News quoted as concluding:

> "The committee from the outset felt that senior football on the North Wales Coast is drifting to its doom. Senior clubs are going into junior football and if this is allowed to go unchecked it will mean an end to Junior football too.
>
> It is the unanimous decision of this committee that we adopt, in principle, the Zone Scheme so aptly propounded by Col. J. Llewelyn Williams.
>
> We sincerely believe that every town that has had a senior club should again carry a senior club before it is allowed to run merely a junior club."

They then listed a number of clubs that "should be compelled to enter the Zone Scheme which should be divided into two sections".

It was a revolutionary but complex system which was originally put forward. Clubs in Section A would have the option of playing in Section B and vice-versa but ten clubs would be compelled to play in both sections!

Three clubs not in the ten, namely Pwllheli, Portmadoc and Blaenau Ffestiniog would also be allowed to play in the Cambrian League (sic).

FAW Secretary Ted Robbins set a timetable for the next two meetings within tight schedules. The first, held at Rhyl was of the Management Committee. The officials in place included Joint Secretaries – W.F. Morris and H.R. Williams.

A meeting of the North Wales Coast Football League formally adopted the proposals the same week

Further meetings were held to resolve differences but it was not until June 1935 that matters came to a head when two of the Junior leagues the Vale of Conwy and Flintshire expressed reservations on the effect on junior football of the rules being imposed within the new system. They were joined in their concerns by the Bangor & District League and the Anglesey League. These leagues were criticised by Col. Williams as lacking in vision and the Bangor & District League, who had decided to run independently was told in no uncertain terms to toe the line or not to be allowed to function at all.

The Flintshire Amateur Football League wrote to the new Welsh League and the FAW stating their intention to manage their own affairs for the coming term.

The Welsh League, which covered Denbighshire and Flintshire, was quite a successful league and three of its clubs, namely Flint Town, Denbigh Mental Hospital and Ruthin, were the chief objectors, having been virtually forced to join the top division. So far, a rough ride for the new system.

As it stood at this point the end of July 1935, the three zones of the top division remained in the frame with the Flintshire League First Division forming Division II and the area leagues, Bangor, Anglesey, Conway, Mold, Dyserth plus the Second Division of the Flintshire League would form Division III. And it would appear that the Welsh League was to be, as described by Mr J. Lloyd Kearns (Denbigh) at the League's AGM in Rhyl on July 13th, "washed away".

The arguing continued but eventually the Division II and III set-up was adopted at a meeting in Llandudno Junction in September 1935. The Welsh League disbanded. Denbigh Mental Hospital and Flint Town opted to join the senior League which eventually kicked off at the end of the month.

Llanddulas and Abergele went into the Dyserth League whilst the fate of Prestatyn Town, Llysfaen and Ruthin are not known although Llysfaen reappeared in the Vale of Conwy League in 1938.

A senior division eventually took shape and comprised of eleven clubs: Bangor City, Blaenau Ffestiniog FC, Colwyn Bay FC, CPD Porthmadog, Denbigh Mental Hospital, Flint Town, Holyhead Town, Llandudno FC, Llanfairfechan Town, Penrhyn Quarry FC and Rhyl FC.

The first season was something of a failure with original dissenters Flint Town and Denbigh Mental Hospital failing to complete their fixtures, the season closing with fourteen fixtures unplayed and Llandudno FC taking the title.

Llanfairfechan and Denbigh Mental Hospital dropped out at the end of the first term and Pwllheli British Legion entered the fray and together with the remaining nine clubs continued into the second season.

The League continued to flourish with regional second divisions being formed in 1948 which continued until a single 18-club division format returned in 1960.

It was to be the most successful league in the history of North Wales football, running uninterrupted (bar the war) for forty-nine years until its transition into the Welsh Alliance League in 1985.

WELSH LEAGUE (NORTH) TABLES
1935-36

Llandudno FC	20	14	2	4	71	37	30
Colwyn Bay FC	20	11	4	5	65	47	26
Fflint Town	14	9	2	3	49	26	20
Llanfairfechan Town	20	9	2	9	47	43	20
Rhyl FC	20	9	2	9	50	65	20
CPD Porthmadog	16	8	3	5	53	37	19
Blaenau Ffestiniog FC	16	7	2	7	40	32	16
Holyhead Town	16	6	2	8	36	44	14
Bangor City	20	5	2	13	60	65	12
Penrhyn Quarry FC	18	4	1	13	21	63	9
Denbigh Mental Hospital	12	2	2	8	20	36	6

Fixtures not completed

WELSH LEAGUE (NORTH) TABLES
1936-37

Llandudno FC	18	16	1	1	83	15	33
Fflint Town	17	12	1	4	71	32	25
Pwllheli FC	18	11	1	6	42	31	23
Penrhyn Quarry FC	18	10	2	6	44	37	22
CPD Porthmadog	18	7	2	9	58	43	16
Holyhead Town	18	7	1	10	43	66	15
Blaenau Ffestiniog FC	17	6	2	9	52	60	14
Colwyn Bay FC Reserves	18	6	2	10	46	66	14
Bangor City Reserves	18	4	2	12	33	62	10
Rhyl FC Reserves	18	3	0	15	21	78	6

One match was not played.

WELSH LEAGUE (NORTH) TABLES
1937-38

CPD Porthmadog	20	13	5	2	57	23	31
Pwllheli FC	20	14	2	4	66	34	30
Llandudno FC	20	12	3	5	75	33	27
Blaenau Ffestiniog FC	20	11	3	6	55	32	25
Caernarfon Town	20	11	3	6	42	34	25
Bangor City	20	10	2	8	57	46	22
Penrhyn Quarry FC	20	9	1	10	47	56	19
Rhyl FC Reserves	20	6	2	12	51	62	14
Royal Air Force Penrhos	20	6	2	12	40	57	14
Colwyn Bay FC Reserves	20	1	5	14	28	80	7
Holyhead Town	20	1	4	15	31	92	6

WELSH LEAGUE (NORTH) TABLES
1938-39

Llandudno FC	20	17	2	1	74	22	36
Pwllheli FC	20	11	4	5	62	37	26
CPD Porthmadog	20	12	1	7	55	25	25
Caernarfon Town	20	11	3	6	67	40	25
Penrhyn Quarry FC	20	10	2	8	56	41	22
Blaenau Ffestiniog FC	20	8	4	8	53	37	20
Holyhead Town	20	8	1	11	42	75	17
Llanrwst Town	20	6	3	11	41	60	15
Rhyl FC Reserves	20	6	2	12	54	86	14
Bangor City Reserves	20	5	3	12	33	55	13
Royal Air Force Penrhos	20	3	1	16	27	86	7

WELSH LEAGUE (NORTH) TABLES
1939-40

Western Area

Caernarfon Town (78%)	14	10	2	2	47	16	22
Llandudno FC (72%)	11	8	0	3	37	23	16
Penmaenmawr FC (75%)	6	4	1	1	18	12	9
Llysfaen FC	8	4	1	3	18	19	9
Llanfairfechan FC	10	4	1	5	20	25	9
Conway Borough	12	4	1	7	26	39	9
Bangor City	7	3	0	4	21	26	6
Llandudno Junction	4	0	0	4	18	12	0
Royal Air Force Penrhos	4	0	0	4	6	12	0
Rhyl FC	2	0	0	2	5	11	0

Eastern (Fflintshire) Area

Connahs Quay St. Davids	18	14	1	3	90	40	29
Connahs Quay Rangers	18	14	1	3	72	37	29
Sandycroft FC	18	13	0	5	71	37	26
Connahs Quay Albion	18	10	2	6	69	39	22
Treuddyn Villa	18	10	2	6	69	33	22
Caer Estyn Wanderers	18	6	1	11	35	66	13
Mancot FC	18	6	1	11	47	59	13
Mold Hotspurs	18	5	2	11	48	71	12
Sealand Tennants	18	4	2	12	24	72	6
Queensferry St. Andrews	18	2	1	15	35	98	5

The League did not operate between 1940 and 1945 due to the war.

WELSH LEAGUE (NORTH) TABLES
1945-46

H.M.S. Glendower	20	15	0	5	110	42	30
Colwyn Bay FC	19	15	0	4	76	44	30
Bangor City Reserves	19	12	2	5	87	40	26
Caernarfon Town	19	12	0	7	76	37	24
5th Cheshire Regiment	12	10	0	2	66	16	20
Llanfairfechan Town	19	9	0	10	54	70	18
Rhyl FC Reserves	19	7	1	11	50	73	15
Blaenau Ffestiniog FC	18	6	1	11	27	76	13
Penrhyn Quarry FC	20	5	0	15	59	83	10
CPD Porthmadog	19	4	1	14	33	94	9
Holyhead Town	20	4	1	15	32	95	9

5th Cheshire Regiment withdrew due to being disbanded. Their ecord was not expunged.
H.M.S. Glendower were awarded the championship.

WELSH LEAGUE (NORTH) TABLES
1946-47

Caernarfon Town	22	15	1	6	86	38	31
Llandudno Junction FC	22	14	3	5	82	45	31
Rhyl FC Reserves	22	15	0	7	78	47	30
Llandudno FC	22	13	2	7	57	34	28
Penrhyn Quarry FC	22	14	0	8	81	73	28
Llanfairfechan Town	22	11	2	9	84	64	24
Colwyn Bay FC	22	8	4	10	68	63	20
Blaenau Ffestiniog FC	22	9	1	12	47	71	19
Bangor City Reserves	22	8	0	14	54	75	16
Pwllheli British Legion	22	8	0	14	71	96	16
CPD Porthmadog	22	5	1	16	53	103	11
Holyhead Town	22	4	2	16	41	95	10

WELSH LEAGUE (NORTH) TABLES
1947-48

Penrhyn Quarry FC	26	18	3	5	105	44	39
Rhyl FC Reserves	26	17	2	7	101	47	36
Llandudno Junction FC	26	16	3	7	84	49	35
Caernarfon Town	26	14	4	8	83	64	32
Llandudno FC	26	14	4	8	67	54	32
Llanfairfechan Town	26	13	3	10	99	79	29
Pwllheli British Legion	26	11	5	10	72	81	27
Colwyn Bay FC	26	11	4	11	70	63	26
Holyhead Town	26	11	0	15	69	72	22
Penmaenmawr FC	26	7	7	12	72	97	21
Blaenau Ffestiniog FC	26	7	6	13	70	84	20
Conwy Borough FC	26	7	3	16	45	77	17
Bangor City Reserves	26	7	2	17	49	101	16
CPD Porthmadog	26	5	2	19	39	92	12

WELSH LEAGUE (NORTH) TABLES
1948-49

Division 1

Llandudno Junction FC	26	20	3	3	103	30	43
Conwy Borough FC	26	20	1	5	98	44	41
Pwllheli & District FC	26	16	4	6	87	45	36
Holyhead Town	26	15	3	8	91	49	33
Rhyl FC Reserves	26	16	1	9	86	47	33
Llandudno FC	26	16	1	9	53	37	33
Colwyn Bay FC	26	14	3	9	89	55	31
Bangor City Reserves	26	13	3	10	72	74	29
Caernarfon Town	26	10	2	14	59	66	22
Llanfairfechan Town	26	8	1	17	56	82	17
Blaenau Ffestiniog FC	26	7	0	19	41	96	14
Penmaenmawr FC	26	5	2	19	50	89	12
CPD Porthmadog	26	4	3	19	48	113	11
Penrhyn Quarry FC	26	4	1	21	48	117	9

Division 2 – Western Section

Llanberis FC	18	14	2	2	74	33	30
Menai Bridge Tigers	18	14	1	3	74	34	29
Abersoch FC	18	11	2	5	70	44	24
Criccieth Town	18	8	2	8	60	54	18
Nantlle Vale FC	18	8	0	10	47	62	16
Cookes United	18	6	3	9	53	54	15
Caernarfon Town Reserves	18	7	1	10	50	56	15
Portdinorwic FC	18	5	3	10	48	74	13
CPD Porthmadog Reserves	18	4	3	11	39	55	11
Pwllheli & District Reserves	18	1	3	14	30	66	5

Division 2 – Eastern Section

Denbigh Town	18	12	2	4	76	35	26
Llanddulas FC	18	12	0	6	63	42	25
Llanrwst Town	18	10	2	6	43	47	22
Llandudno Junction Reserves	18	9	3	6	55	43	21
Abergele United	18	9	0	9	67	58	18
Mostyn Y.M.C.A.	18	7	4	7	51	49	18
Colwyn Bay FC Reserves	18	7	2	9	48	53	16
Prestatyn Town	18	5	2	11	36	52	12
Llandudno FC Reserves	18	5	2	11	36	52	12
Conwy Borough Reserves	18	3	4	11	36	69	10

WELSH LEAGUE (NORTH) TABLES 1949-50

Division 1

Holyhead Town	30	22	3	5	105	44	47
Fflint Town United	30	21	1	8	92	46	43
Conwy Borough	30	19	3	8	69	51	41
Pwllheli & District FC	30	17	3	10	75	47	37
Holywell Town	30	15	7	8	97	64	37
Colwyn Bay FC	30	11	13	6	67	50	35
Rhyl FC Reserves	30	12	8	10	82	78	32
Caernarfon Town	30	13	5	12	58	51	31
Llandudno Junction FC	30	13	4	13	63	70	30
Bangor City Reserves	30	13	3	14	67	71	29
Bethesda Athletic	30	8	7	15	83	98	23
Blaenau Ffestiniog FC	30	8	6	16	58	86	22
Llandudno FC	30	10	2	18	40	72	22
Penmaenmawr FC	30	7	6	17	42	69	20
CPD Porthmadog	30	7	5	18	50	82	19
Llanfairfechan Town	30	4	5	21	42	91	13

Division 2 – Western Section

Llanberis	18	15	1	2	72	29	31
Pwllheli & District Reserves	19	13	0	6	58	34	26
Port Dinorwic FC	17	11	2	4	62	29	24
Llechid Celts	19	10	3	6	61	38	23
Llanrug United	17	11	1	5	52	33	23
Nantlle Vale FC	20	6	5	9	45	25	17
CPD Porthmadog Reserves	18	6	5	7	38	45	17
Menai Bridge Tigers	18	7	2	9	42	45	16
Caernarfon Town Reserves	18	6	2	10	57	48	14
Criccieth Town	19	3	4	12	38	60	10
Cookes United	20	2	1	17	20	88	5

The table shown is the latest one found. No later table has been found and nor have any subsequent results so it is possibly the final table.

Division 2 – Eastern Section

Fflint Town United Reserves	12	10	1	1	58	25	21
Llanddulas FC	12	9	2	1	63	27	20
Llanrwst Town	12	8	0	4	42	36	16
Llandudno FC Reserves	12	6	0	6	27	38	12
Denbigh Town	12	3	2	7	33	44	8
Colwyn Bay FC Reserves	12	1	3	8	19	43	5
Llandudno Junction Reserves	12	2	0	10	20	64	4

WELSH LEAGUE (NORTH) TABLES 1950-51

Division 1

Pwllheli & District FC	30	21	4	5	84	26	46
Conwy Borough FC	30	22	2	6	67	32	46
Holyhead Town	30	20	3	7	83	48	43
Blaenau Ffestiniog FC	30	14	6	10	79	60	34
Llandudno Junction FC	30	13	8	9	62	54	34
Holywell Town	30	15	3	12	70	52	33
Bangor City Reserves	30	14	4	12	62	62	32
CPD Porthmadog	30	13	5	12	53	55	31
Penmaenmawr FC	30	11	4	15	55	62	26
Bethesda Athletic	30	11	4	15	76	89	26
Fflint Town United	30	10	5	15	50	54	25
Caernarfon Town	30	10	5	15	49	60	25
Colwyn Bay FC	30	9	6	15	54	67	24
Llandudno FC	30	7	10	13	42	56	24
Rhyl FC Reserves	30	7	4	19	51	82	18
Llanrwst Town	30	5	3	22	29	99	13

Division 2 – Western Section

Port Dinorwic FC	22	15	3	4	75	40	33
Llanrug United	22	13	3	6	75	37	29
Llanberis FC	22	14	0	8	76	46	28
Llandudno FC Reserves	22	13	2	7	76	55	28
Criccieth Town	22	10	5	7	65	50	25
Nantlle Vale FC	22	9	4	9	64	57	22
Bethesda Athletic Reserves	22	9	3	10	43	61	21
CPD Porthmadog Reserves	22	8	3	11	37	59	19
CPD Bl.Ffestiniog Reserves	22	8	2	12	52	72	18
Caernarfon Town Reserves	22	8	1	13	45	57	17
Pwllheli & Dist. Reserves	22	4	6	12	33	63	14
Cookes United	22	4	2	16	38	82	10

Division 2 – Eastern Section

The division did not operate this season.

WELSH LEAGUE (NORTH) TABLES 1951-52

Division 1

Pwllheli & District FC	32	27	4	1	121	39	58
Fflint Town United	32	19	5	8	90	50	43
Bangor City Reserves	32	19	3	10	88	58	41
Holyhead Town	32	20	1	11	75	56	41
Holywell Town	32	16	5	11	82	54	37
Blaenau Ffestiniog FC	32	14	7	11	100	73	35
Colwyn Bay FC	32	14	4	14	56	62	32
Llandudno FC	32	13	5	14	64	68	31
CPD Porthmadog	32	13	5	14	61	73	31
Rhyl FC Reserves	32	12	6	14	67	72	30
Llanrwst Town	32	12	5	15	66	71	29
Penmaenmawr FC	32	10	7	15	62	75	27
Llandudno Junction FC	32	10	3	19	60	93	23
Wrexham FC Reserves	32	9	5	18	54	92	23
Conwy Borough FC	32	7	9	16	43	75	23
Caernarfon Town	32	7	7	18	48	96	21
Bethesda Athletic	32	7	5	20	67	91	19

Division 2 – Western Section

Llanberis FC	20	16	1	3	92	40	33
Nantlle Vale FC	20	15	2	3	75	36	32
Criccieth Town	20	14	1	5	85	34	29
Llanrug United	20	12	3	5	64	38	27
Holyhead Town Reserves	20	10	6	4	62	39	26
Pwllheli & District Reserves	20	9	2	9	44	42	20
Mountain Rangers	20	6	4	10	46	49	16
Abersoch Athletic	20	5	2	13	34	22	12
Caernarfon Town Reserves	20	4	2	14	30	73	10
Cesarea Rovers	20	3	2	15	37	89	8
Talysarn Celts	20	2	3	15	30	112	7

Division 2 – Eastern Section

The division did not operate this season.

WELSH LEAGUE (NORTH) TABLES
1952-53

Division 1

Holywell Town	34	24	6	4	119	56	54
Fflint Town United	34	21	9	4	105	39	51
Blaenau Ffestiniog FC	34	19	4	11	101	63	42
Llandudno FC	34	17	8	9	95	61	42
CPD Porthmadog	34	16	10	8	87	63	42
Pwllheli & District FC	34	17	6	11	74	48	40
Colwyn Bay FC	34	16	8	10	88	76	40
Llanrwst Town	34	16	6	12	84	65	38
55th R.A.Tonfannau	34	14	9	11	81	63	37
Bangor City Reserves	34	14	7	13	102	75	35
Holyhead Town	34	16	3	15	94	90	35
Caernarfon Town	34	12	8	14	76	86	32
Connah's Quay Nomads	34	12	6	16	80	111	30
Penmaenmawr FC	34	11	4	19	57	88	26
Rhyl FC Reserves	34	9	4	21	55	92	22
Llandudno Junction FC	34	6	6	22	53	106	18
Conwy Borough FC	34	5	6	23	47	110	16
Bethesda Athletic	34	3	6	25	54	161	12

Division 2 - Western Section

Nantlle Vale FC	14	12	1	1	55	16	25
Criccieth Town	14	9	1	4	44	32	19
Holyhead Town Reserves	14	6	1	7	44	39	13
Caernarfon Town Reserves	14	5	2	7	33	38	12
Mountain Rangers	14	6	0	8	32	47	12
Llanfairfechan Town	14	4	3	7	30	39	11
Talysarn Celts	14	4	3	7	26	32	11
Llanrug United	14	4	1	9	26	48	9

Division 2 - Eastern Section

Denbigh Town	20	15	1	4	90	39	31
Connah's Quay Albion	20	14	3	3	76	37	31
Holywell Town Reserves	20	13	0	7	75	34	26
Rhos Rangers	20	11	4	5	67	56	26
Fflint Town United Reserves	20	10	3	7	53	44	23
Bagillt United	20	10	2	8	67	46	22
Saltney FC	20	9	2	9	56	54	20
Mancot FC	20	5	4	11	53	73	14
Connah's Quay Nomads Res.	20	5	4	11	39	66	14
Tunnel Sports	20	2	3	15	41	70	7
Rhydymwyn FC	20	2	2	16	29	77	6

WELSH LEAGUE (NORTH) TABLES
1953-54

Division 1

55th R.A. Tonfannau	34	26	2	6	108	38	54
Pwllheli & District FC	34	24	6	4	120	46	54
Holyhead Town	34	24	3	7	134	53	51
Holywell Town	34	21	7	6	91	38	49
Bangor City Reserves	34	22	5	7	101	56	49
Fflint Town United	34	18	6	10	92	67	42
Llandudno FC	34	17	7	10	79	56	41
CPD Porthmadog	34	16	6	12	75	67	38
Blaenau Ffestiniog FC	34	13	5	16	62	57	31
Rhyl FC Reserves	34	13	5	16	62	61	31
Penmaenmawr FC	34	12	7	15	70	77	28
Llanrwst Town	34	9	10	15	69	63	28
Colwyn Bay FC	34	11	6	17	77	104	28
Caernarfon Town	34	10	4	20	49	88	24
Connahs Quay Nomads	34	9	3	22	56	116	21
Conwy Borough	34	7	0	27	45	138	14
Llandudno Junction FC	34	5	4	25	33	113	14
Bethesda Athletic	34	3	6	25	57	112	12

Division 2 - Western Section

In existence but no table has yet been found.

Division 2 - Eastern Section

Denbigh Town	27	20	3	4	117	60	43
Connahs Quay Albion	28	20	1	7	131	49	41
Fflint Town United Reserves	27	18	3	6	104	51	39
Prestatyn Town	27	17	3	7	91	52	37
Rhos Rangers	25	15	1	9	96	61	31
38th T.R.R.A. Kinmel Bay	25	13	3	9	83	69	29
Mancot FC	22	13	2	7	76	41	28
Holywell Town Reserves	26	12	2	12	71	75	26
Connahs Quay Nomads Res.	26	12	2	12	74	84	26
Llandudno FC Reserves	26	10	2	14	67	79	22
Bagillt Hotspurs	26	9	3	14	50	68	21
Saltney FC	26	8	2	16	54	96	18
Colwyn Bay FC Reserves	26	4	1	21	34	106	9
Rhydymwyn FC	26	3	1	22	41	125	7

WELSH LEAGUE (NORTH) TABLES
1954-55

Division 1

Fflint Town United	34	29	3	2	150	34	61
Holywell Town	34	27	1	6	132	56	55
55th R.A. Tonfannau	34	22	6	6	133	58	50
Pwllheli & District FC	34	17	7	10	120	62	41
Llandudno FC	34	18	4	12	87	67	40
Blaenau Ffestiniog FC	34	18	2	14	98	81	38
Holyhead Town	34	17	2	15	96	73	36
Caernarfon Town	34	18	0	16	90	70	36
Connahs Quay Nomads	34	15	5	14	94	106	35
Colwyn Bay FC	34	15	5	14	78	104	35
Rhyl FC Reserves	34	15	4	15	85	87	34
Bangor City Reserves	34	13	4	17	90	80	30
Bethesda Athletic	34	12	4	18	76	100	28
Borough United	34	10	7	17	58	78	27
CPD Porthmadog	34	10	6	18	72	106	26
Llanrwst Town	34	8	4	22	59	126	20
Penmaenmawr FC	34	8	1	25	65	128	17
Llanfairfechan Town	34	1	1	32	33	200	3

Division 2 - Eastern Section

Rhos Rangers	28	23	3	2	151	42	49
38th T.R.R.A. Kinmel Bay	28	21	4	3	149	56	46
Prestatyn Town	28	18	4	6	101	54	40
Denbigh Town	28	18	3	7	124	64	39
Llandudno FC Reserves	28	18	3	7	84	72	39
Fflint Town United Reserves	28	16	3	9	115	73	35
Connahs Quay Nomads Res.	28	11	3	14	93	94	25
Holywell Town Reserves	28	11	3	14	78	104	25
Mancot FC	28	10	3	13	71	91	23
Connahs Quay Albion	28	10	2	16	76	114	22
Greenfield United	28	9	3	16	63	81	21
Buckley Rovers	28	9	1	18	74	81	19
Bagillt Hotspurs	28	9	1	18	59	76	19
Saltney FC	28	9	1	18	73	121	19
Rhydymwyn FC	28	1	3	24	40	170	5

WELSH LEAGUE (NORTH) TABLES 1955-56

Division 1

Fflint Town United	34	25	6	3	125	41	56
Holyhead Town	34	24	5	5	133	53	53
Caernarfon Town	34	23	7	4	149	55	51
Blaenau Ffestiniog FC	34	21	6	7	130	51	48
Borough United	34	22	2	10	88	61	46
Pwllheli & District FC	34	19	4	11	125	57	42
Holywell Town	34	17	5	12	92	58	39
CPD Porthmadog	34	17	5	12	82	63	39
Colwyn Bay FC	34	15	4	15	90	78	34
Llanrwst Town	34	14	6	14	87	99	34
Llandudno FC	34	14	4	16	55	76	32
Rhyl FC Reserves	34	12	4	18	75	103	28
Bangor City Reserves	34	8	5	21	62	102	21
Connahs Quay Nomads	34	8	5	21	58	119	21
Nantlle Vale FC	34	6	8	20	65	115	20
Bethesda Athletic	34	7	4	23	58	111	18
Penmaenmawr FC	34	6	4	24	38	136	16
Llanfairfechan Town	34	5	2	27	44	178	12

Division 2 – Eastern Section

31st T.R.R.A. Kinmel Bay	26	20	4	2	103	29	44
Rhos Rangers	26	18	3	5	91	44	39
38th T.R.R.A. Kinmel Bay	26	18	2	6	110	57	38
Buckley Rovers	26	15	1	10	78	70	31
Denbigh Town	26	12	6	8	81	56	30
Prestatyn Town	26	14	2	10	74	70	30
Mold Alexandra	26	12	1	13	74	71	25
Llandudno FC Reserves	26	10	3	13	78	84	23
Fflint Town United Reserves	26	8	5	13	63	76	21
Connahs Quay Nomads Res.	26	9	3	14	66	109	21
Holywell Town Reserves	26	9	2	15	69	75	20
Saltney R.	26	8	4	14	58	91	20
Connahs Quay Albion	26	6	1	19	56	113	13
Mancot FC	26	5	1	20	52	97	11

WELSH LEAGUE (NORTH) TABLES 1956-57

Division 1

Fflint Town United	34	30	1	3	158	34	61
Caernarfon Town	34	24	3	7	132	61	51
Holyhead Town	34	22	4	8	125	64	48
Pwllheli & District FC	34	23	2	9	106	54	48
Holywell Town	34	18	7	9	92	68	43
Blaenau Ffestiniog FC	34	19	0	15	99	100	38
CPD Porthmadog	34	18	0	16	104	77	36
Borough United	34	14	7	16	82	69	35
Llandudno FC	34	16	3	15	90	86	35
Rhyl FC Reserves	34	15	4	15	86	71	34
Connahs Quay Nomads	34	14	5	15	94	84	33
Colwyn Bay FC	34	12	5	17	102	100	29
Bangor City Reserves	34	12	5	17	65	92	29
Bethesda Athletic	34	12	3	19	70	108	27
Penmaenmawr FC	34	10	5	19	83	118	25
Llanrwst Town	34	7	6	21	73	115	20
Nantlle Vale FC	34	7	2	25	63	134	16
Llanfairfechan Town	34	1	2	31	31	230	4

Division 2 – Eastern Section

31st T.R.R.A. Kinmel Bay	18	15	1	2	81	24	31
Rhyl Colts	18	10	2	6	64	38	24
Buckley Rovers	18	10	4	4	60	40	24
Denbigh Town	18	11	2	5	72	53	24
Fflint Town United Reserves	18	10	3	5	62	41	23
Llandudno FC Reserves	18	6	4	8	48	54	16
Prestatyn Town	18	7	2	9	52	61	16
Holywell Town Reserves	18	5	3	10	28	53	13
38th T.R.R.A. Kinmel Bay	18	3	2	13	38	70	8
Connahs Quay Nomads Res.	18	1	1	16	25	100	3

WELSH LEAGUE (NORTH) TABLES 1957-58

Division 1

Holyhead Town	32	25	3	4	142	45	53
Caernarfon Town	32	25	2	5	112	54	52
Holywell Town	32	23	2	7	136	42	48
Fflint Town United	32	21	4	7	99	42	46
CPD Porthmadog	32	18	5	9	76	67	41
Rhyl FC Reserves	32	16	5	11	103	61	37
Llandudno FC	32	14	4	14	70	78	32
Borough United	32	13	3	16	91	86	29
Connahs Quay Nomads	32	12	5	15	84	91	29
Pwllheli & District FC	32	11	7	14	76	89	29
Nantlle Vale FC	32	13	2	17	75	82	28
Colwyn Bay FC	32	10	6	16	74	113	26
Blaenau Ffestiniog FC	32	10	5	17	61	82	25
Bangor City Reserves	32	7	7	18	55	84	21
Bethesda Athletic	32	8	4	20	72	109	20
Penmaenmawr FC	32	6	8	18	48	100	20
Llanfairfechan Town	32	1	6	25	33	164	8

Division 2 – Eastern Section

Holywell Town Reserves	16	15	0	1	65	19	30
31st T.R.R.A. Kinmel Bay	16	13	1	2	86	31	27
Prestatyn Town	16	11	1	4	56	38	23
Rhyl Colts	16	7	2	7	71	44	16
LLandudno FC Reserves	16	6	2	8	41	54	14
Buckley Rovers	16	6	0	10	35	47	12
Fflint Town United Reserves	16	5	1	10	46	60	11
Connahs Quay Nomads Res.	16	3	1	12	26	76	7
Northop FC	16	3	0	13	35	83	6

WELSH LEAGUE (NORTH) TABLES 1958-59

Division 1

Borough United	34	26	4	4	146	60	56
Llandudno FC	34	24	5	5	131	63	53
Blaenau Ffestiniog FC	34	23	4	7	99	49	50
Holyhead Town	34	24	0	10	139	71	48
Colwyn Bay FC	34	20	3	11	96	70	43
Holywell Town	34	17	5	12	100	99	39
CPD Porthmadog	34	18	3	13	103	77	37
Pwllheli & District FC	34	17	3	14	78	77	37
Wrexham AFC Reserves	34	14	4	16	80	98	32
Bangor City Reserves	34	13	5	16	75	85	31
Nantlle Vale FC	34	12	3	19	76	85	27
Prestatyn Town	34	11	5	18	60	105	27
Connahs Quay Nomads	34	9	8	17	73	89	26
Caernarfon Town	34	12	2	20	76	95	26
Rhyl FC Reserves	34	11	2	21	66	100	24
Fflint Town United	34	9	3	22	63	121	21
Bethesda Athletic	34	7	4	23	43	102	18
Penmaenmawr FC	34	5	5	24	71	135	15

CPD Porthmadog had 2 points deducted.

Division 2 – Eastern Section

31st T.R.R.A. Kinmel Bay	16	11	3	2	68	23	25
Holywell Town Reserves	15	10	2	3	55	30	22
Llandudno FC Reserves	15	7	4	3	44	30	18
38th T.R.R.A. Kinmel Bay	16	6	2	8	41	43	14
Prestatyn Town Reserves	16	0	1	15	22	103	1

It is believed that one match was not played.

WELSH LEAGUE (NORTH) TABLES 1959-60

Division 1

Nantlle Vale AFC	32	20	5	7	96	53	45
Borough United	32	19	4	9	70	39	42
Holywell Town	32	18	6	8	84	62	42
Bethesda Athletic	32	17	8	7	65	56	42
Holyhead Town	32	18	5	9	84	63	41
Caernarfon Town	32	16	6	10	80	46	38
Bangor City Reserves	32	14	8	10	71	51	36
Llandudno FC	32	13	8	11	66	47	34
Colwyn Bay FC	32	13	7	12	68	64	33
Pwllheli & District FC	32	15	3	14	77	73	33
Fflint Town United	32	12	7	13	85	65	31
CPD Porthmadog	32	14	3	15	59	68	31
Blaenau Ffestiniog FC	32	11	6	15	73	73	28
Rhyl FC Reserves	32	11	3	18	49	66	25
Prestatyn Town	32	5	5	22	35	102	15
Wrexham AFC Reserves	32	5	4	23	53	119	14
Penmaenmawr FC	32	5	4	23	37	105	14

Division 2 – Eastern Section

Holywell Town Reserves	14	10	3	1	50	17	23
31st T.R.R.A. Kinmel Bay	14	9	3	2	60	16	21
Rhyl Colts	14	9	2	3	42	18	20
Llandudno FC Reserves	14	7	2	5	38	30	16
Borough United Reserves	14	6	0	8	40	55	12
Fflint Town United Reserves	14	5	1	7	37	57	11
38th T.R.R.A. Kinmel Bay	14	3	1	10	29	56	7
Prestatyn Town Reserves	14	1	0	13	24	67	2

WELSH LEAGUE (NORTH) TABLES 1960-61

Pwllheli & District FC	34	25	6	3	123	49	56
Blaenau Ffestiniog FC	34	23	6	5	101	41	52
Borough United	34	19	8	7	94	51	46
Nantlle Vale FC	34	21	4	9	86	53	46
Caernarfon Town	34	19	4	11	86	66	42
Holywell Town	34	17	7	10	85	85	41
Fflint Town United	34	15	6	13	67	63	36
Bangor City Reserves	34	15	4	15	75	74	34
Prestatyn Town	34	13	7	14	71	84	33
Holyhead Town	34	13	6	15	76	77	32
Colwyn Bay FC	34	12	8	14	59	68	32
CPD Porthmadog	34	12	4	18	63	75	28
Llandudno FC	34	12	4	18	52	70	28
Bethesda Athletic	34	10	7	17	57	70	27
Dolgellau Athletic	34	9	9	16	50	65	27
Wrexham AFC Reserves	34	7	7	20	61	113	21
Penmaenmawr FC	34	8	8	22	52	85	20
Rhyl FC Reserves	34	3	3	26	35	104	11

WELSH LEAGUE (NORTH) TABLES 1961-62

Blaenau Ffestiniog FC	34	23	6	5	89	36	52
Holyhead Town	34	24	3	7	113	31	51
Bangor City Reserves	34	22	3	9	89	47	47
Rhyl FC Reserves	34	20	5	9	63	49	45
Pwllheli & District FC	34	20	4	10	89	47	44
Borough United	34	18	6	10	76	60	42
Caernarfon Town	34	17	5	12	67	67	39
Llandudno FC	34	15	8	11	74	63	38
Nantlle Vale FC	34	14	6	14	77	67	34
Bethesda Athletic	34	15	4	15	67	61	34
CPD Porthmadog	34	11	11	12	70	71	33
Penmaenmawr FC	34	14	4	16	79	93	32
Dolgellau Athletic	34	12	3	19	57	75	27
Holywell Town	34	12	2	20	63	80	26
Wrexham AFC Reserves	34	10	3	21	45	85	23
Prestatyn Town	34	6	6	22	44	88	18
Colwyn Bay FC	34	5	6	23	45	95	16
Fflint Town United	34	5	1	28	39	111	11

WELSH LEAGUE (NORTH) TABLES 1962-63

Borough United	32	27	0	5	117	37	54
Holyhead Town	32	24	4	4	103	43	52
Colwyn Bay FC	32	19	4	9	82	61	42
Blaenau Ffestiniog FC	32	17	5	10	80	56	39
Llandudno FC	32	18	2	12	78	55	38
CPD Porthmadog	32	15	5	12	77	47	35
Dolgellau Athletic	32	16	3	13	78	61	35
Pwllheli & District FC	32	14	5	13	61	48	33
Bangor City Reserves	32	15	3	14	77	62	33
Holywell Town	32	15	3	14	64	66	33
Bethesda Athletic	32	11	3	18	58	76	25
Rhyl FC Reserves	32	8	8	16	57	77	24
Caernarfon Town	32	9	6	17	62	85	24
Wrexham AFC Reserves	32	10	4	18	69	103	24
Nantlle Vale FC	32	9	4	19	64	96	22
Prestatyn Town	32	7	4	21	48	123	18
Penmaenmawr FC	32	4	5	23	41	120	13

WELSH LEAGUE (NORTH) TABLES 1963-64

Holyhead Town	32	27	2	3	123	43	56
Colwyn Bay FC	32	26	1	5	112	49	53
Borough United	32	26	0	6	134	37	52
Pwllheli & District FC	32	20	3	9	110	61	43
Holywell Town	32	17	6	9	96	52	40
Dolgellau Athletic	32	17	6	9	80	58	40
Caernarfon Town	32	13	6	13	91	72	32
Rhyl FC Reserves	32	14	4	14	86	67	32
Bangor City Reserves	32	11	8	13	79	70	30
Bethesda Athletic	32	13	4	15	65	82	30
Llandudno FC	32	11	6	15	53	59	28
CPD Porthmadog	32	12	3	17	66	91	27
Blaenau Ffestiniog FC	32	9	7	16	46	72	25
Wrexham AFC Reserves	32	7	6	19	48	111	20
Penmaenmawr FC	32	5	4	23	54	129	14
Nantlle Vale FC	32	4	4	24	42	131	12
Prestatyn Town	32	4	2	26	38	133	10

WELSH LEAGUE (NORTH) TABLES
1964-65

Team	P	W	D	L	F	A	Pts
Colwyn Bay FC	32	25	3	4	127	34	53
Borough United	32	22	5	5	115	37	49
Bangor City Reserves	32	22	5	5	106	54	49
Caernarfon Town	32	20	6	6	89	46	46
Pwllheli & District FC	32	20	5	7	105	55	45
Llandudno FC	32	18	3	11	98	46	39
Wrexham AFC Reserves	32	12	8	12	84	80	32
Rhyl FC Reserves	32	14	4	14	46	63	32
Nantlle Vale FC	32	13	5	14	67	69	31
Holyhead Town	32	10	7	15	74	66	27
Blaenau Ffestiniog FC	32	11	4	17	54	76	26
CPD Porthmadog	32	8	7	17	64	79	23
Dolgellau Athletic	32	10	5	17	64	88	23
Holywell Town	32	9	2	21	46	110	20
Penmaenmawr FC	32	7	5	20	46	99	19
Prestatyn Town	32	7	5	20	40	107	19
Bethesda Athletic	32	3	3	26	26	142	9

Dolgellau Athletic had 2 points deducted.

WELSH LEAGUE (NORTH) TABLES
1967-68

Team	P	W	D	L	F	A	Pts
CPD Porthmadog	30	27	2	1	99	33	56
Pwllheli & District FC	30	21	4	5	95	41	46
Bethesda Athletic	30	19	4	7	73	39	42
Holyhead Town	30	18	5	7	89	49	41
Blaenau Ffestiniog FC	30	18	5	7	73	46	41
Bangor City Reserves	30	17	1	12	87	59	35
Caernarfon Town	30	12	6	12	71	71	30
Rhyl FC Reserves	30	13	4	13	63	68	30
Penmaenmawr FC	30	11	7	12	59	60	29
Wrexham AFC Reserves	30	11	5	14	56	63	27
Prestatyn Town	30	11	2	17	59	62	24
Connahs Quay Nomads	30	9	5	16	69	77	23
U.C.N.W. Bangor	30	11	0	19	50	92	22
Nantlle Vale FC	30	7	2	21	28	71	16
Colwyn Bay FC	30	4	3	23	38	101	11
Llandudno FC	30	3	1	26	34	111	7

WELSH LEAGUE (NORTH) TABLES
1965-66

Team	P	W	D	L	F	A	Pts
Caernarfon Town	28	24	1	3	100	34	49
CPD Porthmadog	28	22	2	4	87	41	44
Colwyn Bay FC	28	18	4	6	80	48	40
Pwllheli & District FC	28	18	4	6	80	49	34
Borough United	28	12	7	9	65	40	31
Holyhead Town	28	14	6	8	58	54	30
Rhyl FC Reserves	28	9	7	12	44	46	25
Nantlle Vale FC	28	8	7	13	51	66	23
Llandudno FC	28	10	2	16	59	68	22
Penmaenmawr FC	28	7	7	14	55	77	21
Wrexham FC Reserves	28	8	4	16	51	65	20
Bangor City Reserves	28	8	4	16	48	64	20
Bethesda Athletic	28	6	6	16	44	91	18
Blaenau Ffestiniog FC	28	7	2	19	51	85	16
Holywell Town	28	6	3	19	45	90	15

CPD Porthmadog had 2 points deducted.
Holyhead Town had 4 points deducted.
Pwllheli & District FC had 6 points deducted.

WELSH LEAGUE (NORTH) TABLES
1968-69

Team	P	W	D	L	F	A	Pts
CPD Porthmadog	32	24	4	4	135	41	52
Blaenau Ffestiniog FC	32	22	6	4	91	51	50
Wrexham AFC Reserves	32	20	7	5	68	32	47
Bethesda Athletic	32	21	5	6	94	44	47
Bangor City Reserves	32	19	4	9	93	55	42
Holyhead Town	32	20	1	11	92	60	41
Prestatyn Town	32	17	3	12	74	57	37
Nantlle Vale FC	32	14	6	12	68	59	34
Connahs Quay Nomads	32	13	6	13	87	71	32
Rhyl FC Reserves	32	11	5	16	63	103	27
Queensferry Wanderers	32	9	7	16	55	77	25
Pwllheli & District FC	32	10	4	18	63	103	24
Colwyn Bay FC	32	9	5	18	53	82	23
Penmaenmawr FC	32	8	4	20	59	88	20
U.C.N.W. Bangor	32	5	7	20	54	105	17
Caernarfon Town	32	6	5	21	39	89	17
Llandudno FC	32	4	1	27	27	98	9

WELSH LEAGUE (NORTH) TABLES
1966-67

Team	P	W	D	L	F	A	Pts
CPD Porthmadog	30	25	4	1	104	27	54
Holyhead Town	30	21	5	4	87	36	47
Pwllheli & District FC	30	19	6	5	100	46	44
Borough United	30	14	6	10	66	43	34
Penmaenmawr FC	30	13	8	9	64	65	34
Caernarfon Town	30	12	6	12	70	54	30
Blaenau Ffestiniog FC	30	10	9	11	55	58	29
Llandudno FC	30	12	4	14	51	51	28
Connahs Quay Nomads	30	10	6	14	55	79	26
Bangor City Reserves	30	10	5	15	63	60	25
Colwyn Bay FC	30	10	5	15	46	79	25
Nantlle Vale FC	30	8	9	13	47	62	25
Prestatyn Town	30	9	6	15	43	71	24
Rhyl FC Reserves	30	9	4	17	46	73	22
Wrexham AFC Reserves	30	7	4	19	43	73	18
Bethesda Athletic	30	5	5	20	25	88	15

WELSH LEAGUE (NORTH) TABLES
1969-70

Team	P	W	D	L	F	A	Pts
Holyhead Town	32	26	3	3	110	38	55
Connahs Quay Nomads	32	25	2	5	98	47	52
CPD Porthmadog	32	22	4	6	105	30	48
Bethesda Athletic	32	20	8	4	110	51	48
Bangor City Reserves	32	20	5	7	74	37	45
Wrexham AFC Reserves	32	15	10	7	58	31	40
Blaenau Ffestiniog FC	32	16	6	10	91	50	38
Nantlle Vale FC	32	14	7	11	68	55	35
Llandudno FC	32	12	7	13	50	58	31
Prestatyn Town	32	11	6	15	61	65	28
Pwllheli & District FC	32	11	6	15	59	72	28
Queensferry Wanderers	32	10	4	18	51	92	24
Penmaenmawr FC	32	8	7	17	48	78	23
Caernarfon Town	32	6	6	20	46	98	18
U.C.N.W. Bangor	32	5	3	24	32	83	13
Colwyn Bay FC	32	3	5	24	32	112	11
Rhyl FC Reserves	32	3	1	28	18	114	7

WELSH LEAGUE (NORTH) TABLES
1970-71

	P	W	D	L	F	A	Pts
Bethesda Athletic	30	23	3	4	112	38	49
Connahs Quay Nomads	30	21	5	4	92	37	47
Wrexham AFC Reserves	30	22	2	6	117	35	46
Blaenau Ffestiniog FC	30	20	5	5	81	29	45
CPD Porthmadog	30	19	3	8	98	47	41
Pwllheli & District FC	30	16	5	9	77	53	37
Llandudno FC	30	14	8	8	54	40	36
Holyhead Town	30	15	1	14	61	71	31
Nantlle Vale FC	30	11	5	14	64	78	27
Bangor City Reserves	30	10	4	16	50	67	24
Penmaenmawr FC	30	9	5	16	43	87	23
Prestatyn Town	30	8	5	17	52	76	21
Caernarfon Town	30	7	4	19	44	96	18
Colwyn Bay FC	30	4	4	22	44	111	12
Rhyl FC Reserves	30	4	4	22	38	99	12
U.C.N.W. Bangor	30	2	7	21	26	89	11

WELSH LEAGUE (NORTH) TABLES
1971-72

	P	W	D	L	F	A	Pts
Blaenau Ffestiniog FC	30	22	3	5	95	27	47
Bethesda Athletic	30	20	3	7	83	31	43
Wrexham AFC Reserves	30	18	6	6	94	38	42
CPD Porthmadog	30	17	8	5	68	43	42
Connahs Quay Nomads	30	15	11	4	57	30	41
Caernarfon Town	30	16	6	8	70	51	38
Holyhead Town	30	16	5	9	74	51	37
Hawarden Rangers	30	12	6	12	57	57	30
Colwyn Bay FC	30	11	7	12	52	56	29
Rhyl FC Reserves	30	12	1	17	63	57	25
Bangor City Reserves	30	9	5	16	56	63	23
Pwllheli & District FC	30	8	4	18	39	111	20
Penmaenmawr FC	30	7	5	18	37	67	19
Nantlle Vale FC	30	5	6	19	44	74	16
U.C.N.W. Bangor	30	7	2	21	46	116	16
Llandudno FC	30	4	4	22	27	88	12

WELSH LEAGUE (NORTH) TABLES
1972-73

	P	W	D	L	F	A	Pts
Blaenau Ffestiniog FC	30	24	3	3	100	21	51
Caernarfon Town	30	22	5	3	90	26	49
Wrexham AFC Reserves	30	19	6	5	105	36	41
Nantlle Vale FC	30	17	7	6	101	31	41
CPD Porthmadog	30	17	5	8	74	32	39
Pwllheli & District	30	17	5	8	85	37	39
Bethesda Athletic	30	17	5	8	77	42	39
Connahs Quay Nomads	30	13	7	10	66	43	33
Colwyn Bay FC	30	11	3	16	74	86	25
Rhyl FC Reserves	30	10	4	16	46	78	24
U.C.N.W. Bangor	30	9	5	16	59	96	23
Penmaenmawr FC	30	10	2	18	47	66	22
Bangor City Reserves	30	8	3	19	44	93	19
Holyhead Town	30	7	3	20	37	112	17
Llandudno Swifts	30	4	4	22	36	124	12
Llandudno FC	30	1	1	28	21	140	3

WELSH LEAGUE (NORTH) TABLES
1973-74

	P	W	D	L	F	A	Pts
Blaenau Ffestiniog FC	32	27	3	2	122	19	57
Bethesda Athletic	32	25	3	4	127	24	53
CPD Porthmadog	32	24	2	6	141	29	50
Wrexham AFC Reserves	32	24	2	6	119	32	50
Nantlle Vale FC	32	21	5	6	114	37	47
Pwllheli & District FC	32	21	4	7	138	43	46
Connahs Quay Nomads	32	17	4	11	86	67	38
Bangor City Reserves	32	18	2	12	83	67	38
Colwyn Bay FC	32	15	3	14	87	58	33
Caernarfon Town	32	12	3	17	71	93	27
Rhos Aelwyd FC	32	10	6	16	70	84	26
Holyhead Town	32	7	6	19	49	97	22
Rhyl FC Reserves	32	8	2	22	65	112	18
Penmaenmawr FC	32	8	2	22	55	116	18
U.C.N.W. Bangor	32	8	1	23	38	110	17
Llandudno Swifts	32	2	0	30	27	226	4
Llandudno FC	32	1	0	31	22	200	2

WELSH LEAGUE (NORTH) TABLES
1974-75

	P	W	D	L	F	A	Pts
CPD Porthmadog	26	22	3	1	104	16	47
Wrexham AFC Reserves	26	18	6	2	85	20	42
Nantlle Vale FC	26	17	4	5	78	23	38
Pwllheli & District FC	26	16	6	4	103	33	38
Caernarfon Town	26	15	6	5	98	39	36
Bethesda Athletic	26	13	7	6	93	32	33
Blaenau Ffestiniog FC	26	15	2	9	57	43	32
Rhyl FC Reserves	26	11	4	11	62	59	26
Colwyn Bay FC	26	9	5	12	51	45	23
Bangor City Reserves	26	9	1	16	64	63	19
Holyhead Town	26	5	2	19	37	91	12
Rhos Aelwyd FC	26	5	0	21	21	125	10
Llandudno Swifts	26	2	0	24	24	162	4
U.C.N.W. Bangor	26	2	0	24	18	144	4

WELSH LEAGUE (NORTH) TABLES
1975-76

	P	W	D	L	F	A	Pts
CPD Porthmadog	20	14	3	3	59	24	31
Nantlle Vale FC	20	13	4	3	48	14	30
Bethesda Athletic	20	13	4	3	61	21	30
Caernarfon Town	20	13	2	5	71	36	28
Blaenau Ffestiniog FC	20	7	7	6	39	31	21
Wrexham AFC Reserves	20	7	5	8	40	37	19
Pwllheli & District FC	20	7	4	9	40	32	18
Bangor City Reserves	20	7	4	9	37	37	18
Colwyn Bay FC	20	4	8	8	38	35	16
Rhyl FC Reserves	20	3	3	14	24	64	9
Llandudno Swifts	20	0	0	20	11	137	0

Auxilliary Competition – Group A

	P	W	D	L	F	A	Pts
Bethesda Athletic	10	9	1	0	45	5	19
Wrexham AFC Reserves	10	6	3	1	31	4	15
Bangor City Reserves	10	4	2	4	20	19	10
Colwyn Bay FC	10	3	1	6	16	27	7
Rhyl FC Reserves	10	3	1	6	13	37	7
Llandudno Swifts	10	1	0	9	7	46	2

Auxiliary Competition – Group B

	P	W	D	L	F	A	Pts
CPD Porthmadog	8	6	1	1	21	7	13
Nantlle Vale FC	8	5	1	2	20	11	11
Pwllheli & District FC	8	3	2	3	10	13	8
Caernarfon Town	8	2	1	5	13	20	5
Blaenau Ffestiniog FC	8	1	1	6	7	20	3

Auxilliary Shield Final

Bethesda Athletic v CPD Porthmadog   2-0
(Played at Bangor)

WELSH LEAGUE (NORTH) TABLES
1976-77

Bethesda Athletic	18	10	6	2	61	21	26
CPD Porthmadog	18	11	4	3	48	17	26
Pwllheli & District FC	18	10	3	5	43	18	23
Nantlle Vale FC	18	9	5	3	37	28	23
Bangor City Reserves	18	8	4	6	33	33	20
Wrexham AFC Reserves	18	7	4	7	30	38	18
Colwyn Bay FC	18	6	5	7	30	38	17
Rhyl FC Reserves	18	4	4	10	23	39	12
Blaenau Ffestiniog FC	18	3	4	11	23	47	10
Llandudno Swifts	18	2	1	15	15	79	5

Auxilliary Competition – Group A

Bangor City Reserves	10	7	1	2	29	19	15
Wrexham AFC Reserves	10	7	0	3	31	12	14
Rhyl FC Reserves	10	5	3	2	27	15	13
Colwyn Bay FC	10	2	4	4	12	18	8
Blaenau Ffestiniog FC	10	3	1	6	17	19	7
Llandudno Swifts	10	1	1	8	11	43	3

Auxiliary Competition – Group B

Pwllheli & District FC	6	3	2	1	10	5	8
Bethesda Athletic	6	3	0	3	9	10	6
CPD Porthmadog	6	2	2	2	7	11	6
Nantlle Vale FC	6	2	0	4	12	12	4

Auxiliary Competition – Final

Bangor City Reserves v Pwllheli & District	5-1

(Played at Bethesda)

WELSH LEAGUE (NORTH) TABLES
1977-78

Caernarfon Town	22	14	7	1	63	20	35
CPD Porthmadog	22	12	6	4	72	25	30
Nantlle Vale FC	22	12	5	5	53	23	29
Wrexham AFC Reserves	22	11	7	4	37	21	29
Conwy United	22	11	7	4	41	31	29
Colwyn Bay FC	22	10	7	5	53	33	27
Blaenau Ffestiniog FC	22	10	2	10	40	40	22
Bangor City Reserves	22	10	1	11	36	37	21
Rhos United	22	6	4	12	33	45	16
Rhyl FC Reserves	22	7	2	13	33	50	16
Pwllheli & District FC	22	2	4	16	24	53	8
Llandudno Swifts	22	0	2	20	14	121	2

WELSH LEAGUE (NORTH) TABLES
1978-79

Caernarfon Town	20	15	5	0	77	11	35
Pwllheli & District FC	20	14	4	2	47	20	32
CPD Porthmadog	20	13	4	3	85	21	30
Colwyn Bay FC	20	9	6	5	51	30	24
Nantlle Vale FC	20	10	3	7	58	21	23
Conwy United	20	8	5	7	40	38	21
Blaenau Ffestiniog FC	20	6	6	8	32	40	18
Bangor City Reserves	20	5	6	9	34	42	16
Rhos United	20	6	1	13	24	55	13
Rhyl FC Reserves	20	0	3	17	11	78	3
Llandudno Swifts	20	1	3	16	11	114	3

Llandudno Swifts had 2 points deducted.

WELSH LEAGUE (NORTH) TABLES
1979-80

Blaenau Ffestiniog FC	18	12	4	2	47	21	28
Caernarfon Town	18	12	3	3	26	13	27
Colwyn Bay FC	18	10	4	4	40	14	24
Pwllheli & District FC	18	9	5	4	37	20	23
Llandudno Amateurs	18	8	3	7	24	27	19
CPD Porthmadog	18	9	0	9	34	40	18
Nantlle Vale FC	18	5	4	9	30	36	14
Conwy United	18	5	3	10	17	32	13
Bangor City Reserves	18	4	3	11	26	43	11
Rhyl FC Reserves	18	1	1	16	13	48	3

WELSH LEAGUE (NORTH) TABLES
1980-81

Colwyn Bay FC	22	17	5	0	48	16	39
Fflint Town United	22	16	5	1	46	12	37
Pwllheli & District FC	22	13	4	5	48	18	30
Llandudno Amateurs	22	9	6	7	51	34	24
CPD Porthmadog	22	8	5	9	43	34	21
Caernarfon Town Reserves	22	6	9	7	32	28	21
Blaenau Ffestiniog FC	22	8	5	9	41	40	21
Conwy United	22	9	2	11	34	43	20
Holyhead United Juniors	22	8	2	12	34	44	18
Bangor City Reserves	22	3	5	14	35	65	11
Rhyl FC Reserves	22	5	1	16	27	64	11
Menai Bridge Tigers	22	4	3	15	19	60	11

WELSH LEAGUE (NORTH) TABLES
1981-82

Courtaulds FC Greenfield	26	19	3	4	81	31	41
Blaenau Ffestiniog FC	26	17	6	3	68	33	40
Colwyn Bay FC	26	18	3	5	70	36	39
Conwy United	26	15	5	6	41	30	35
Llandudno Amateurs	26	9	10	7	49	45	28
Fflint Town United	26	7	9	10	49	54	23
Pwllheli & District FC	26	8	6	12	35	42	22
U.C.N.W. Bangor	26	9	4	13	39	46	22
Caernarfon Town Reserves	26	8	6	12	43	59	22
Bangor City Reserves	26	7	6	13	50	59	20
CPD Porthmadog	26	8	4	14	54	65	20
Menai Bridge Tigers	26	5	9	12	30	47	19
Rhyl FC Reserves	26	5	7	14	30	57	17
Holyhead United Juniors	26	5	6	15	31	66	16

WELSH LEAGUE (NORTH) TABLES
1982-83

Colwyn Bay FC	22	16	4	2	66	27	36
U.C.N.W. Bangor	22	14	3	5	54	30	31
Llandudno Amateurs	22	14	1	7	67	45	29
Courtaulds FC Greenfield	22	11	6	5	47	21	28
Rhos United	22	9	4	9	28	30	22
Blaenau Ffestiniog FC	22	10	2	10	36	45	22
Conwy United	22	7	7	8	33	26	21
Rhyl FC Reserves	22	7	7	8	34	42	21
Fflint Town United	22	6	7	9	34	44	19
Bangor City Reserves	22	5	5	12	33	44	15
Pwllheli & District FC	22	2	9	11	30	54	13
Caernarfon Town Reserves	22	3	1	18	22	78	7

WELSH LEAGUE (NORTH) TABLES
1983-84

Colwyn Bay FC	18	13	4	1	48	18	30
Pwllheli & District FC	18	13	4	1	41	15	30
Llandudno Amateurs	18	10	1	7	41	35	21
Conwy United	18	7	7	4	32	23	19
Rhos United	18	7	3	8	25	32	17
Bangor City Reserves	18	6	3	9	30	34	15
Caernarfon Town Reserves	18	5	5	8	28	35	15
Rhyl FC Reserves	18	4	5	9	22	24	13
Blaenau Ffestiniog FC	18	3	5	9	23	39	11
U.C.N.W. Bangor	18	1	5	12	16	45	7

Conwy United had 2 points deducted.

Auxilliary Competition – Group A

Pwllheli & District FC	8	6	1	1	26	11	13
Bangor City Reserves	8	4	0	4	23	20	8
Caernarfon Town	8	3	2	3	14	17	8
Blaenau Ffestiniog FC	8	3	1	4	15	18	7
U.C.N.W. Bangor	8	1	2	5	11	23	4

Auxilliary Competition – Group B

Rhos United	8	5	2	1	14	4	12
Colwyn Bay FC	8	4	3	1	15	7	11
Conwy United	8	2	3	3	14	11	7
Llandudno Amateurs	8	3	2	2	8	14	6
Rhyl FC Reserves	8	0	2	6	5	21	2

LLandudno Amateurs had 2 points deducted.

Auxilliary Competition – Final

Pwllheli & District FC v Rhos United	3-0

(Played at Blaenau Ffestiniog)

The league was formally disbanded and then reborn as the Welsh Alliance League.

WELSH ALLIANCE LEAGUE

Formation

By the mid-1980s the Welsh League (Northern Section) had so reduced in membership that an Auxiliary competition was needed to create sufficient fixtures. With only ten member clubs it was clear that a re-think was needed for the North Wales Coast area's most senior league.

At the 1984 Annual General Meeting of the Welsh League (Northern Section) held on July 7th at the Park Hall Hotel, Conwy, a new structure was adopted. The new Welsh Alliance Football League (North) was to encompass the whole of North and Mid-Wales, incorporating clubs from the old league, the Mid-Wales League and the Welsh National League (Wrexham Area). It was meant to counterbalance the long established Welsh Football League in the south with the intention of both champions playing off for the all-Wales title.

The idea was visionary but did not convince clubs from outside the area of the old League although five new clubs were admitted: CPD Porthmadog, Llanrwst United, an amalgamation of Llanrwst Town and Llanrwst Athletic, Bethesda Athletic, CPD Y Felinheli, and Llanfairpwll FC. The last three opted for membership following the collapse of the Gwynedd Football League.

The League continued the long established Cookson Cup and Alves Cup competitions run by the old Welsh League (Northern Section) and also administered the younger Barritt Cup established in 1977.

The vision never materialised as far as the Welsh Alliance League was concerned but the idea eventually bore fruit in 1990 when the Cymru Alliance League was set up, demoting the WAL to the second level. The League continues to act as one of three feeder leagues to the Cymru Alliance but with the creation of the League of Wales in 1992, the WAL now occupies the third tier of the pyramid.

It has recovered its membership level following departures during the setting up of the Cymru Alliance and has operated two divisions since 2010.

WELSH ALLIANCE LEAGUE 1984-85

Team	P	W	D	L	F	A	Pts
Conwy United	28	21	3	4	107	34	45
Bethesda Athletic	28	19	5	4	72	19	43
CPD Y Felinheli	28	20	2	6	72	39	42
CPD Porthmadog	28	17	5	6	59	37	39
Llanfairpwll FC	28	15	6	7	63	39	36
Pwllheli & District FC	28	14	3	11	68	52	31
Caernarfon Town Reserves	28	12	5	11	55	50	29
Llanrwst United	28	11	6	11	49	51	28
Bangor City Reserves	28	12	3	13	65	53	27
Blaenau Ffestiniog FC	28	10	6	12	68	82	26
Rhos United	28	6	9	13	40	67	21
Llandudno Amateurs	28	6	8	14	35	52	20
Rhyl FC Reserves	28	7	6	15	45	72	20
U.C.N.W. Bangor	28	2	3	23	35	109	7
Colwyn Bay FC Reserves	28	2	2	24	30	106	6

WELSH ALLIANCE LEAGUE 1985-86

Team	P	W	D	L	F	A	Pts
Conwy United	30	21	6	3	88	31	48
Bethesda Athletic	30	21	3	6	77	28	45
Caernarfon Town Reserves	30	19	4	7	80	36	42
Llanfairpwll FC	30	16	10	4	57	28	42
CPD Y Felinheli	30	15	7	8	58	45	37
Holyhead United	30	13	5	12	64	58	31
Blaenau Ffestiniog FC	30	11	9	10	62	59	31
Pwllheli & District FC	30	12	5	13	63	62	29
Rhyl FC Reserves	30	10	7	13	39	50	27
Bangor City Reserves	30	9	8	13	48	63	26
Rhos United	30	9	8	13	48	63	26
Llanrwst United	30	8	9	13	53	72	25
Llandudno Amateurs	30	6	8	16	36	69	20
Colwyn Bay FC Reserves	30	6	7	17	30	60	19
Mochdre FC	30	6	6	18	47	71	18
CPD Porthmadog	30	4	6	21	34	67	14

WELSH ALLIANCE LEAGUE 1986-87

Team	P	W	D	L	F	A	Pts
Bethesda Athletic	26	20	5	1	80	19	45
Llanfairpwll FC	26	20	4	2	70	17	44
Caernarfon Town Reserves	26	15	7	4	59	29	37
Pilkingtons FC St. Asaph	26	14	7	5	63	33	35
Bangor City Reserves	26	14	4	8	69	32	32
CPD Porthmadog	26	12	2	12	56	55	26
Rhyl FC Reserves	26	10	5	11	51	52	25
Conwy United	26	9	5	12	38	55	23
Llanrwst United	26	8	4	14	41	68	20
Rhos United	26	4	9	13	35	42	17
CPD Y Felinheli	26	6	5	15	36	66	17
Colwyn Bay FC Reserves	26	6	5	15	25	60	17
Mochdre FC	26	7	2	17	39	63	16
Llandudno Amateurs	26	3	4	19	36	79	10

WELSH ALLIANCE LEAGUE 1987-88

Team	P	W	D	L	F	A	Pts
Llanfairpwll FC	30	23	4	3	68	14	50
Bethesda Athletic	30	20	9	1	69	21	49
CPD Porthmadog	30	21	7	2	75	29	49
Connahs Quay Nomads	30	18	5	7	86	36	41
Caernarfon Town Reserves	30	16	6	8	74	47	38
Pilkingtons FC St. Asaph	30	13	6	11	55	53	32
Llanrwst United	30	14	3	13	60	62	31
CPD Y Felinheli	30	13	5	12	54	72	31
Colwyn Bay FC Reserves	30	10	5	15	55	66	25
Mochdre FC	30	9	4	17	48	63	22
Rhos United	30	9	4	17	31	64	22
Conwy United	30	8	5	17	57	76	21
Fflint Town United	30	7	7	16	44	60	21
Llandudno FC	30	7	3	20	39	66	17
Bangor City Reserves	30	6	7	17	39	78	17
Rhyl FC Reserves	30	4	6	20	26	73	13

Bangor City Reserves had 2 points deducted.

WELSH ALLIANCE LEAGUE 1988-89

Team	P	W	D	L	F	A	Pts
Fflint Town United	32	23	4	5	72	26	73
Rhyl FC Reserves	32	22	4	6	67	36	70
Nantlle Vale FC	32	20	6	6	85	42	66
CPD Porthmadog	32	16	10	6	85	60	58
Holywell Town	32	16	3	13	65	64	51
Connahs Quay Nomads	32	15	5	12	58	42	50
Llanfairpwll FC	32	15	4	13	54	51	49
Bethesda Athletic	32	12	10	10	57	56	46
CPD Y Felinheli	32	12	8	12	48	55	44
Conwy United	32	11	10	11	58	55	43
Bangor City Reserves	32	12	6	14	57	57	40
Llanrwst United	32	12	3	17	55	69	39
Caernarfon Town Reserves	32	10	7	15	47	49	37
Mochdre FC	32	9	8	15	50	66	35
Llandudno FC	32	7	2	23	35	68	23
Pilkingtons FC St. Asaph	32	4	9	19	37	76	21
Colwyn Bay FC Reserves	32	5	3	24	42	100	18

Bangor City Reserves had 2 points deducted.

WELSH ALLIANCE LEAGUE 1989-90

Team	P	W	D	L	F	A	Pts
CPD Porthmadog	34	26	4	4	98	26	82
Bangor City Reserves	34	23	10	1	90	30	79
Connahs Quay Nomads	34	23	4	7	89	39	73
Nantlle Vale FC	34	20	7	7	81	47	67
Bethesda Athletic	34	18	6	10	89	53	60
CPD Locomotive Llanberis	34	17	8	9	89	72	59
Fflint Town United	34	16	5	13	61	54	53
Llanfairpwll FC	34	16	3	15	70	66	51
Conwy United	34	14	6	14	70	61	48
Llandudno FC	34	13	6	15	76	74	45
CPD Y Felinheli	34	12	8	14	56	68	44
Rhyl FC Reserves	34	12	6	16	45	61	39
Mochdre FC	34	9	7	18	49	82	34
Holywell Town	34	8	8	18	44	68	29
Pilkingtons FC St. Asaph	34	7	7	20	53	78	28
Llanrwst United	34	6	9	19	46	85	27
Colwyn Bay FC Reserves	34	5	5	24	43	108	20
Caernarfon Town Reserves	34	4	5	25	38	115	17

Rhyl FC Reserves and Holywell Town each had 3 points deducted.

WELSH ALLIANCE LEAGUE 1990-91

Team	P	W	D	L	F	A	Pts
Llangefni Town	28	19	6	3	102	32	63
Caernarfon Town Reserves	28	19	3	6	84	41	60
Bethesda Athletic	28	18	5	5	79	38	59
Rhydymwyn FC	28	15	6	7	59	41	51
Llanfairpwll FC	28	14	7	7	70	47	49
Rhyl FC Reserves	28	14	7	7	46	34	49
Mochdre FC	28	10	9	9	58	59	39
CPD Y Felinheli	28	9	7	12	47	52	34
Llandudno FC	28	8	10	10	41	54	34
Bangor City Reserves	28	10	6	12	50	53	33
Pilkingtons FC St. Asaph	28	10	5	13	57	74	32
Connahs Quay Nomads Res.	28	7	6	15	52	63	27
Llanrwst United	28	8	3	17	38	79	27
CPD Locomotive Llanberis	28	6	6	16	49	73	24
Nantlle Vale FC	28	0	0	28	26	118	0

Bangor City Reserves and Pilkingtons FC St. Asaph each had 3 points deducted.

WELSH ALLIANCE LEAGUE 1991-92

Llangefni Town	28	21	3	4	84	27	66
CPD Y Felinheli	28	20	5	3	70	35	65
Bangor City Reserves	28	18	4	6	70	37	58
Cemaes Bay FC	28	16	5	7	58	37	53
Llandudno FC	28	15	7	6	74	41	52
Llanfairpwll FC	28	12	5	11	60	51	41
Pilkingtons FC St. Asaph	28	9	8	11	40	44	35
Rhydymwyn FC	28	8	9	11	40	47	33
Conwy United Reserves	28	7	10	11	29	41	31
Connahs Quay Nomads Res.	28	9	6	13	35	51	30
Mochdre FC	28	7	6	15	40	54	27
CPD Locomotive Llanberis	28	7	5	16	29	62	26
Rhyl FC Reserves	28	7	3	18	28	65	24
Nantlle Vale FC	28	5	7	16	41	58	22
Llanrwst United	28	5	5	18	26	71	20

Connahs Quay Nomads Reserves had 3 points deducted.

WELSH ALLIANCE LEAGUE 1992-93

Cemaes Bay FC	32	23	6	3	113	30	75
Llanfairpwll FC	32	22	4	6	73	42	70
Llangefni Town	32	21	6	5	97	45	69
Llandudno FC	32	21	4	7	86	47	67
Pilkingtons FC St. Asaph	32	18	6	8	78	57	60
Rhydymwyn FC	32	16	4	12	58	46	52
Nefyn United	32	13	8	11	61	64	47
CPD Locomotive Llanberis	32	11	12	9	71	68	45
Bangor City Reserves	32	13	6	13	61	57	45
Nantlle Vale FC	32	12	6	14	74	79	42
Llanrwst United	32	11	5	16	58	82	38
Llandyrnog United	32	9	7	16	50	71	34
Connahs Quay Nomads Res.	32	9	6	17	47	84	33
CPD Y Felinheli	32	7	10	15	52	64	31
Conwy United Reserves	32	6	5	21	49	78	23
Rhyl FC Reserves	32	5	4	23	48	103	19
Penmaenmawr Phoenix	32	3	5	24	33	104	14

WELSH ALLIANCE LEAGUE 1993-94

Llangefni Town	34	25	3	6	141	51	78
Llanfairpwll FC	34	24	6	4	105	39	78
Rhydymwyn FC	34	24	6	4	75	31	78
CPD Locomotive Llanberis	34	23	8	3	85	39	77
Nefyn United	34	17	6	11	76	66	57
Llanfairfechan Town	34	17	5	12	80	45	56
Bangor City Reserves	34	16	5	13	86	53	53
Nantlle Vale FC	34	15	7	12	81	78	51
Prestatyn Town	34	14	7	13	74	60	49
Connahs Quay Nomads Res.	34	14	6	14	65	70	48
Holyhead Town	34	14	3	17	92	101	45
Llandyrnog United	34	12	5	17	64	67	41
Rhyl FC Reserves	34	12	4	18	61	71	40
St. Asaph City	34	9	9	16	65	80	39
CPD Y Felinheli	34	9	5	20	45	73	32
Llanrwst United	34	8	3	23	57	102	27
Conwy United Reserves	34	3	3	28	42	138	12
Penmaenmawr Phoenix	34	2	3	29	33	133	9

WELSH ALLIANCE LEAGUE 1994-95

Rhydymwyn FC	34	23	6	5	118	40	75
Prestatyn Town	34	22	5	7	91	52	71
CPD Glantraeth	34	19	8	7	77	52	65
Denbigh Town	34	18	10	6	84	45	64
Llanfairpwll FC	34	19	5	10	95	55	62
Llangefni Town	34	17	7	10	84	62	58
Bangor City Reserves	34	17	5	12	74	57	56
CPD Locomotive Llanberis	34	15	10	9	64	53	55
Caernarfon Athletic	34	14	8	12	50	41	50
Connahs Quay Nomads Res.	34	11	11	12	73	81	44
Rhyl FC Reserves	34	12	8	14	66	75	44
Nefyn United	34	12	7	15	69	81	43
Llandyrnog United	34	11	7	16	55	77	40
Nantlle Vale FC	34	10	7	17	55	80	37
Llanfairfechan Town	34	8	8	18	49	77	32
Llanrwst United	34	8	4	22	57	94	28
Holyhead Town	34	6	2	26	43	126	20
CPD Y Felinheli	34	3	4	27	29	79	13

WELSH ALLIANCE LEAGUE 1995-96

Denbigh Town	28	20	3	5	60	30	63
Prestatyn Town	28	19	3	6	70	31	60
Llanfairpwll FC	28	18	4	6	74	41	58
CPD Glantraeth	28	17	2	9	66	50	53
CPD Porthmadog Reserves	28	15	2	11	46	35	52
CPD Locomotive Llanberis	28	15	2	11	46	35	47
Llandyrnog United	28	14	4	10	53	48	46
Llangefni Town	28	13	3	12	55	51	42
Bangor City Reserves	28	12	5	11	45	38	41
Nantlle Vale FC	28	9	6	13	53	56	33
Halkyn United	28	10	3	15	46	50	33
Connahs Quay Nomads Res.	28	6	3	19	48	80	21
Caernarfon Town Reserves	28	6	3	19	27	60	21
Nefyn United	28	5	4	19	38	86	19
Rhyl FC Reserves	28	4	3	21	28	80	15

WELSH ALLIANCE LEAGUE 1996-97

CPD Glantraeth	26	20	2	4	96	29	62
Llanfairpwll FC	26	17	6	3	62	30	57
Conwy United Reserves	26	19	6	5	61	39	47
CPD Locomotive Llanberis	26	12	8	6	52	31	44
Halkyn United	26	12	7	7	53	33	43
Saltney Community Centre FC	26	12	4	10	61	54	40
Porthmadog FC Reserves	26	12	2	12	44	48	36
Nantlle Vale FC	26	10	8	10	54	59	36
Prestatyn Town	26	8	9	9	44	30	33
Rhyl FC Reserves	26	8	3	15	42	68	27
Caernarfon Town Reserves	26	4	11	11	36	53	23
Bangor City Reserves	26	6	5	5	38	63	23
Llangefni Town	26	5	3	18	23	69	18
Llandyrnog United	26	4	4	18	23	70	16

WELSH ALLIANCE LEAGUE 1997-98

Holyhead Hotspur	26	23	1	2	102	32	70
Colwyn Bay YMCA	26	17	3	6	71	41	54
CPD Locomotive Llanberis	26	15	5	6	71	50	50
Halkyn United	26	15	2	9	60	40	47
Llangefni United	26	12	6	8	73	46	42
Prestatyn Town	26	13	3	10	50	34	42
Bangor City Reserves	26	12	4	10	72	53	40
Nantlle Vale FC	26	11	5	10	41	49	38
Llanfairpwll FC	26	8	5	13	38	51	29
Caernarfon Town Reserves	26	9	1	16	46	61	28
Saltney Community Centre FC	26	7	7	12	40	60	28
Rhyl FC Reserves	26	6	5	15	33	63	23
Conwy United Reserves	26	5	2	19	48	108	17
Llandyrnog United	26	2	5	19	29	86	11

WELSH ALLIANCE LEAGUE 1998-99

Team							
Llangefni Town	18	12	3	3	49	25	39
CPD Locomotive Llanberis	18	12	3	3	43	31	39
Colwyn Bay YMCA	18	11	5	2	45	22	38
Amlwch Town	18	10	3	6	48	36	33
Llanfairpwll FC	18	6	5	7	39	30	23
Rhyl Delta	18	6	3	9	37	37	21
Halkyn United	18	6	3	9	29	40	21
Rhyl FC Reserves	18	5	5	8	28	44	20
Bangor City Reserves	18	5	1	12	37	50	16
Llandyrnog United	18	1	1	16	22	72	4

WELSH ALLIANCE LGE. 1999-2000

Team							
Halkyn United	24	19	5	0	70	23	62
Colwyn Bay YMCA	24	15	6	3	49	26	51
Llanfairpwll FC	24	14	6	4	30	46	48
Glan Conwy FC	24	13	4	7	74	33	43
Llandudno Junction FC	24	11	4	9	67	51	37
Bangor City Reserves	24	10	6	8	65	52	36
Prestatyn Town	24	11	2	11	48	54	35
CPD Locomotive Llanberis	24	10	4	10	59	47	34
Amlwch Town	24	10	2	12	76	53	33
Rhyl Athletic	24	8	4	12	51	59	28
Rhyl Delta	24	6	4	14	42	68	22
Penmaenmawr Phoenix	24	2	8	14	37	71	14
Llandyrnog United	24	1	1	22	22	147	4

WELSH ALLIANCE LEAGUE 2000-01

Team							
Llanfairpwll FC	26	18	4	4	75	38	58
Glan Conwy FC	26	18	2	6	92	49	56
Amlwch Town	26	16	4	6	91	41	52
Bethesda Athletic	26	12	8	6	64	45	44
Rhyl FC Reserves	26	13	4	9	50	52	43
Prestatyn Town	26	12	4	10	48	56	40
Abergele Town	26	11	6	9	58	52	39
Bangor City Reserves	26	9	6	11	48	55	33
Llandudno Junction FC	26	8	6	12	69	71	30
Colwyn Bay YMCA	26	9	2	15	48	62	29
CPD Locomotive Llanberis	26	8	4	14	50	56	28
Caerwys FC	26	4	9	13	35	68	21
Conwy United	26	4	8	14	38	86	20
Penmaenmawr Phoenix	26	4	5	17	55	90	17

WELSH ALLIANCE LEAGUE 2001-02

Team							
Amlwch Town	24	20	3	1	94	28	63
Conwy United	24	18	2	4	57	28	56
Rhyl FC Reserves	24	13	5	6	43	31	44
CPD Y Felinheli	24	13	4	7	44	34	43
Llandudno Junction FC	24	13	3	8	52	30	42
Bangor City Reserves	24	12	3	9	63	41	39
Bethesda Athletic	24	11	4	9	60	40	37
CPD Locomotive Llanberis	24	10	4	10	58	57	34
Prestatyn Town	24	8	5	11	40	49	29
Rhydymwyn FC	24	9	2	13	50	60	29
Penmaenmawr Phoenix	24	3	4	17	39	79	13
Glan Conwy FC	24	2	4	18	38	79	10
Caerwys FC	24	1	3	20	32	96	6

WELSH ALLIANCE LEAGUE 2002-03

Team							
CPD Glantraeth	28	19	5	4	118	33	62
CPD Bodedern	28	18	7	3	65	19	61
Denbigh Town	28	17	5	6	64	31	56
Bethesda Athletic	28	17	2	9	74	44	53
Rhyl FC Reserves	28	15	6	7	62	31	51
CPD Locomotive Llanberis	28	12	7	9	47	42	43
Llandudno Junction FC	28	12	7	9	57	53	43
Rhydymwyn FC	28	11	6	11	52	54	39
Sealand Leisure FC	28	10	6	12	44	63	36
CPD Y Felinheli	28	10	4	14	44	60	31
Caerwys FC	28	9	4	15	57	78	31
Prestatyn Town	28	7	7	14	32	58	28
Glan Conwy FC	28	4	8	16	42	89	17
Penmaenmawr Phoenix	28	4	5	19	35	83	17
Conwy United	28	4	3	21	31	86	15

WELSH ALLIANCE LEAGUE 2003-04

Team							
Rhyl FC Reserves	30	26	2	2	101	27	80
Llandyrnog United	30	22	1	7	77	35	67
Prestatyn Town	30	21	3	6	72	28	66
CPD Bodedern	30	19	7	4	71	24	64
Rhydymwyn FC	30	19	1	10	73	35	58
Bethesda Athletic	30	13	7	10	58	60	46
CPD Locomotive Llanberis	30	12	6	12	75	59	42
Glan Conwy FC	30	13	3	14	49	54	42
Sealand Leisure FC	30	10	9	11	59	58	39
Llanrug United	30	12	3	15	55	69	39
Llandudno Junction	30	12	1	17	69	62	37
Denbigh Town	30	11	3	16	62	66	36
Conwy United	30	8	1	21	44	89	25
Penmaenmawr Phoenix	30	7	4	19	51	106	25
Caerwys FC	30	3	5	22	32	105	14
CPD Y Felinheli	30	4	0	26	33	104	12

WELSH ALLIANCE LEAGUE 2004-05

Team							
CPD Bodedern	30	21	4	5	77	32	67
Rhydymwyn FC	30	20	6	4	69	37	66
Bethesda Athletic	30	18	8	4	100	42	62
Rhyl FC Reserves	30	18	7	5	80	31	61
Conwy United	30	19	4	7	70	42	61
Prestatyn Town	30	16	5	9	61	45	53
Llanrwst United	30	12	7	11	45	36	43
Denbigh Town	30	13	3	14	54	65	42
CPD Llanberis	30	10	7	13	44	47	37
Sealand Leisure FC	30	10	5	15	39	53	35
Glan Conwy FC	30	9	8	13	43	58	35
Llandudno Junction FC	30	10	3	17	65	56	33
Llanrug United	30	6	8	16	36	65	25
Caerwys FC	30	7	4	19	40	82	25
Penmaenmawr Phoenix	30	6	5	19	37	85	20
CPD Y Felinheli	30	2	2	26	28	112	8

WELSH ALLIANCE LEAGUE 2005-06

Team							
Prestatyn Town	30	25	5	0	114	28	80
Denbigh Town	30	23	2	5	90	31	71
Bethesda Athletic	30	22	3	5	101	43	69
Rhyl FC Reserves	30	21	5	4	94	36	68
Llanrwst United	30	19	3	8	74	35	60
Nefyn United	30	16	2	12	60	57	50
Llandudno Junction	30	12	7	11	53	53	43
Llanrug United	30	12	6	12	47	57	42
Llanberis	30	12	4	14	55	55	40
Rhydymwyn	30	11	3	16	48	69	36
Caerwys FC	30	11	0	19	60	83	33
Conwy United	30	9	5	16	41	50	32
Glan Conwy FC	30	6	5	19	38	72	23
Sealand Rovers	30	6	2	22	40	92	20
Cemaes Bay	30	5	3	22	38	127	18
Penmaenmawr Phoenix	30	1	3	26	37	102	3

WELSH ALLIANCE LEAGUE 2006-07

Denbigh Town	28	23	2	3	82	23	71
Rhyl FC Reserves	28	21	5	2	81	29	68
Llanrwst United	28	17	4	7	56	36	55
Glan Conwy	28	16	6	6	52	36	54
Pwllheli FC	28	14	5	9	78	46	47
Bethesda Athletic	28	13	7	8	69	50	46
Llanrug United	28	10	10	8	68	45	40
Rhydymwyn	28	11	6	11	57	53	39
Conwy United	28	11	4	13	58	70	37
Holywell Town	28	8	8	12	59	63	32
Nefyn United	28	9	2	17	41	61	29
Llandudno Junction	28	7	4	17	44	80	25
CPD Llanberis	28	5	7	16	46	68	22
Halkyn United	28	6	2	20	28	74	20
Caerwys FC	28	3	0	25	39	124	9

WELSH ALLIANCE LEAGUE 2007-08

Bethesda Athletic	28	23	2	3	104	26	71
Glan Conwy	28	19	3	6	77	32	60
Rhyl FC Reserves	28	14	5	9	74	40	47
Llanrwst United	28	14	4	10	50	45	46
Conwy United	28	14	3	11	69	58	45
Llanrug United	28	12	8	8	78	65	44
Pwllheli FC	28	11	7	10	53	57	40
Nantlle Vale	28	11	5	12	41	60	38
CPD Llanberis	28	8	9	11	47	58	33
Nefyn United	28	10	4	14	48	68	31
Rhydymwyn FC	28	8	5	15	48	54	29
Holywell Town	28	8	6	14	44	70	27
Amlwch Town	28	6	7	15	50	80	25
Halkyn United	28	6	7	15	37	68	25
Llandudno Junction	28	6	5	17	38	77	23

Nefyn United and Holywell Town each had 3 points deducted.

WELSH ALLIANCE LEAGUE 2008-09

Bethesda Athletic	32	27	1	4	146	35	82
Rhydymwyn FC	32	20	6	6	83	45	63
Rhyl Reserves	32	19	4	9	82	43	61
Llanrwst United	32	19	4	9	76	45	61
Glan Conwy FC	32	19	3	10	106	53	60
Llandudno Junction	32	17	5	10	86	54	56
Nefyn United	32	16	6	10	65	58	54
Llanrug United	32	16	4	12	84	66	52
Pwllheli FC	32	16	4	12	59	54	52
Barmouth & Duffryn United	32	14	5	13	85	71	47
Halkyn United	32	15	3	14	79	79	45
Conwy United	32	12	4	16	63	64	37
CPD Llanllyfni	32	11	4	17	62	89	37
Holywell Town	32	10	3	19	64	80	33
CPD Llanberis	32	7	5	20	40	82	26
Amlwch Town	32	0	2	30	20	190	2
Nantlle Vale	32	1	3	28	31	123	0

Rhydymwyn FC, Halkyn United and Conwy United each had 3 points deducted.
Nantlle Vale had 6 points deducted.

WELSH ALLIANCE LEAGUE 2009-10

Rhydymwyn	30	21	4	5	81	30	67
Glan Conwy	30	20	3	7	88	53	63
Llandudno Junction	30	17	6	7	83	36	57
Barmouth & Dyffryn United	30	17	5	8	66	38	56
Conwy United	30	14	11	5	71	36	53
Pwllheli	30	15	7	8	73	37	52
Llanrwst United	30	14	7	9	53	44	49
Llanrug United	30	14	6	10	65	51	48
Llanberis	30	13	8	9	71	64	47
Holywell Town	30	13	7	10	72	43	46
Nefyn United	30	12	5	13	50	59	41
Blaenau Ffestiniog Amateurs	30	10	3	17	62	75	33
Llandyrnog United	30	7	7	16	42	66	28
Nantlle Vale	30	3	4	23	28	100	13
Amlwch Town	30	4	1	25	30	116	13
Halkyn United	30	3	2	25	36	123	8

Halkyn United had 3 points deducted.

WELSH ALLIANCE LEAGUE 2010-11

Division 1

Conwy United	30	25	2	3	89	30	77
Holyhead Hotspur	30	20	6	4	82	36	66
Holywell Town	30	17	3	10	68	40	54
Denbigh Town	30	13	7	10	53	52	46
Caernarfon Town	30	13	4	13	57	59	43
Llanfairpwll	30	12	6	12	57	52	42
Gwalchmai	30	10	10	10	47	48	40
Nefyn United	30	10	7	13	40	55	37
Bethesda Athletic	30	10	7	13	57	82	37
Pwllheli	30	10	9	11	42	46	36
Glan Conwy	30	10	6	14	47	50	36
Llanrwst United	30	9	8	13	50	60	35
Llanrug United	30	11	2	17	62	75	35
Barmouth & Dyffryn United	30	10	5	15	58	75	35
Llandudno Junction	30	8	10	12	54	65	34
Llanberis	30	4	4	22	42	81	16

Pwllheli had 3 points deducted.

Division 2

Caernarfon Wanderers	20	15	1	4	63	29	46
Bodedern Athletic	20	14	3	3	55	25	45
Connahs Quay Town.	20	13	2	5	49	26	41
Llandyrnog United	20	12	1	7	54	28	37
Amlwch Town	20	8	4	8	43	49	28
Greenfield	20	7	5	8	42	38	26
Penmaenmawr Phoenix	20	6	3	11	43	48	21
Nantlle Vale	20	6	1	13	23	55	19
Halkyn United	20	5	3	12	31	52	18
Gaerwen	20	5	3	12	41	64	15
Blaenau Ffestiniog Amateurs	20	5	2	13	32	62	14

Gaerwen and Blaenau Ffestiniog Amateurs each had 3 points deducted.

WELSH ALLIANCE LEAGUE 2011-12

Division 1

Holyhead Hotspur	30	25	1	4	87	28	73
Holywell Town	30	23	3	4	77	29	72
Pwllheli	30	19	6	5	57	32	63
Caernarfon Town	30	19	3	8	67	36	60
Bethesda Athletic	30	16	6	8	69	52	54
Llanrug United	30	14	5	11	74	54	47
Denbigh Town	30	14	4	12	58	47	46
Barmouth & Dyffryn United	30	11	3	16	59	83	36
Gwalchmai	30	10	5	15	54	65	35
Llandudno Junction	30	9	7	14	60	71	34
Bodedern Athletic	30	9	9	12	46	52	33
Glan Conwy	30	9	2	19	46	68	29
Nefyn United	30	7	4	19	35	70	25
Llanrwst United	30	4	11	15	45	69	23
Llanfairpwll	30	6	5	19	46	78	23
Caernarfon Wanderers	30	6	4	20	46	91	22

Holyhead Hotspur and Bodedern Athletic each had 3 points deducted.

Division 2

Glantraeth	22	19	1	2	97	27	58
Llanberis	22	17	1	4	53	28	52
Kinmel Bay	22	17	3	2	73	25	51
Llandyrnog United	22	16	2	4	56	18	50
Greenfield	22	10	2	10	46	54	29
Penmaenmawr Phoenix	22	8	4	10	36	39	28
Nantlle Vale	22	7	0	15	36	62	21
Blaenau Ffestiniog Amateurs	22	7	2	13	27	48	18
Connahs Quay Town	22	6	3	13	27	48	18
Amlwch Town	22	3	9	10	33	63	18
Gaerwen	22	5	2	15	34	61	17
Halkyn United	22	2	1	19	29	73	7

Kinmel Bay, Greenfield and Connahs Quay Town each had 3 points deducted.
Blaenau Ffestiniog Amateurs had 5 points deducted.

WELSH ALLIANCE LEAGUE 2012-13

Division 1

Caernarfon Town	28	21	3	4	91	30	66
Denbigh Town	28	20	4	4	89	39	64
Holywell Town	28	18	7	3	98	38	61
Barmouth & Dyffryn United	28	14	5	9	60	59	47
Llanrug United	28	14	4	10	70	43	46
Llanberis	28	13	5	10	65	51	44
Llanrwst United	28	10	8	10	55	42	38
Gwalchmai	28	11	5	12	53	55	38
Glantraeth	28	11	2	15	57	59	35
Pwllheli	28	10	5	13	45	66	35
Glan Conwy	28	8	8	12	45	58	32
Bodedern Athletic	28	9	2	17	40	60	29
Nefyn United	28	8	4	16	40	81	28
Llandudno Junction	28	8	2	18	42	69	26
Llangefni Town	28	2	2	24	18	118	8

Division 2

Llandyrnog United	24	18	4	2	66	29	58
Llanfairpwll	24	18	3	3	66	26	57
Penrhyndeudraeth	24	15	3	6	73	32	48
Kinmel Bay	23	14	4	5	47	32	43
Meliden	24	13	3	8	73	38	42
Greenfield	24	11	4	9	75	55	37
Penmaenmawr Phoenix	24	10	4	10	47	50	34
Halkyn United	24	8	6	10	45	48	30
Blaenau Ffestiniog Amateurs	24	7	4	13	48	79	25
Connahs Quay Town	23	6	5	12	38	74	23
Gaerwen	24	4	4	16	38	65	16
Amlwch Town	24	3	5	16	21	67	14
Nantlle Vale	24	2	3	19	39	81	9

Kinmel Bay had 3 points deducted.

WELSH ALLIANCE LEAGUE 2013-14

Division 1

Denbigh Town	28	25	3	0	96	18	78
Holywell Town	28	20	5	3	103	23	65
Llanrug United	28	18	5	5	76	43	59
Barmouth & Dyffryn United	28	14	4	10	53	58	46
Glantraeth	28	14	4	10	67	61	43
Llanberis	28	12	3	13	69	65	39
Bodedern Athletic	28	10	7	11	49	53	37
Gwalchmai	28	10	5	13	55	74	35
Glan Conwy	28	8	10	10	48	64	34
Llanrwst United	28	8	5	15	52	69	29
Nefyn United	28	9	1	18	34	73	28
Llandudno Junction	28	6	9	13	46	66	27
Pwllheli	28	7	4	17	37	69	25
Llanfairpwll	28	7	3	18	51	70	24
Llandyrnog United	28	7	2	19	37	67	23

Glantraeth had 3 points deducted.

Division 2

Penrhyndeudraeth	24	22	1	1	114	23	67
Kinmel Bay Sports	24	16	5	3	92	38	53
Trearddur Bay United	24	15	4	5	79	37	49
St. Asaph City	24	15	4	5	77	33	46
Nantlle Vale	24	13	3	8	69	48	42
Halkyn United	24	12	2	10	67	57	38
Meliden	24	11	2	11	60	55	35
Greenfield	24	9	4	11	51	57	31
Penmaenmawr Phoenix	24	9	2	13	54	68	29
Blaenau Ffestiniog Amateurs	24	7	1	16	61	95	22
Amlwch Town	24	6	2	16	31	72	20
Gaerwen	24	3	1	20	24	87	10
Bethesda Athletic	24	1	3	20	16	125	6

St. Asaph City had 3 points deducted.

WELSH ALLIANCE LEAGUE 2014-15

Division 1

Holywell Town	26	23	2	1	119	19	71
Llandudno Junction	26	17	5	4	77	39	56
Glantraeth	26	16	4	6	62	33	52
Llanrug United	26	14	6	6	66	43	48
Penrhyndeudraeth	26	12	6	8	55	44	42
Kinmel Bay	26	10	5	11	55	50	35
Gwalchmai	26	9	7	10	46	47	34
Barmouth & Duffyn United	26	9	7	10	44	52	34
Llanberis	26	10	3	13	50	48	33
Pwllheli	26	10	3	13	58	70	33
Llandyrnog United	26	8	4	14	34	51	28
Glan Conwy	26	7	5	14	49	65	26
Llanrwst United	26	7	3	16	33	70	24
Llanfairpwll	26	0	0	26	17	134	0

Nefyn United and Bodedern both withdrew from the league during the season.

Division 2

St. Asaph City	30	23	3	4	105	27	72
Llangefni Town	30	23	3	4	106	34	72
Trearddur Bay	30	22	3	5	93	39	69
Nantlle Vale	30	21	4	5	101	52	67
Llanerchymedd	30	21	4	5	81	32	67
Mynydd Llandegai	30	12	7	11	64	66	43
Greenfield	30	12	6	12	75	69	42
Blaenau Ffestiniog Amateurs	30	11	6	13	72	67	39
Meliden	30	10	4	16	68	71	34
Bethesda Athletic	30	10	2	18	72	104	32
Halkyn United	30	9	3	18	59	82	30
Amlwch Town	30	9	3	18	59	96	30
Gaerwen	30	8	2	20	54	108	26
Mochdre Sports	30	7	3	20	43	87	24
Penmaenmawr Phoenix	30	6	4	20	45	107	22
Pentraeth	30	6	3	21	50	106	21

WELSH ALLIANCE LEAGUE 2015-16

Division 1

Trearddur Bay United	30	22	7	1	85	31	73
Llandudno Junction	30	21	7	2	86	37	70
Llangefni Town	30	19	5	6	65	44	62
Glantraeth	30	18	6	6	65	42	57
Llanrug United	30	16	7	7	68	36	55
Penrhyndeudraeth	30	15	5	10	81	53	50
Glan Conwy	30	13	2	15	71	67	41
Abergele Town	30	12	3	15	41	51	39
Gwalchmai	30	11	3	16	43	61	36
Barmouth & Duffryn United	30	11	2	17	37	59	35
Llanberis	30	8	9	13	46	48	33
St. Asaph City	30	10	3	17	57	65	33
Llanrwst United	30	9	5	16	39	61	32
Pwllheli	30	7	8	15	45	66	26
Llandyrnog United	30	7	5	18	41	72	23
Llanfairpwll	30	1	3	26	20	97	6

Glantraeth, Pwllheli and Llandyrnog United each had 3 points deducted.

Division 2

Greenfield	24	21	2	1	94	36	65
Nantlle Vale	24	18	2	4	77	39	56
Llanllyfni	24	13	7	4	76	46	46
Mynydd Llandegai	24	13	3	8	59	61	42
Pentraeth	24	11	5	8	75	47	38
Prestatyn Sports	24	11	4	9	72	57	37
Mochdre Sports	24	8	6	10	46	59	30
Meliden	24	9	2	13	59	65	29
Amlwch Town	24	8	4	12	44	59	28
Penmaenmawr Phoenix	24	7	5	12	49	54	26
Llannerchymedd	24	7	3	14	33	58	24
Blaenau Ffestiniog Amateurs	24	7	0	17	55	100	21
Gaerwen	24	0	3	21	35	93	0

Bethesda Athletic and Halkyn United both withdrew from the league during the season.
Gaerwen had 3 points deducted.

WELSH ALLIANCE LEAGUE 2016-17

Division 1

Glantraeth	30	23	4	3	90	29	73
Llandudno Junction	30	18	3	9	79	47	57
Llangefni Town	30	17	6	7	69	37	57
Llanrug United	30	16	6	8	77	52	54
Greenfield	30	15	5	10	57	44	50
Penrhyndeudraeth	30	14	7	9	66	46	49
Trearddur Bay United	30	14	4	12	58	58	46
Llandyrnog United	30	12	8	10	55	55	44
Nantlle Vale	30	11	6	13	67	64	39
St. Asaph City	30	11	5	14	60	61	38
Llanberis	30	10	5	15	44	59	35
Abergele Town	30	10	7	13	45	62	34
Pwllheli	30	9	5	16	61	76	32
Barmouth & Dyffryn United	30	9	5	16	51	79	32
Llanrwst United	30	7	5	18	28	68	26
Glan Conwy	30	2	3	25	35	105	9

Division 2

Llandudno Albion	26	20	1	5	90	36	61
Mynydd Llandegai	26	19	1	6	90	50	58
Prestatyn Sports	26	17	2	7	93	51	50
Mochdre Sports	26	15	3	8	52	37	48
Amlwch Town	26	13	5	8	54	39	44
Meliden	26	13	3	10	61	54	42
Penmaenmawr Phoenix	26	13	1	12	56	59	40
Gaerwen	26	11	5	10	53	55	38
Cemaes Bay FC	26	9	5	12	53	58	32
Y Felinheli	26	8	3	13	47	57	29
Llanfairpwll	26	8	1	17	40	77	25
Pentraeth	26	6	2	18	37	73	20
Llanerchymedd	26	5	4	17	35	67	19
Blaenau Ffestiniog Amateurs	26	5	2	19	28	76	17

Prestatyn Sports had 3 points deducted.
Llanllyfni FC resigned from the league and their record was expunged.

WELSH ALLIANCE LEAGUE 2017-18

Division 1

Conwy Borough	28	20	4	4	107	37	64
Llangefni Town	28	19	4	5	68	25	61
Llanrug United	28	12	12	4	64	51	48
Llanberis	28	14	4	10	43	55	46
Greenfield	28	14	5	9	82	53	44
Llanrwst United	28	12	8	8	63	54	44
Llandudno Albion	28	13	6	9	76	52	42
Penrhyndeudraeth	28	11	5	12	55	49	38
Barmouth & Dyffryn United	28	12	2	14	38	49	38
Mynydd Llandegai	28	10	5	13	57	72	35
Llandyrnog United	28	8	6	14	51	63	30
St. Asaph City	28	7	8	13	49	60	29
Nantlle Vale	28	6	5	17	32	74	23
Trearddur Bay	28	7	1	20	42	83	22
Pwllheli	28	6	3	19	47	97	21

Llandudno Albion had 3 points deducted for non-fulfilment of a fixture.
Greenfield had 3 points deducted after fielding an ineligible player.

Division 2

Prestatyn Sports	28	24	3	1	117	30	72
Bodedern Athletic	28	21	1	6	78	41	64
Glan Conwy	28	19	2	7	74	35	59
Llannefydd	28	15	7	6	65	35	52
Amlwch Town	28	16	4	8	67	48	52
Y Felinheli	28	16	1	11	71	49	49
Meliden	28	12	4	12	70	67	40
Gaerwen	28	12	3	13	47	58	39
Aberffraw	28	11	2	15	53	61	35
Penmaenmawr Phoenix	28	10	4	14	58	59	34
Blaenau Ffestiniog	28	9	4	15	70	98	31
Pentraeth	28	8	4	16	40	67	28
Mochdre Sports	28	7	3	18	53	84	24
Llannerchymedd	28	4	2	22	19	78	14
Llanfairpwll	28	2	4	22	26	98	10

GWYNEDD FOOTBALL LEAGUE

Formation

During the late 1970s and early 1980s football administrators continually attempted to persuade clubs in the area leagues to seek higher status in Division I of the Welsh League (Northern Section) but with little success.

Area Leagues such as the Anglesey League, Caernarfon & District League and the Vale of Conway League were regarded as Division III of the Welsh League; there was no Division II. The Area Leagues were all financially sound, well administered, thriving competitive Leagues; successful clubs were happy to be "big fish in small pools" and were unwilling to venture into the higher League and its extra financial demands. Supporters were also content to have their club battling it out season after season against the same opponents with the N.W.C.F.A. Junior Cup being the top prize. This was the period when clubs such as Bethesda Athletic, Llanberis, Llanfairpwll, Llanrug United and Machno United dominated the area league football in Gwynedd.

In Clwyd the former Dyserth League and Halkyn League had amalgamated to form three divisions of a new Clwyd Football League. Having a similar set-up in Gwynedd had proved unacceptable to the area leagues, but their management committees responded positively when the formation of a totally separate league as a Division II of the Welsh League was mooted.

A Steering Committee comprising representatives from the Welsh League (Northern Section) and all the area leagues in Gwynedd was formed and approaches were made to successful area league clubs with adequate facilities, but few were interested in membership of the proposed league. An open invitation to all clubs in Gwynedd proved to be more successful, and steering committee meetings were held in April and May 1983, which resulted in the Management committee of the Welsh League (Northern Section) deciding to form a Gwynedd League.

The Steering Committee proceeded to hold a meeting at the Menai Bridge Tigers Sports and Recreation Club, Wood Street, Menai Bridge on Tuesday, 23rd June 1983, and the Gwynedd Football League was born. Admitted into the membership were: Benllech & District, Bethesda Athletic, Conwy United, Llandudno Amateurs, Llanfairpwll, Menai Bridge Tigers, Porthmadog and Y Felinheli. Robert Owen of Llanddoged (Chairman of the Vale of Conwy League) was elected chairman of the new league and requested to form a Management Committee and elect administration officers as soon as possible. The first Management Committee of the Gwynedd League was held at the board room of Bangor City FC on Tuesday, 19th July 1983, and the club representatives appointed R. Brian Jones (Penygroes) as Secretary, J.O. Hughes (Rhostrehwfa) as Treasurer and Robert Edwards (Llangefni) as Registration Secretary. Gwyn Pierce Owen (Pentraeth) was to be responsible for appointing referees.

League fixtures commenced on Saturday 20th August, 1983, but internal problems at Portmadog led to the club withdrawing from the League without playing a single match. When the students returned to College in October, Bangor University accepted an invitation to replace Portmadog as founder members of the League.

The League's founder President, Mr Trevor Owen of Bangor donated a league championship trophy which was won during the opening season by Y Felinheli, who withstood the challenge of Llanfairpwll to take the title by the smallest possible margin, one single goal.

The N.W.C.F.A. invited the League to field a representative team in the revived Tucker Shield competition staged at The Oval, Llandudno, on Saturday, 24th March, 1984. Mr Bryan Owen of Llanfairpwll FC was appointed team manager and after thrilling matches with the Clwyd League and the Anglesey Area, the magnificent shield was won by the Gwynedd League.

At the end-of-season presentation evening much satisfaction was expressed with the standard of the league and the following season was anticipated with relish. But it was not to be. The standards set proved to be too high and the anticipated flood of membership applications did not materialize. Area League clubs felt unable to compete with the clubs in membership. Menai Bridge Tigers resigned because of financial difficulties.

The Welsh League (Northern Section) endeavoured to form a new Welsh Alliance League to include clubs from North East Wales and Central Wales, but failed to attract sufficient clubs. Realising the Gwynedd League would be unable to provide enough matches, champions Y Felinheli and runners-up Llanfairpwll opted for the new Welsh Alliance League. Bangor University, Bethesda Athletic and Conwy United followed suit once they realised there was no hope of attracting ample clubs to the Gwynedd League, but all five clubs participated in a limited League programme and in the Cwpan Gwynedd and Eryri Shield competitions.

Although the League organised no competitions during season 1985-86 the League Management Committee continued to make plans for the following season, and with a much less demanding ground criteria nine clubs were attracted into membership. Locomotive Llanberis emerged as champions.

The League continued to grow in successive seasons but it was still Division II of the Welsh Alliance League, the umbrella body for all Leagues in the area of the N.W.C.F.A. All rule amendments had to be confirmed by the A.G.M. of the Alliance League, all appeals against League Management Committee decisions were made to the Alliance League.

At an historic A.G.M. at Penmachno in July 1988, the Gwynedd League clubs supported a Management Committee decision to break away from the Welsh Alliance League and become independent. But the change of rules had to be sanctioned by the N.W.C.F.A. The Association deferred a decision several times, but on 21st September 1988, on the casting vote of the President, the N.W.C.F.A. Council refused to even consider the ratification of Gwynedd League Rule Amendments, despite a plea from the league's representative that certain amendments had no bearing on the decision to be independent.

An appeal was made to the F.A.W. whose commission had to sit twice before ruling that the Gwynedd League had acted perfectly properly in breaking away from their parent body, the Welsh Alliance League – and they could stay independent. This decision justified the stand made by the Gwynedd League Management Committee.

The F.A.W. ruled that "The leagues in the N.W.C.F.A. area shall register only with the area associated and shall not affiliate to any other league."

This gave the all clear to the remaining leagues – Clwyd, Anglesey, Caernarfon & District and the Vale of Conwy – to break their links with the Welsh Alliance and they too became independent leagues, able to manage their own affairs without having to be answerable to another league.

With a stable management committee, now Presided over by the irrepressible Gwyn Pierce Owen, the League has now established itself in the fourth level of the Welsh pyramid system. Champions regularly move up into the Welsh Alliance whilst the Anglesey and Caernarfon & District League are well respected feeder leagues from below.

In 2003 the Gwynedd League accepted the clubs from the wound-up Vale of Conwy League as a second division the remnants of whom were absorbed into the top division in 2004.

Source: Article provided by Gwynedd League Chairman Bob Owen for "A Coast of Soccer Memories 1894-1994" by Gareth M Davies.

Additional material by Mel Thomas.

GWYNEDD LEAGUE 1983-84

CPD Y Felinheli	14	9	4	1	46	11	22
Llanfairpwll FC	14	8	6	0	42	8	22
Bethesda Athletic	14	7	6	1	35	14	20
Conwy United	14	5	4	5	34	25	14
Benllech & District FC	14	5	2	7	32	29	12
Llandudno Amateurs	14	5	1	8	27	44	11
U.C.N.W. Bangor	14	3	2	9	23	47	8
Menai Bridge Tigers	14	1	1	12	11	72	3

GWYNEDD LEAGUE 1984-85

Bethesda Athletic	8	6	1	1	21	6	13
CPD Y Felinheli	8	5	0	3	24	13	10
Conwy United	8	4	1	3	20	16	9
Llanfairpwll FC	8	3	1	4	18	15	7
U.C.N.W. Bangor	8	0	1	7	11	40	1

1985-1986 NO COMPETITION

GWYNEDD LEAGUE 1986-87

CPD Locomotive Llanberis	16	15	1	0	53	17	31
Llanrug United	16	11	2	3	51	26	24
CPD Coleg Normal Bangor	16	7	2	7	44	49	16
Machno United	16	6	3	7	40	39	15
Harlech Town	16	6	2	8	33	42	14
CPD Llanerchymedd	16	4	5	7	38	42	13
U.C.N.W. Bangor	16	6	1	9	25	37	13
Llanfairpwll FC	16	4	2	10	36	45	10
Conwy United	16	2	4	10	23	46	8

GWYNEDD LEAGUE 1987-88

Nantlle Vale FC	24	20	2	2	105	35	42
CPD Locomotive Llanberis	24	15	7	2	64	32	37
Machno United	24	14	4	6	58	30	32
Nefyn United	24	14	4	6	57	38	32
CPD Bro Goronwy	24	13	5	6	57	34	31
Llanfairpwll FC	24	12	3	9	52	47	27
CPD Llanerchymedd	24	9	5	10	41	38	23
Hotpoint FC Llandudno Junct.	24	7	6	11	50	60	20
Llanrug United	24	8	4	12	49	61	20
CPD Penrhyndeudraeth	24	6	4	15	57	71	16
U.C.N.W. Bangor	24	5	4	15	31	78	14
CPD Coleg Normal Bangor	24	3	4	17	31	81	10
Harlech Town	24	1	6	17	32	79	8

GWYNEDD LEAGUE 1988-89

Llangefni Town	26	20	4	2	108	34	44
CPD Locomotive Llanberis	26	18	5	3	83	42	41
CPD Llanerchymedd	26	16	4	6	86	44	36
Nefyn United	26	15	4	7	64	42	34
Holyhead Town	26	16	2	8	85	33	32
Hotpoint FC Llandudno Junct.	26	14	3	9	75	54	31
Machno United	26	13	2	11	58	45	28
Llanrug United	26	12	3	11	63	53	27
CPD Coleg Normal Bangor	26	12	2	12	57	73	26
Blaenau Amateurs	26	4	9	13	62	66	22
CPD Penrhyndeudraeth	26	6	8	12	45	70	20
CPD Bontnewydd	26	3	4	19	42	108	10
U.C.N.W. Bangor	26	3	2	21	36	105	8
Harlech Town	26	1	1	24	30	125	3

Holyhead Town had 2 points deducted.

GWYNEDD LEAGUE 1989-90

Llangefni Town	24	22	0	2	110	20	46
Nefyn United	24	16	5	3	75	32	37
Llanrug United	24	14	4	6	65	34	32
Blaenau Amateurs	24	11	5	8	65	34	27
Caernarfon Borough	24	10	6	8	50	44	26
Hotpoint FC Llandudno Junct.	24	11	2	11	43	43	24
Llanfairfechan Town	24	10	3	11	52	58	23
CPD Llanerchymedd	24	10	3	11	48	68	23
Machno United	24	7	5	12	40	52	19
Pwllheli Borough	24	6	5	13	37	60	17
U.C.N.W. Bangor	24	7	3	14	36	68	17
CPD Penrhyndeudraeth	24	3	6	15	37	74	12
Harlech Town	24	3	3	18	37	83	9

GWYNEDD LEAGUE 1990-91

Llanrug United	28	22	3	3	88	27	47
Machno United	28	23	1	4	95	40	47
Llanfairfechan Town	28	19	3	6	75	31	41
Penmaenmawr Phoenix	28	16	5	7	58	45	37
Caernarfon Borough	28	15	5	8	60	40	35
Pwllheli Borough	28	13	4	11	51	42	30
Hotpoint FC Llandudno Junct.	28	12	6	10	44	46	30
Holyhead United	28	12	3	13	75	67	27
U.C.N.W. Bangor	28	9	6	13	50	91	24
CPD Penrhyndeudraeth	28	10	1	17	49	69	21
CPD Glantraeth	28	8	4	16	53	69	20
Blaenau Amateurs	28	8	4	16	43	60	20
Nefyn United	28	7	6	15	55	75	20
CPD Llanerchymedd	28	6	4	18	45	62	15
Pwllheli & District FC	28	3	0	25	29	106	6

GWYNEDD LEAGUE 1991-92

Nefyn United	26	20	4	2	93	23	44
Llanrug United	26	20	2	4	61	26	42
Holyhead United	26	15	4	7	67	60	34
CPD Glantraeth	26	15	3	8	63	39	33
CPD Penrhyndeudraeth	26	13	6	7	62	45	32
Llanfairfechan Town	26	12	5	9	62	44	29
Penrhos United	26	12	5	9	59	52	29
CPD Llanerchymedd	26	10	6	10	39	36	26
U.C.N.W. Bangor	26	11	4	11	41	67	24
Penmaenmawr Phoenix	26	10	3	13	47	46	23
Blaenau Amateurs	26	6	8	12	48	60	20
Pwllheli Borough	26	6	0	20	34	73	12
Hotpoint FC Llandudno Junct.	26	3	2	21	28	70	8
Pwllheli & District FC	26	2	2	22	25	88	6

U.N.C.W. Bangor had 2 points deducted.

GWYNEDD LEAGUE 1992-93

Holyhead Town	32	23	4	5	114	43	50
Mountain Rangers	32	23	3	6	110	43	49
Llanfairfechan Town	32	20	8	4	92	40	48
CPD Porthmadog Reserves	32	21	3	8	81	48	43
CPD Glantraeth	32	19	3	10	85	56	41
Penrhosgarnedd United	32	17	4	11	76	61	38
Llanrug United	32	14	10	8	76	66	38
Bangor Waterloo	32	12	8	12	68	57	32
Blaenau Amateurs	32	14	4	14	79	71	32
Pwllheli Borough	32	10	9	13	64	72	29
Hotpoint FC Llandudno Junct.	32	10	8	14	53	61	28
Pwllheli & District FC	32	8	10	14	57	75	26
U.C.N.W. Bangor	32	8	5	19	59	79	21
CPD Penrhyndeudraeth	32	8	5	19	49	82	21
CPD Llanerchymedd	32	7	5	20	47	105	19
Crosville SC Llandudno Junct.	32	6	6	20	51	102	18
CPD Coleg Normal Bangor	32	4	3	25	58	158	11

GWYNEDD LEAGUE 1993-94

CPD Glantraeth	34	27	2	5	153	44	83
Caernarfon Athletic	34	25	7	2	101	31	82
CPD Porthmadog Reserves	34	25	4	5	138	40	79
Mountain Rangers	34	23	2	9	127	57	71
Penrhosgarnedd United	34	22	5	7	128	62	71
Llandegfan FC	34	18	7	9	85	56	61
Llangefni Athletic	34	17	7	10	104	79	58
Hotpoint FC Llandudno Junct.	34	17	5	12	92	71	56
CPD Llanechymedd	34	17	2	15	105	97	53
Pwllheli & District FC	34	14	4	16	81	72	46
Crosville SC Llandudno Junct.	34	14	4	16	92	99	46
Blaenau Amateurs	34	9	4	21	70	116	31
CPD Coleg Normal Bangor	34	9	3	22	72	141	30
Pwllheli Borough	34	8	5	21	62	112	29
Llanrug United	34	7	4	23	86	120	25
CPD Penrhyndeudraeth	34	5	7	22	47	112	22
U.C.N.W. Bangor	34	3	9	22	49	109	18
Barmouth & Dyffryn United	34	4	3	27	45	220	15

GWYNEDD LEAGUE 1994-95

CPD Porthmadog Reserves	28	21	4	3	83	32	67
Mountain Rangers	28	21	1	6	94	44	64
Hotpoint FC Llandudno Junct.	28	20	3	5	89	39	63
Blaenau Amateurs	28	15	4	9	62	54	49
Pwllheli FC	28	15	3	10	70	55	48
Caernarfon Borough	28	12	4	12	53	47	40
Conwy United Reserves	28	12	2	14	65	69	38
Llandegfan FC	28	11	5	12	51	52	38
Llangefni Athletic	28	12	2	14	65	69	38
Llanrug United	28	10	5	13	51	74	35
Barmouth & Dyffryn United	28	10	3	15	56	63	33
Crosville SC Llandudno Junct.	28	9	5	14	47	66	32
CPD Penrhyndeudraeth	28	9	4	15	62	74	31
Penmaenmawr Phoenix	28	6	1	21	40	87	19
CPD Coleg Normal Bangor	28	4	2	22	46	120	14

GWYNEDD LEAGUE 1995-96

Conwy United Reserves	30	25	3	2	98	27	78
Hotpoint FC Llandudno Junct.	30	21	4	5	99	49	67
Llanrwst United	30	21	3	6	94	48	66
CPD Deiniolen	30	20	4	6	85	57	64
Barmouth & Dyffryn United	30	18	1	11	101	64	55
CPD Y Felinheli	30	13	8	9	75	60	47
Mountain Rangers	30	13	5	12	79	78	42
CPD Penrhyndeudraeth	30	11	8	11	68	72	41
Blaenau Amateurs	30	12	3	15	80	80	39
Pwllheli FC	30	10	8	12	66	66	38
Llandegfan FC	30	10	6	14	58	71	36
Llanrug United	30	6	7	17	50	84	25
Llangefni Athletic	30	7	4	19	53	93	25
Llanfairfechan Town	30	6	5	19	37	87	23
Caernarfon Borough	30	5	5	20	35	72	17
Holyhead Town	30	5	0	25	46	117	15

Mountain Rangers had 2 points deducted.
Caernarfon Borough had 3 points deducted

GWYNEDD LEAGUE 1996-97

Holyhead Hotspur	24	17	2	5	82	34	53
Hotpoint FC Llandudno Junct.	24	15	2	7	78	39	47
Caernarfon Borough	24	13	7	4	66	47	46
Pwllheli	24	14	3	7	56	40	45
Llanrwst United	24	12	6	6	77	34	42
CPD Penrhyndeudraeth	24	13	2	9	50	43	41
CPD Deiniolen	24	9	5	10	57	55	32
Barmouth & Dyffryn United	24	9	4	11	55	62	31
Llanrug United	24	8	5	11	40	55	29
CPD Y Felinheli	24	6	4	14	40	58	22
Llandegfan FC	24	5	5	14	49	86	20
Talysarn Celts	24	6	1	17	50	82	19
Llangefni Athletic	24	5	2	17	43	107	17

GWYNEDD LEAGUE 1997-98

Amlwch Town	24	23	1	0	107	21	70
Llanrwst United	24	18	2	4	94	35	56
CPD Penrhyndeudraeth	24	15	2	7	93	46	47
CPD Deiniolen	24	14	4	6	70	44	46
Llandegfan FC	24	15	0	9	57	47	45
Pwllheli	24	10	4	10	52	55	34
Llanfairfechan Athletic	24	9	5	10	56	60	32
Llanrug United	24	9	2	13	52	67	29
Llangefni Athletic	24	8	3	13	59	69	27
CPD Y Felinheli	24	6	4	14	34	65	19
Barmouth & Dyffryn United	24	4	6	14	39	87	18
University of Wales Bangor	24	5	2	17	43	96	17
Talysarn Celts	24	2	1	21	30	94	7

GWYNEDD LEAGUE 1998-99

Glan Conwy	26	22	1	3	104	32	67
CPD Penrhyndeudraeth	26	18	2	6	85	47	56
Llanfairfechan Athletic	26	17	2	7	73	62	53
Bethesda Athletic	26	16	2	8	60	34	50
CPD Deiniolen	26	16	2	8	60	46	50
Pwllheli	26	13	2	11	62	54	41
Barmouth & Dyffryn United	26	12	3	11	64	68	39
Llanrwst United	26	12	3	11	70	76	39
Llanrug United	26	12	2	12	60	50	38
Llangefni Athletic	26	9	2	15	63	73	29
CPD Y Felinheli	26	6	4	16	37	60	22
University of Wales Bangor	26	5	4	17	31	65	19
Holyhead Hotspur Reserves	26	4	4	18	39	77	16
Llandegfan FC	26	2	3	21	30	94	9

GWYNEDD LEAGUE 1999-2000

Bethesda Athletic	28	24	4	0	82	20	76
Llangefni Town Reserves	28	21	2	5	103	42	65
Bodedern FC	28	19	2	7	78	41	59
Caernarfon Town Reserves	28	16	7	5	72	33	55
Llanrug United	28	17	3	8	63	30	54
CPD Penrhyndeudraeth	28	14	4	10	77	72	46
Pwllheli	28	12	5	11	62	60	41
Blaenau Amateurs	28	13	2	13	64	72	41
CPD Y Felinheli	28	10	4	14	47	58	34
Llanrwst United	28	10	3	15	43	73	33
Holyhead Hotspur	28	10	0	18	47	77	30
Barmouth & Dyffryn United	28	7	5	16	58	80	26
CPD Deiniolen	28	6	1	21	50	97	19
University of Wales Bangor	28	4	3	21	36	70	15
Llandegfan FC	28	2	3	21	29	86	9

GWYNEDD LEAGUE 2000-01

CPD Y Felinheli	26	18	6	2	75	27	60
Llanrug United	26	19	3	4	78	33	60
Pwllheli	26	17	5	7	80	38	56
Bodedern FC	26	16	4	6	87	30	52
Blaenau Amateurs FC	26	13	4	9	52	59	43
Nefyn United	26	12	4	10	64	60	40
Llanrwst United	26	10	7	9	45	44	37
CPD Deiniolen	26	11	1	14	52	68	34
Holyhead Hotspur	26	10	2	14	55	62	32
University of Wales Bangor	26	10	2	14	46	59	32
Caernarfon Town Reserves	26	9	4	13	50	44	31
Cemaes Bay Reserves	26	7	6	13	43	65	27
Barmouth & Dyffryn United	26	4	4	18	36	104	16
CPD Penrhyndeudraeth	26	0	0	26	15	116	0

Llangefni Town Reserves withdrew during the season and their record was expunged.

GWYNEDD LEAGUE 2001-02

Team	P	W	D	L	F	A	Pts
Bodedern FC	24	18	4	2	96	23	58
Pwllheli	24	18	1	5	74	40	55
Llanrwst United	24	15	5	4	61	32	50
Nantlle Vale FC	24	15	4	5	73	42	49
Caernarfon Town Reserves	24	13	3	8	63	43	42
Nefyn United	24	11	4	9	82	57	37
Blaenau Amateurs FC	24	10	4	10	76	61	34
Llanrug United	24	10	4	10	56	57	34
Cemaes Bay FC Reserves	24	7	1	16	45	82	22
Holyhead Hotspur Reserves	24	6	4	14	33	81	22
University of Wales Bangor	24	5	2	17	53	87	17
Llangefni-Glantraeth Reserves	24	5	2	17	51	91	17
CPD Deiniolen	24	3	2	19	35	103	11

GWYNEDD LEAGUE 2002-03

Premier Division

Team	P	W	D	L	F	A	Pts
Llanrug United	24	18	4	2	69	24	58
Beaumaris Town	24	18	2	4	95	38	56
CPD Porthmadog Reserves	24	15	3	6	78	44	48
Pwllheli	24	14	4	6	78	41	46
Llanrwst United	24	14	2	8	45	40	44
Nefyn United	24	13	3	8	75	57	42
Nantlle Vale FC	24	12	3	9	57	52	39
Blaenau Amateurs	24	10	3	11	61	58	33
Caernarfon Town Reserves	24	8	0	16	53	69	24
Holyhead Hotspur Reserves	24	6	3	15	36	77	21
University of Wales Bangor	24	5	2	17	42	72	17
Llanfairfechan Town	24	3	3	18	30	87	12
CPD Deiniolen	24	3	2	19	39	99	10

Division 1

Team	P	W	D	L	F	A	Pts
Llandudno Cricketers	10	10	0	0	50	15	30
Machno United	10	5	2	3	28	27	17
University of Wales Bangor Res.	10	5	1	4	37	35	16
Llanrwst United Reserves	10	2	3	5	16	28	9
Conwy United Reserves	10	2	2	6	38	40	8
Llandudno Junction Reserves	10	1	2	7	18	42	5

GWYNEDD LEAGUE 2003-04

Premier Division

Team	P	W	D	L	F	A	Pts
Llanrwst United	26	19	4	3	68	26	61
Nefyn United	26	17	4	5	68	31	55
University of Wales Bangor	26	16	3	7	81	54	51
CPD Porthmadog Reserves	26	15	5	6	88	43	50
Nantlle Vale FC	26	15	4	7	72	48	49
Barmouth & Dyffryn United	26	12	6	8	60	45	42
Llangefni Town Reserves	26	12	3	11	72	47	39
Blaenau Amateurs	26	10	3	13	77	69	33
Beaumaris Town	26	9	4	13	55	55	31
Caernarfon Town Reserves	26	8	3	15	53	80	27
Llandudno Cricketers	26	8	2	16	46	76	26
Pwllheli	26	7	4	15	53	65	25
Holyhead Hotspur Reserves	26	7	2	17	43	101	23
Llanfairfechan Town	26	3	1	22	31	127	10

Division 1

Team	P	W	D	L	F	A	Pts
Llanrwst United Reserves	12	9	1	2	36	11	28
University of Wales Bangor Res.	12	7	2	3	27	16	23
Llandudno Junction Reserves	12	4	4	4	23	20	16
Betws-y-coed FC	12	0	3	9	12	51	3

At the end of this season Division 1 was disbanded. UWBangor Reserves moved to the Angelsey League. Betws-y-coed FC moved to the Caernarfon & District League whilst Llanrwst United Reserves and Llandudno Junction Reserves were absorbed into the Premier Division.

GWYNEDD LEAGUE 2004-05

Team	P	W	D	L	F	A	Pts
CPD Porthmadog Reserves	28	22	2	4	90	40	68
Nefyn United	28	19	7	2	99	38	64
Blaenau Amateurs	28	20	3	5	86	35	63
Pwllheli	28	16	6	6	88	48	53
Llangefni Town Reserves	28	13	5	10	76	62	44
Beaumaris Town	28	12	4	12	85	82	40
University of Wales Bangor	28	12	4	12	45	49	40
Llandudno Alexandra	28	9	8	11	56	57	35
Nantlle Vale FC	28	10	4	14	71	68	34
Barmouth & Dyffryn United	28	10	4	14	48	56	34
Holyhead Hotspur Reserves	28	10	1	17	51	78	31
CPD Bethel	28	7	9	12	47	60	30
Llanfairfechan Town	28	9	2	17	47	70	29
Llanrwst United Reserves	28	4	4	20	40	97	16
Llandudno Junction Reserves	28	5	1	22	50	137	16

GWYNEDD LEAGUE 2005-06

Team	P	W	D	L	F	A	Pts
Pwllheli FC	30	24	2	4	107	39	74
Llangefni Town Reserves	30	17	6	7	73	53	57
Barmouth & Dyffryn United	30	18	2	10	85	51	56
University of Wales Bangor	30	17	1	12	60	37	52
Bontnewydd	30	16	4	10	71	55	52
Nantlle Vale	30	15	5	10	84	61	50
Gaerwen	30	14	5	11	63	56	47
Beaumaris Town	30	13	4	13	60	51	43
Bethel	30	13	4	13	55	62	43
Holyhead Hotspur Reserves	30	12	4	14	84	85	40
Blaenau Amateurs	30	10	6	14	53	63	36
CPD Porthmadog Reserves	30	10	6	14	55	67	36
Llanfairfechan	30	10	5	15	62	76	35
West Shore	30	7	4	19	37	96	25
Llanrwst United Reserves	30	6	5	19	29	84	23
CPD Y Felinheli	30	5	3	22	42	84	18

GWYNEDD LEAGUE 2006-07

Team	P	W	D	L	F	A	Pts
Barmouth & Dyffryn United	30	24	2	4	124	40	74
Amlwch Town	30	21	4	5	100	49	67
Nantlle Vale	30	19	5	6	92	49	62
Beaumaris Town	30	19	2	9	95	59	59
Holyhead Hotspur Reserves	30	16	5	9	89	66	53
CPD Porthmadog Reserves	30	17	1	12	87	54	52
Blaenau Ffestiniog Amateurs	30	16	4	10	91	67	52
Llangefni Town Reserves	30	15	5	10	92	57	50
Bontnewydd	30	11	4	15	70	62	35
Bethel	30	10	5	15	70	62	35
Llanllyfni	30	9	8	13	60	82	35
Gaerwen	30	7	11	12	76	87	32
Llanfairfechan Town	30	8	7	15	71	93	31
Real Llandudno	30	5	7	18	47	81	22
University of Wales Bangor	30	5	6	19	36	89	21
Cemaes Bay	30	0	0	30	12	188	0

GWYNEDD LEAGUE 2007-08

CPD Llanllyfni	30	24	1	5	78	38	73
Barmouth & Dyffryn United	28	22	0	6	87	32	66
CPD Bethel	30	21	2	7	99	55	65
CPD Porthmadog Reserves	30	18	3	9	99	59	57
Beaumaris Town	30	17	6	7	81	54	57
Blaenau Ffestiniog Amateurs	30	18	1	11	78	53	55
CPD Llanystumdwy	30	15	4	11	75	60	49
Llangefni Town Reserves	30	13	4	13	73	68	43
CPD Bodedern	30	12	5	13	51	51	41
Gaerwen FC	30	12	4	14	60	61	40
Holyhead Hotspurs Reserves	30	12	3	15	74	74	39
Llanfairfechan Town	30	10	1	19	62	97	31
University of Wales Bangor	28	9	3	16	47	59	30
CPD Bontnewydd	30	6	5	19	44	73	23
Real Llandudno	30	5	4	21	48	97	19
Cemaes Bay FC	30	0	2	28	17	146	2

Both matches between University of Wales Bangor and Barmouth & Dyffryn United were not played.

GWYNEDD LEAGUE 2008-09

Blaenau Ffestiniog Amateurs	28	20	3	5	82	32	63
Holyhead Hotspur Reserves	28	16	6	6	66	41	54
CPD Gwalchmai	28	16	5	7	54	32	53
CPD Bethel	28	17	1	10	90	55	52
CPD Llanystumdwy	28	16	3	9	80	56	51
CPD Bodedern Athletic	28	14	5	9	67	48	47
Llangefni Town Reserves	28	13	6	9	68	44	45
CPD Gaerwen	28	10	8	10	56	47	38
CPD Porthmadog Reserves	28	13	5	10	17	62	38
CPD Bontnewydd	28	9	5	14	39	59	32
CPD Rhiwlas	28	9	3	16	51	73	30
University of Wales Bangor	28	8	5	15	46	64	26
Llanfairfechan Town	28	8	1	19	56	75	25
Beaumaris Town	28	7	1	20	52	91	22
Real Llandudno	28	5	1	22	36	131	16

CPD Porthmadog reserves had 6 points deducted.
University of Wales Bangor had 3 points deducted.

GWYNEDD LEAGUE 2009-10

Gwalchmai	22	16	5	1	65	25	53
Bodedern Athletic	22	16	4	2	60	19	52
Holyhead Reserves	22	14	0	8	40	32	42
Beaumaris Town	22	12	3	7	66	46	39
Caernarfon Wanderers	22	11	6	5	53	38	39
Bethel	22	10	5	7	63	44	35
Gaerwen	22	9	8	5	40	39	35
CPD Porthmadog Reserves	22	8	5	9	45	50	30
Llanfairfechan Town	22	4	4	14	31	57	16
University of Wales Bangor	22	3	3	16	31	57	12
Llanystumdwy	22	2	5	15	31	73	11
Bontnewydd	22	1	4	17	20	65	7

Pentraeth Nurseries withdrew from the League.

GWYNEDD LEAGUE 2010-11

Bro Goronwy	18	13	2	3	77	30	41
Glantraeth	18	13	1	4	57	28	40
Beaumaris Town	18	11	4	3	57	26	37
Holyhead Hotspur Reserves	18	10	4	4	40	26	34
Llanfairfechan	18	7	4	7	43	34	25
University of Wales Bangor	18	5	7	6	34	36	22
Bethel	18	7	0	11	42	55	21
Llanystumdwy	18	6	3	9	41	57	21
Bangor City Reserves	18	2	4	12	28	58	10
Bontnewydd	18	0	3	15	17	86	3

GWYNEDD LEAGUE 2011-12

Penrhyndeudraeth	24	20	3	1	104	33	63
Trearddur Bay	24	18	3	3	97	47	57
Bro Goronwy	24	16	2	6	83	54	50
Llanllyfni	24	14	4	8	72	44	46
Holyhead Town	24	14	3	7	62	47	45
Llanystumdwy	24	13	2	9	82	63	41
Holyhead Hotspur Reserves	24	10	0	14	58	65	30
Beaumaris Town	24	8	4	12	66	74	28
Bontnewydd	24	9	1	14	51	73	28
Llanfairfechan Town	24	9	2	13	69	79	26
Bangor City Reserves	24	6	1	17	52	77	19
University of Wales Bangor	24	4	2	18	47	84	14
Bethel	24	1	1	22	18	122	4

Llanfairfechan Town had 3 points deducted.

GWYNEDD LEAGUE 2012-13

Trearddur Bay	22	20	2	0	79	24	62
Waunfawr	22	13	5	4	63	37	44
Llanerchymedd	22	13	3	6	59	35	42
Beaumaris Town	22	12	3	7	67	42	39
Bro Goronwy	22	11	3	8	69	53	36
Bethel	22	10	3	9	58	40	33
Llanllyfni	22	8	3	11	56	66	27
Holyhead Hotspur Reserves	22	7	5	10	37	45	26
University of Wales Bangor	22	9	4	9	51	49	25
Llanystumdwy	22	6	2	14	49	59	20
Llanfairfechan Town	22	4	4	0	18	38	105	9
Bontnewydd	22	1	3	18	23	94	6

Llanfairfechan Town had 3 points deducted.
Holyhead Town withdrew from the League.

GWYNEDD LEAGUE 2013-14

Llanerchymedd	20	17	2	1	73	21	53
Holyhead Hotspur Reserves	20	14	2	4	51	25	44
Myn Llandegai	20	12	3	5	52	34	39
Beaumaris Town	20	10	3	7	46	41	33
University of Wales Bangor	20	10	8	47	29	32
Llanystumdwy	20	9	5	6	51	35	32
Waunfawr	20	7	2	11	36	43	23
Pentraeth	20	7	2	11	43	54	23
Bontnewydd	20	5	4	11	24	60	16
Llanfairfechan Town	20	3	1	16	34	71	7
Llanllyfni	20	1	4	15	22	66	4

Bontnewydd, Llanfairfechan Town and Llanllyfni each had 3 points deducted.

GWYNEDD LEAGUE 2014-15

Llanllyfni	28	22	2	4	87	39	68
Bontnewydd	28	20	2	6	69	48	62
Y Felinheli	28	19	4	5	92	46	61
Llanystumdwy	28	19	2	7	102	44	59
Menai Bridge Tigers	28	14	6	8	99	59	48
Nefyn United	28	13	4	11	71	64	43
Waunfawr	28	13	3	12	66	49	42
Llanberis	28	11	7	10	71	69	40
Holyhead Hotspur Reserves	28	11	4	13	63	46	37
Llanrug United	28	12	1	15	64	67	37
Aberffraw	28	9	7	12	53	57	34
University of Wales Bangor	28	7	4	17	46	83	25
Harlech Town	28	7	3	18	52	89	24
Talysarn Celts	28	5	4	19	34	67	19
Beaumaris Town	28	1	1	26	28	170	4

GWYNEDD LEAGUE 2015-16

Y Felinheli	24	17	2	5	64	39	53
Llanystumdwy	24	15	4	5	78	42	49
Cemaes Bay	24	14	3	7	63	34	45
Menai Bridge Tigers	24	14	3	7	69	47	45
Nefyn United	24	14	2	8	70	39	44
Aberffraw	24	13	3	8	62	41	42
Bodedern	24	11	6	7	66	37	39
Waunfawr	24	11	2	11	57	47	35
Bontnewydd	24	10	4	10	57	60	34
Talysarn Celts	24	8	5	11	52	68	29
Beaumaris Town	24	4	3	17	48	118	15
Harlech Town	24	4	2	18	39	86	14
University of Wales Bangor	24	1	1	22	34	101	4

GWYNEDD LEAGUE 2016-17

Bodedern Athletic	22	18	2	2	81	25	56
Aberffraw	22	18	0	4	73	31	54
Bontnewydd	22	15	5	2	77	34	50
Bro Goronwy	22	11	5	6	52	45	38
Menai Bridge Tigers	22	10	4	8	57	49	34
Nefyn United	22	10	4	8	59	59	34
Llanystumdwy	22	9	4	9	62	49	31
Waunfawr	22	6	6	10	41	41	24
Beaumaris Town	22	6	3	13	46	75	21
Talysarn Celts	22	6	1	15	36	56	19
Harlech Town	22	2	6	14	33	65	12
Bethesda Athletic	22	0	2	20	26	114	2

GWYNEDD LEAGUE 2017-18

Holyhead Town	22	17	1	4	95	40	52
Bro Goronwy	22	16	3	3	87	32	51
Llanystumdwy	22	14	2	6	83	48	44
Bontnewydd	22	14	0	8	67	35	42
Gwalchmai	22	13	3	6	60	38	42
Nefyn United	22	11	4	7	58	34	37
Waunfawr	22	9	2	11	58	59	29
Llangoed & District	22	9	2	11	45	58	29
Menai Bridge Tigers	22	7	5	10	48	50	26
Talysarn Celts	22	7	0	15	34	72	21
Beaumaris Town	22	2	4	16	40	91	7
Llanllyfni	22	0	0	22	18	136	0

Bethesda & Harlech withdrew from the League.
Beaumaris Town had 3 points deducted.

WELSH FOOTBALL
THE NATIONAL FOOTBALL MAGAZINE OF WALES

"25 years of independent publishing in an independent football nation"

For over 25 years *Welsh Football* has celebrated everything that is unique and special about football in Wales.

Coverage includes the national team and the Welsh Premier through all levels of the Welsh pyramid, with regular analysis, club features, programme and book reviews, history features etc. as well as a comprehensive statistics supplement withy every issue, containing league tables, cup draws and results etc.

Welsh Football magazine is published 8 times a year

UK Subscription rate only £27.00 - overseas rates on application.

Essential reading for everyone with an interest in football in Wales.

email for further details:

info@welsh-football.net